ROCK AND ICE CLIMBING
ROCKY MOUNTAIN NATIONAL PARK

THE HIGH PEAKS

ROCK AND ICE CLIMBING
ROCKY MOUNTAIN
NATIONAL PARK

THE HIGH PEAKS

Richard Rossiter

Chockstone Press
Evergreen, Colorado

ROCK AND ICE CLIMBING ROCKY MOUNTAIN NATIONAL PARK:
THE HIGH PEAKS

Cover: Rappelling from the summit of the Petit Grepon. Photo by Richard Rossiter.

Back photo is of John Marrs on Dr. Wazz. John Marrs collection.

Unless noted otherwise, all photos are the property of the author.

ISBN: 0-934641-66-8

PUBLISHED AND DISTRIBUTED BY:
Chockstone Press, Inc.
Post Office Box 3505
Evergreen, Colorado 80437-3505

WARNING: CLIMBING IS A SPORT WHERE YOU MAY BE SERIOUSLY INJURED OR DIE. READ THIS BEFORE YOU USE THIS BOOK.

This guidebook is a compilation of unverified information gathered from many different climbers. The author cannot assure the accuracy of any of the information in this book, including the topos and route descriptions, the difficulty ratings, and the protection ratings. These may be incorrect or misleading and it is impossible for any one author to climb all the routes to confirm the information about each route. Also, ratings of climbing difficulty and danger are always subjective and depend on the physical characteristics (for example, height), experience, technical ability, confidence and physical fitness of the climber who supplied the rating. Additionally, climbers who achieve first ascents sometimes underrate the difficulty or danger of the climbing route out of fear of being ridiculed if a climb is later down-rated by subsequent ascents. Therefore, be warned that you must exercise your own judgment on where a climbing route goes, its difficulty and your ability to safely protect yourself from the risks of rock climbing. Examples of some of these risks are: falling due to technical difficulty or due to natural hazards such as holds breaking, falling rock, climbing equipment dropped by other climbers, hazards of weather and lightning, your own equipment failure, and failure or absence of fixed protection.

You should not depend on any information gleaned from this book for your personal safety; your safety depends on your own good judgment, based on experience and a realistic assessment of your climbing ability. If you have any doubt as to your ability to safely climb a route described in this book, do not attempt it.

The following are some ways to make your use of this book safer:

1. Consultation: You should consult with other climbers about the difficulty and danger of a particular climb prior to attempting it. Most local climbers are glad to give advice on routes in their area and we suggest that you contact locals to confirm ratings and safety of particular routes and to obtain first-hand information about a route chosen from this book.

2. Instruction: Most climbing areas have local climbing instructors and guides available. We recommend that you engage an instructor or guide to learn safety techniques and to become familiar with the routes and hazards of the areas described in this book. Even after you are proficient in climbing safely, occasional use of a guide is a safe way to raise your climbing standard and learn advanced techniques.

3. Fixed Protection: Many of the routes in this book use bolts and pitons which are permanently placed in the rock. Because of variances in the manner of placement, weathering, metal fatigue, the quality of the metal used, and many other factors, these fixed protection pieces should always be considered suspect and should always be backed up by equipment that you place yourself. Never depend for your safety on a single piece of fixed protection because you never can tell whether it will hold weight, and in some cases, fixed protection may have been removed or is now absent.

Be aware of the following specific potential hazards which could arise in using this book:

1. Misdescriptions of Routes: If you climb a route and you have a doubt as to where the route may go, you should not go on unless you are sure that you can go that way safely. Route descriptions and topos in this book may be inaccurate or misleading.

2. Incorrect Difficulty Rating: A route may, in fact, be more difficult than the rating indicates. Do not be lulled into a false sense of security by the difficulty rating.

3. Incorrect Protection Rating: If you climb a route and you are unable to arrange adequate protection from the risk of falling through the use of fixed pitons or bolts and by placing your own protection devices, do not assume that there is adequate protection available higher just because the route protection rating indicates the route is not an "X" or an "R" rating. Every route is potentially an "X" (a fall may be deadly), due to the inherent hazards of climbing – including, for example, failure or absence of fixed protection, your own equipment's failure, or improper use of climbing equipment.

THERE ARE NO WARRANTIES, WHETHER EXPRESS OR IMPLIED, THAT THIS GUIDEBOOK IS ACCURATE OR THAT THE INFORMATION CONTAINED IN IT IS RELIABLE. THERE ARE NO WARRANTIES OF FITNESS FOR A PARTICULAR PURPOSE OR THAT THIS GUIDE IS MERCHANTABLE. YOUR USE OF THIS BOOK INDICATES YOUR ASSUMPTION OF THE RISK THAT IT MAY CONTAIN ERRORS AND IS AN ACKNOWLEDGMENT OF YOUR OWN SOLE RESPONSIBILITY FOR YOUR CLIMBING SAFETY.

Gail Effron on pitch 2, *Directissima*, Longs Peak.

TABLE OF CONTENTS

Preface

I decided to write a guide book to Rocky Mountian National Park during the summer of 1984. It is embarrassing to admit that I have been working on it for more than a decade, but I can marginally excuse myself by having written five other guidebooks during the same period and established a private training and sports injury center. Still, this project may qualify me for life-time membership in the Dull Men's Club. Toward the end, I wouldn't do any-thing with anyone if it didn't have something to do with this book. It always seemed that the book would be ready the following spring, but it never was. Then I thought I would just write a "selected climbs" guide and save myself an enormous amount of work, but there was no "complete" book from which it might be drawn. Further, no one in the last two decades had put much effort into capturing the historical aspect of climbing in the park. My fate was sealed. The only way out was through. I lost my wife, I lost my friends, I took up motorcycle racing, and blew my hard drive. The last chapter was written in blood. But I pressed on to the end.

Acknowledgments

Many of the names and dates of first ascents before 1980 are borrowed from A Climber's Guide to the Rocky Mountain National Park Area by Walter Fricke, Jr., The High Peaks by Richard DuMais, and Lumpy Ridge, Estes Park Rock Climbs by Scott Kimball. First ascent information for newer routes is from personal research and from the many climbers who submitted information and addenda to the interim version of this book.

I wish to thank the following people for contributing route information, topos, photos, and/or first ascent data: Roger Briggs, Jeff Lowe, Greg Davis, Lou Dawson, Michael Gilbert, Ed Webster, The Crusher, Charlie Fowler, Dan Hare, George Bracksieck, John Marrs, Larry Coats, Randy Joseph, Bob Bradley, Richard DuMais, Malcom Daly, Alec Sharp, Kris Walker, Michael Bearzi, Eric Winkelman, Jeff Achey, Roy McClenahan, Greg Sievers, Gary Neptune, Kyle Copeland, Gene Ellis, Terry Murphy, Joe Burke, Mike Caldwell, Peter Hubbel, Morris Hershoff, Craig Luebben, Lawrence Steumke, Todd Swain, Jim Detterline, Clay Jackson, Bernard Gillett, Doug Redosh, Dr. Roger Clark, David Speyrer, Paul Kunasz, Doug Allcock, Bruce Hildenbrand, Ron Olson, Dan Bradford, and the late great Derek Hersey. Most of these climbers worked with me in person, pouring over photos and topos of routes they knew well or of which they had made first ascents. No effort was spared in the name of accuracy. Bonnie Von Grebe was a tremendous help with production aspects the book.

Greg Carelli on *Keyhole Ridge*, Longs Peak.

INTRODUCTION

The high peaks are the scenic heart of Rocky Mountain National Park and offer some of the finest alpine climbing in North America. This area has so many outstanding features that one could spend a lifetime exploring the established routes and still not climb them all. For a guide book writer, it is no small challenge to assimilate the ever-expanding sea of data and present it to his readers in a comprehensible and useful form.

The peaks are catalogued from left to right as they are normally viewed or approached, that is, peaks approached from the eastern slope are listed from south to north. Peaks approached from the west are listed from north to south. Routes are listed from left to right across (or counterclockwise around) each feature. For those unfamiliar with Rocky Mountain National Park, a map of the roads and trails will prove useful.

Park Policy

The high country of Rocky Mountain National Park supports a fragile ecosystem that is not immune to the intrepidations of human beings. To preserve the alpine and tundra areas of the park, the National Park Service has found it necessary to develope a policy of limited use. Climbers do not need to register for ascents, but all overnight camps and bivouacs require a backcountry permit which must be obtained in person from the backcountry office or from a ranger station. There are strict regulations regarding fires, pets, the use of tents, et cetera. Make sure you are familiar with these policies before venturing into the backcountry...lest you be busted.

Equipment

Appropriate climbing hardware can vary drastically from one route to another, and what a climber chooses to carry is a matter of style and experience. There is, however, at least in terms of crack width, a general array of devices that most parties would want to carry. Thus, a "standard rack" (SR) might consist of the following gear:

> A set of RPs
> Wired stoppers up to 1 inch
> Two or three slung stoppers or Tri-cams
> Various camming devices up to 3 inches
> Six or seven quick draws (QDs)
> Three to five runners long enough to wear over the shoulder
> One double-length runner
> Six to eight unoccupied carabiners (usually with the runners)

On some routes this rack would be overkill; on others, it might be weak in certain areas. Snow and ice climbs typically will require crampons, ice ax(es), snow pickets or flukes, and ice screws as well as some part of the rock climbing gear listed above and perhaps a few pitons. Equipment suggestions are given with some route descriptions; in some cases gear requirements are not known; otherwise, the gear listed above may serve as a general guideline.

Ratings

The system used for rating difficulty in this book is a streamlined version of the so-called Yosemite Decimal System. That is, the class five designation is assumed, so that 5.0 through 5.14 is written as 0 through 14 without the 5. prefix. Aid climbing is rated A0 through A6. The Welzenbach classes 2 through 4 have been retained and appear in route descriptions as (cl3), (cl4), and appear with route names as Class 3 or Class 4. The Roman numeral grades I through VI for overall difficulty are also retained but are not applied to crag routes. The water ice rating system WI1 through WI6 is used for winter ice climbs. Alpine snow and ice climbs are rated AI1 through AI6. Mixed ice and rock is rated M1 through M6, a system initiated by Michael Bearzi.

The potential for a long leader fall is indicated by an **s** (serious) or **vs** (very serious) after the rating of difficulty. A climb rated **s** will have at least one notable run-out and the potential for a scary fall. A climb rated **vs** typically will have poor protection for hard moves and the potential for a very serious fall. The absence of these letters indicates a relatively safe climb providing it is within the leader's ability. Difficulty for runout sections is shown in parentheses when it is less than the maximum difficulty of a climb.

Note: The rating of a climb represents an informal consensus of opinion from some of the climbers who have completed a route. Some of the routes in this book may never have been repeated, which makes their ratings extremely subjective. But even the ratings of long established routes are debated, which indicates that numerical ratings have no absolute value and must be taken as approximations.

Weather and Snow Conditions

Climbing in the high peaks is done primarily from June through September. During this period one can expect sunny mornings, comfortable to hot daytime temperatures, and afternoon thundershowers. Until July, many peak climbs involve snow travel, thus an ice ax and mountain boots may be useful for some part of the approach, climb, or descent. From mid-July through August, the weather is usually hot during the day and many climbs can be done without snow travel. Temperatures cool in September, but it is still reasonable to climb on warm days, even on the Diamond. By October the first serious snows come and windows of opportunity for rock climbing are rare; however, the alpine ice gullies are at their best. In November it gets cold and the winter ice climbs begin to form up. Winter ascents of the Diamond and other major features are not uncommon, but it's a whole different ball game than during summer. Spring is avalanche time in the Rockies.

A word of caution: Violent thunderstorms with heavy precipitation including rain, hail, and even snow are average fare during the summer. Which is to say, a warm sunny morning can go totally industrial by early afternoon. A climb should be started as early as possible so that one is off the route before the ax falls. Sometimes the storms hit early and you get chopped anyway. Always carry storm gear.

Environmental Considerations

Rocky Mountain National Park, which includes Lumpy Ridge, is one of the cleanest and best maintained parks in the country. To preserve the natural beauty and ecological integrity of our climbing environment, a few suggestions are offered.

Use restrooms or outdoor toilets where possible. Otherwise, deposit solid human waste far from the cliffs and away from paths of approach and descent. Do not cover solid waste with a rock but leave it exposed to the elements where it will deteriorate more quickly. Carry used toilet paper out in a plastic bag or use a stick or Douglas fir cone. Do not leave man-made riffraff lying about: If you pack it in, pack it out. Take care to preserve trees and other plants on approaches and climbs. Scree gullies and talus fields usually have sections that are more stable; thrashing up and down loose scree causes erosion and destroys plant life. Always use trails and footpaths where they have been developed, and demonstrate human evolution by removing obstructions, stacking loose rocks along trail sides, and picking up trash. When hiking across tundra, follow footpaths or step on rocks to avoid crushing the fragile plant life.

Fixed Protection

Fixed protection has become a major point of contention with park managers and powerful wilderness lobbies such as the Audubon Society. The very concept of "climbing management" and resultant closures and restrictions has developed around climbers' use of bolts and other forms of fixed anchors, especially in high-profile areas. If we are to have access to public lands and preserve the freedom we have enjoyed in the past, it is critical that we promote a sensible and responsible public image. Climber organizations such as the Access Fund do much to help this cause, but our actions in the field are even more important.

Bolts, pitons, and slings that can be seen from the ground (or through binoculars) are easy targets for complaint. Dangling slings are highly visible and should be kept to an absolute minimum. Bolt hangers should be camouflaged. For those in the first ascent business, it is wiser to place bolts in the most useful possible position for someone leading the route. Bolts that are hard to reach or those that precede long, unprotected cruxes usually have slings hanging from them. Bolt anchors are best fitted with lap links or cold shuts because they are permanent and much less visible than slings.

Knowing that every bolt and piton we place will be counted and documented by some regulatory agency or wildlife organization, it is obvious that some restraint on our part is necessary. As for new free climbs requiring bolts: Only the very best lines should be developed. Contrived and mediocre routes can be left to obscurity or a toprope. When the decision is made to place bolts on a new route, only the best gear should be used so it is reliable and permanent. Whether bolts are placed on rappel or on the lead is irrelevant. The emphasis should not fall on the first ascent but on the resultant route. Regarding that a good route will be climbed thousands of times, and that holes drilled in the rock will last for millenia, it is obvious that the quality and positioning of fixed gear must take precedence over other considerations. Note: The use of power drills is currently banned inside Rocky Mountain National Park, presumably with the hope of limiting the application of bolts. Climbers are still permitted to use hand drills.

The Greater Horizon

"Once Chuang Chou dreamt he was a butterfly, a butterfly flitting and fluttering around, happy with himself and doing as he pleased. He didn't know he was Chuang Chou. Suddenly he woke up and there he was, solid and unmistakable Chuang Chou. But he didn't know if he was Chuang Chou who had dreamt he was a butterfly, or a butterfly dreaming he was Chuang Chou."

"If so were really so, it would differ so clearly from not so, there would be no need for argument. Forget time, forget distinctions. Leap into the boundless and make it your home."
—Chuang Chou

ROCKY MOUNTAIN NATIONAL PARK AREA
(East Side)

Crag Locator
A.   Thumb and Needle
B.   DeVille Rocks
C.   The Crags
D.   The Fin
E.   Cottontail Crag
F.   The Lost World
G.   Rock of Ages
H.   Deer Mountain
     Buttress
I   McGregor Slab
J.   Window Rock
K.   Sundance Buttress
L.   The Book
M.   Twin Owls
N.   Sheep Mountain Rock
O.   Eagle Rock
P.   Crosier Dome
Q.   Combat Rock
R.   Seam Rock

Ice Climb Locator ★
1.   Hidden Falls
2.   Ouzel Falls
3.   Dream Weaver
4.   Columbine Falls
5   Notch Couloir
6.   Black Lake Ice
7.   Big Mac Couloir
8.   Hourglass Couloir
9.   All Mixed Up
10. Necrophilia
11. Thatchtop-Powel Ice
12. Taylor Glacier
13. Dragon Tail Couloir
14. Emerald Lake Ice
15. Ptarmigan Glacier
16. Grace Falls
17. Jaws
18. Y Couloir

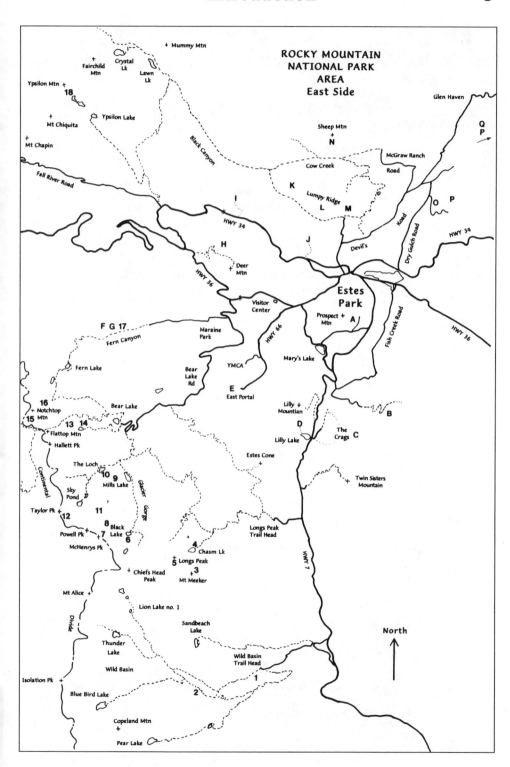

Moe Hershoff on *Main Vein,* **North Face of Mount Meeker.**
Photo: Steve McCorkel

WILD BASIN

Wild Basin occupies the southeast corner of Rocky Mountain National Park. Its remote peaks, lakes, and vast meadows of wildflowers are terra incognita to most climbers. Even Mount Alice, which has a formidable east face reminiscent of the Diamond, is little known and seldom visited. The walk into the basin is pleasant but long and likely accounts for the lack of activity in this area. The profound solitude above tree line and the immense alpine beauty certainly do not keep people away. Aside from the approach, Wild Basin is a peak bagger's paradise with six summits above 13000 feet and several others above 12000. Nearly all of the technical climbing is on Mount Alice and can be summed up in a few great routes.

To reach Wild Basin trailheads from Boulder, take Highway 36 to Lyons and drive to the T intersection at the west end of town. Turn left on Highway 7 and follow it for about 24 miles to the Wild Basin Road which is on the left. The road is initially a section of old highway; follow this for 0.4 mile, then turn right to Copeland Lake and continue along an unpaved road to the various trailheads. From Estes Park, drive 13.1 miles south on Highway 7 to reach Wild Basin Road.

Sandbeach Lake Trail. The trail begins from the road just northeast of Copeland Lake and provides access to the southern slopes of Mount Meeker, Longs Peak, Pagoda Mountain, and Chiefs Head Peak. The trail reaches Sandbeach Lake at 4.0 miles.

Finch Lake Trail. The trail begins from Wild Basin Road 1.8 miles west of Copeland Lake and provides access to Mount Copeland, Elk Tooth, Ogalalla Peak, and Cony Lake Cirque. The trail reaches Finch Lake at 4.6 miles, then continues westward to Pear Lake at 6.6 miles. There are three junctions along this trail; bring a map and read the trail signs carefully. To reach the Cony Lake Cirque from Pear Lake, hike south to Cony Creek and follow the drainage west past several small lakes into the cirque.

Thunder Lake Trail. The trail begins from the west end of the road (2.1 miles from Copeland Lake) and provides access to Bluebird Lake Trail, Lion Lake Trail, Pilot Mountain, Tanima Peak, and reaches Thunder Lake at 6.8 miles.

Bluebird Lake Trail. The trail begins from the Thunder Lake Trail at 3.3 miles and provides access to Mount Copeland, Ouzel Peak, Mahana Peak, and reaches Bluebird Lake at 6.3 miles from the trailhead.

Lion Lake Trail. The trail begins from the Thunder Lake Trail at 5.0 miles and provides access to Mount Alice, Chiefs Head Peak, and the Lion Lake Cirque. It reaches Lion Lake Number 1 at 6.8 miles, after which a footpath continues northwest to Lion Lake Number 2 and Snowbank Lake.

ELK TOOTH

The rugged Elk Tooth (12848) is located southeast of Cony Lake and about 0.7 mile east of Ogalalla Peak along the ridge that forms the divide between Cony Creek and South Saint Vrain Creek. Approach via the Finch Lake trail and hike into the Cony Lake Cirque. Elk Tooth also may be approached via a four-wheel-drive road along Middle Saint Vrain Creek, which is a shorter hike if you drive to the end of the road. From there, follow the Saint Vrain Glacier Trail until southeast of the peak at 10800 feet.

East Ridge   II Class 3

From either drainage, scramble up to a shoulder on the east ridge at 12100 feet and continue up the ridge to the summit. Any obstacles along the ridge can be bypassed on the north side.

OGALALLA PEAK

Ogalalla Peak (13138) is the southernmost summit along the Continental Divide within Rocky Mounatin National Park. The northeast and southeast faces are precipitous and challenging. A long east ridge connects with the summit of Elk Tooth and provides a classic scramble. The west side of the peak is gentle in the manner of many divide summits. Approach as for Elk Tooth (above). The easiest descent from the summit into Wild Basin is via the *North Face* route on Ouzel Peak (below).

MOUNT COPELAND

Mount Copeland (13176) lies 1.3 miles east of the Continental Divide and about 1 mile north of the Elk Tooth. It is a fairly large peak, similar in shape and size to Thatchtop Mountain above Glacier Gorge. Side by side, it would dwarf the likes of Chiefs Head or Hallett Peak. Copeland's northeast slope rises 3000 feet from the shores of Ouzel Lake. Its pinnacled west ridge extends to a col called Cony Pass, then climbs abruptly to the Continental Divide. The north face is steep and broken and does not provide any obvious line of ascent. The only known routes ascend the northeast shoulder begin-ning from Pear Lake to the south or Ouzel Lake to the north. It appears that the summit could be reached as well from Cony Lake to the southwest. Hike the Finch Lake Trail to reach Pear Lake or Cony Lake. Hike the Thunder Lake Trail for 3.3 miles, and then the Bluebird Lake Trail for 1.5 miles to reach Ouzel Lake.

OUZEL PEAK

Ouzel Peak (12716) lies along the Continental Divide roughly midway between Ogalalla Peak and Isoation Peak. It rises only 300 feet or so along the Continental Divide, but as with many Rocky Mountain summits looks more like a mountain from the east. Approach via Bluebird Lake Trail. Scramble up the northeast ridge from Bluebird Lake (cl3) or straight up the north face from Pipit Lake (cl2).

ISOLATION PEAK

Isolation Peak (13118) straddles the Continental Divide some 1.3 miles north of Ouzel Peak and presides over four drainages. The precipitous north face reigns over Fifth Lake at the head of East Inlet and is visible from the summit of Aiguille de Fleur and Andrews Peak. To the southwest is the clandestine valley of Paradise Creek. The broad east face towers above Mahana Peak and the drainages of Ouzel Creek and the Moomaw Glacier. Isolation Peak, worthy of its name, is a grand objective for the well-conditioned peak bagger. An excellent east-side circuit is to ascend the *North Ridge* route from Thunder Lake and Boulder-Grand Pass, then descend the *Southeast Slope* and return via the Bluebird Lake Trail.

1 **Southeast Slope   II Class 2 ★**
    This is the easiest and most often climbed route on the peak. Hike the Thunder Lake Trail for 3.3 miles, then continue on Bluebird Lake Trail for another 3.0 miles to Bluebird Lake. Hike west along the inlet for another mile to Pipit Lake, then hike west-northwest to Isolation Lake (c. 12000 feet). Veer west and ascend steep grassy slopes to the summit.

2 **North Ridge   II 2 ★**
    This route is most easily approached via Boulder-Grand Pass which may be reached from Fourth Lake at the head of East Inlet or from Thunder Lake in Wild Basin. The ridge crest also may be reached from Indigo Pond on the south side of Tanima Peak: This option places one on the crest just south of The Cleaver, a rock tower on the crest of the ridge. The ascent from Boulder-Grand Pass brings one to the north side of The Cleaver, which is most easily passed on its east side. From the col on the south side of The Cleaver, scramble south and pass a northeast-facing cliff on the west side (crux). Continue along the narrow crest passing above the Eagles Beak and the Moomaw Glacier (below to the east) to a broad easy section. The final push to the summit is Class 3.

3 **North Face   II Class 4 AI3**
    From Fifth Lake, the north face of Isolation Peak gives the appearance of a giant tooth recessed between the north and west ridges. It is unquestionably the most imposing aspect of the mountain and does not appear that its midsection might be ascended with only moderate difficulty. Approach via the East Inlet Trail and hike to Fourth Lake. Continue around the west end of the lake and follow a faint trail southeast to Fifth Lake. Hike up to the bottom of the north face and identify a prominent couloir a bit right from the middle of the face. Climb the couloir for several hundred feet, then go left on a large ramp that angles up and left across the face. Follow the ramp on snow or scree to where it joins the north ridge (12950) and scramble to the summit (cl3). This route is probably best done as a snow climb during late June or early July, as the ramp tends to be wet and to hold a lot of loose rock.

4 **West Ridge   II Class 4 ★**
    The high and lonely west ridge of Isolation Peak offers a climb of solitude amid exceptional scenery. It is also a formidable test piece for the alpine marathonist as a one-day, 22-mile, 5000-foot, lung ripper. Hike to

Fifth Lake as for the *North Face* route, but from the lake, hike southwest and gain a saddle at the base of the west ridge (c. 11890) about a mile from the summit. Hike and scramble up the west ridge, past some low towers, to the summit.

TANIMA PEAK

The summit of Tanima Peak (12420) sits just east of the Continental Divide about midway between Isolation Peak and Mount Alice and a short way south of Boulder-Grand Pass. The peak is long and narrow on an east-west axis and presents a beautiful profile from the Lion Lakes basin to the northeast.

1   **East Ridge   II Class 3**
From the east end of Thunder Lake, bushwhack south and gain the crest of the ridge which is followed for a mile to the summit.

2   **West Slopes   I Class 2**
From Thunder Lake, hike to Boulder-Grand Pass, then head southeast to the summit.

PILOT MOUNTAIN

Pilot Mountain (12160+) is a minor summit along an eastern spur of the Continental Divide about a half mile south of Mount Alice. Its 900-foot south face forms the north side of the cirque above Falcon Lake and provides a couple of interesting moderate routes.

Approach. To reach the south face, hike the Thunder Lake Trail to Thunder Lake and continue around to the northwest shore. Follow a faint trail west-northwest up the drainage to Falcon Lake (about five hours from the trail-head) and scramble up talus to the bottom of the face. Use the Lion Lake Trail to reach the northeast side.

Descent. From the summit, reverse the *Northeast Slope* route (below). It is also possible to scramble west to the Continental Divide (an elevation gain of 800 feet) and return to Wild Basin via Boulder-Grand Pass: This is the best route if return to Falcon Lake is desired. It is difficult to reach Falcon Lake by descending the *Northeast Slope.*

1   **Granite Wall   II 6**
FA: Paul Mayrose and Norman Harthill, 1966.
This long route ascends the 1000-foot head wall northwest of Falcon Lake and tops out on the Continental Divide. The difficulties consist largely of short steep cliffs between ledges and low-angle sections. Begin at the base of the wall west-northwest of Falcon Lake and head for "an apparent knob." The exact line of the route is not known.

2   **Schist Wall   II 7 ★**
FA: Mayrose and Harthill, 1966.
This route ascends the center of the south face in five long pitches on good rock. From Falcon Lake, scramble north to the bottom of the wall. Climb straight up on steep knobby schist with good belay ledges and continue directly to the summit of Pilot Mountain.

3 Northeast Slope   II Class 4

This is the easiest route to the summit of Pilot Mountain and is the easiest line of descent. Hike the Lion Lake Trail to Lion Lake Number 1.
From the north end of the lake, hike west across spectaular alpine
meadows to the east side of Pilot Mountain. Scramble up the steepening
slope to the saddle northwest of the summit (cl3), then follow the ridge
southeast to the top (cl4). Steep sections of the ridge can be passed on
the north side. It also is possible to traverse along the exposed southern side of the summit ridge and ascend a gully to the top (cl4).

MOUNT ALICE

Mount Alice (13310) is the monarch of Wild Basin and is among the highest
and most visually striking peaks in Rocky Mountain National Park. It would
undoubtedly be very popular except, like everything in Wild Basin, it is a
long way from the nearest trailhead. Despite an 8-mile approach, a good
number of routes have been completed on Alice's steep, Diamond-like east
face, and its north ridge has become a peak bagger's classic. Still, this great
mountain is visted by few.

Approach. Hike the Thunder Lake Trail for five miles, then go right on the
Lion Lake Trail and follow it for a long mile and a half to Lion Lake Number
1. Walk around the east side of the lake, then continue west-northwest cross-
country for another mile and a half to Mount Alice.

Descent. The quickest descent from the summit is to scramble down the
steep, broad, east-facing talus gully south of the east face. It also is possible
to descend *Hourglass Ridge,* or to follow the ridge crest south to Boulder-
Grand Pass, and then hike east to Thunder Lake.

1 South Ridge   I Class 2 ★

While hiking up the gentle but spectacular south ridge of Mount Alice,
one may be reminded of John Muir's famous proclamation, "Go to the
mountains and get their good tidings." From the west side of Thunder
Lake, follow a path westward past Lake of Many Winds and gain
Boulder-Grand Pass (12061). Turn north and follow the south ridge 1.1
miles to the summit. A longer and perhaps less convenient method is to
reach Boulder-Grand Pass from East Inlet, then hike north to the summit: a 22-mile round trip.

EAST FACE

The east face of Mount Alice is more than 1000 feet high and has three
notable aspects: The south (left) side is characterized by chimneys, buttresses, and deep gullies and is less continuous than the right side which is steeper, sheerer, and much larger. Between the two is a steep ramp (the Central
Ramp) that slashes up and right toward the summit and provides the
"Standard Route" on the east side of the mountain. At the bottom of the ramp
and several hundred feet above the talus, is a large, grassy terrace. This may
be reached from a conspicuous snow tongue on the left or from a long ramp
that angles in from the right (cl3).

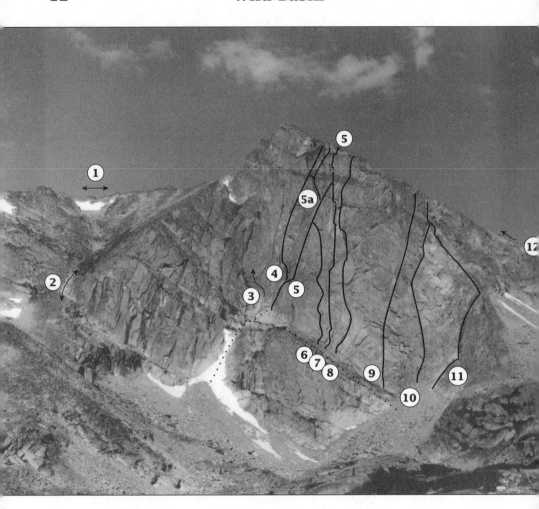

Mount Alice, East Face

1	South Ridge I Class 2 ★	6	Left Side IV 10a ★
2	Southeast Face I Class 2	7	Culp-Turner V 11c ★
3	Central Pillar IV 9 A3	8	Jabberwock V 10 A4
4	Central Crack III 6 A1	9	Good Vibrations V 9 A3 ★
5	Central Ramp III 8 or 7 A2 ★	10	Beyer's Solo V 9 A2
5a	Variation	11	Northeast Ridge IV 7 A1
5b	Variation	12	Hourglass Ridge I Class 3 ★

2 Southeast Face   I Class 2

The easiest way to reach the summit from the Lion Lakes Basin is via the broad curving gully just south of the east face. This is also the easiest return to the bottom of the east face. Hike Lion Lake Trail and gain the cirque beneath the east face, then scramble up the steep, broad gully at the south side of the east face and reach the south ridge very near the summit.

3 Central Pillar   IV 9 A3

This route ascends the large buttress to the left of the Central Ramp. Begin up and left from the bottom of the pillar and follow a system of cracks just left of the prow. Pass a white, left-facing dihedral two-thirds of the way up. Once on top of the pillar, traverse a knife-edged ridge (8) to easier terrain near the summit.

4 Central Crack   III 6 A1

FA: Walker, Fedson, Brooks, and Ehlert, 1958.

This route ascends the middle of three possible crack and chimney systems between the *Central Pillar* and the *Central Ramp* routes. Climb to the top of the snow tongue, then continue up the large gully left of the Central Ramp for several hundred feet to the base of the crack system. Follow the crack for four moderate leads, pass a pegmatite band, and belay beneath a roof where the terrain steepens. Turn the roof on the right and gain a section of slabs. Work up the slabs, then traverse left and regain the crack system (crux). Several more moderate pitches lead to the easy summit ridge.

5 Central Ramp   III 8 or 7 A2 ★

FA: Bob Culp and Larry Dalke, 1966.

This fine route ascends the steep ramp along the left edge of the main east face. For its position and moderate rating it is likely the most popular technical route on the peak.

Climb the snow or the ramp on the right and gain the grassy terrace described above, then scramble up a slab to a broken area below the Central Ramp.

1. Climb a chimney through the broken area to the more continuous part of the ramp (5).
2. and 3. Climb cracks for two long pitches up the Central Ramp to an area of ledges at its top (7).
4. Climb up to the highest ledge and belay to the right beneath a left-facing dihedral (6).
5. Climb the dihedral to a large roof in a long band of dark rock (7), aid right around the roof (A2), then work up and right and climb a slot (A1) to a ledge. It also is possible to climb a difficult crack past the left side of the roof (10).
6. Step left over loose rock and climb a chimney behind a huge flake (6).

Scramble to the summit.

5a Variation

From the left end of the ledges at the top of the fourth pitch, climb a right-facing dihedral through the band of dark rock and belay at its top.

Climb a V-shaped corner and jam up a left-leaning, 2-inch crack to a ramp (8). A final corner leads to the top of the face (7). Scramble to the summit.

5b   Variation

From the highest ledges above the ramp, traverse left along the band of dark rock for about 80 feet to an arête. Climb a short dihedral (8) and continue to a ledge. Climb a short face and bottomless chimney to the top of the face.

6   Left Side   IV 10a ★

This superior route ascends the left side of the main east face, then joins the upper part of the *Central Ramp*. It is steep and sustained on excellent rock.

Scramble up the long, diagonal ramp described above but stop about 200 feet from the top beneath the farthest left of a long series of right-facing flake/dihedrals.

1. Work up and right and gain the left-most right-facing corner. Undercling around a roof and climb up to merge with the next corner on the right, then continue to a ledge on the left (10a, 150 feet).

2. Climb the left side of a narrow flake to its top, then face climb up to a stance in a right-facing corner (9).

3. Climb through a squeeze chimney and continue up the corner to a long ledge/fault that runs across the face (8). Move the belay about 30 feet right to the bottom of a long right-facing dihedral system.

4. Climb straight up the dihedral and belay where it leans to the left (10a, 160 feet).

5. Follow the corner up and left past a roof (10a) and onward (8) to belay around on the *Central Ramp*. Follow that route to the top.

7   Culp-Turner   V 11c ★

FA: Bob Culp and Jack Turner (V 5.9 A3), 1972. FFA: Greg Davis and Kevin Cooney.

This dramatic route ascends a series of very steep right-facing dihedrals just right of *Left Side*. If by no other feature, the route may be identified as beginning directly beneath the left of two white (lichen-free) dihedrals high on the wall, through which the route passes on its fifth pitch. Note that the free climb described here varies from the original aid line in that it is slightly more direct and fewer belays are utilized.

Climb the initial ramp as for *Left Side* and belay directly beneath the dihedrals at the beginning of that route.

1. Climb up and right to gain the right of two right-leaning, right-facing dihedrals and climb it to a good ledge (11a).

2. Climb a steep crack above the belay ledge and belay at a stance beneath a roof (8).

3. Turn the roof and continue over moderate terrain to the big ledge/fault that runs across the face (8). Move the belay about 50 feet right until beneath a long right-facing dihedral system that leads to a big roof.

4. Climb the right of three merging dihedrals and belay at their top (10d).

5. Climb a wide crack and turn the roof at its top, then tackle the crux white dihedral. Near the top of the corner, move to the dihedral on the left and belay beneath the big roof.

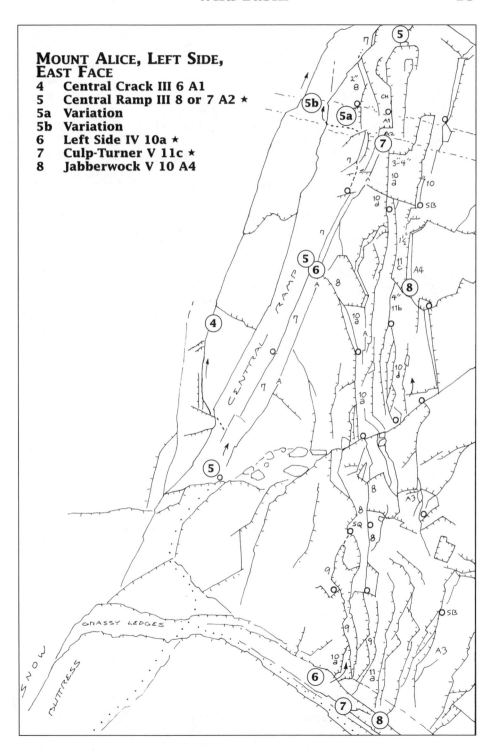

MOUNT ALICE, LEFT SIDE, EAST FACE

4   **Central Crack III 6 A1**
5   **Central Ramp III 8 or 7 A2 ★**
5a   **Variation**
5b   **Variation**
6   **Left Side IV 10a ★**
7   **Culp-Turner V 11c ★**
8   **Jabberwock V 10 A4**

6. Turn the roof, then continue up the right-facing dihedral system past another roof and belay at the bottom of a large flake.

Finish as for the *Central Ramp.*

8   Jabberwock   V 10 A4

FA: Joe Hladick and Keith Loeber, 1979. Rack should include a few hooks, RURPS, pitons, and nuts up to 4 inches.

This very steep and difficult aid route has not received a free ascent. It follows the first major dihedral system to the right of the *Culp-Turner* and passes through the right of the two white dihedrals described under that route.

Begin from the ramp as for the previous routes but set the initial belay about 100 feet down and right from the *Culp-Turner.* The first pitch begins at the left of two large flakes (the right flake forms a chimney at its top).

1. Work up and right along the flake/dihedrals for a rope length and belay in slings (10 A3).
2. Continue to the top of the dihedral system, then work up and left past a squarish flake and belay on a sloping ledge.
3. Climb up through a roof (A3) and climb a curving right-facing dihedral to the ledge/fault system that runs up and right across the face.
4. Climb a left-facing dihedral to a ledge and belay. This is the logical place for a bivouac.
5. Traverse left and gain a white (lichen-free), right-facing dihedral with a thin crack. Climb this to a roof and continue to a sling belay at the bottom of a long right-facing dihedral (A4).
6. Climb the dihedral past a small roof (possible belay for previous pitch).
7. Climb a wide crack through the roof (10) and, after a short way, tension right and climb up to a good ledge in a large, left-facing dihedral.
8. Climb the dihedral, pass a roof at its top (9), and continue easily to the top of the face.

9   Good Vibrations   V 9 A3

FA: Harry Kent and Mike Neri, 1976.

This route begins a short way up the ramp system and beneath some large angular roofs several hundred feet up on the wall, which are the primary charcteristics of the climb. The line goes up and left through these roofs to gain a prominent crack system that leads to the top of the wall.

1. Climb up and right along a broken, grassy ramp system (6).
2. Climb up and slightly left to a V-shaped break in the initial roofs.
3. Aid through the V, then free climb up and left beneath the next tier of roofs (8).
4. Cut back right and climb the face to the right of a thin crack to a ledge.
5 - 8. Climb the long, right-leaning crack system to grassy ledges near the top of the wall.
9. Work up and left and climb a right-facing dihedral to the top of the face.

10 Beyer's Solo   V 9 A2
FA: Jim Beyer, 1978.
This route follows a long, left-leaning, left-facing dihedral on the right
side of the face, then leans right along the left edge of a light-colored
area to reach grassy ledges near the top of the face.
Begin about 100 feet up and right from the beginning to the long ramp
that runs up and left toward the Central Ramp. Climb a short corner
(cl4) and scramble up and right along a grassy ramp to the highest of
several ledges.
1. Climb difficult loose rock past some roofs and gain the bottom of the
long, left-facing dihedral.
2. Climb up and left to a loose rock horn, traverse left, then work
straight up to a small, grassy ramp that leads back into the dihedral.
3 - 5. Mixed aid and free climbing lead to a pedestal at the top of the
dihedral, then climb a short wall to a big ledge.
6. Climb up and right along short right-facing corners and roofs to a
good ledge.
7. Angle up and left to a grassy ledge and traverse right to the bottom
of a chimney that breaches the final cliff band.
8. Climb the chimney (7) and gain the northeast ridge, which may be
followed to the summit. Note that this chimney is the last steep pitch of
the *Northeast Ridge* route.

11 Northeast Ridge   IV 7 A1
FA: Greg Davis and Jeff Sherman, 1974.
This route ascends the large left-facing corner formed by a buttress at
the lower right side of the east face, then continues up a knife-edged
ridge along the margin of the east face. To the right of the *Beyers Solo*
dihedral, scramble up and right along a ramp and gain the bottom of a
big left-facing dihedral.
1. Climb an easy pitch and belay after 100 feet.
2. Continue up the dihedral and belay after about 100 feet (7).
3. A long pitch leads to the crest of the southeast ridge (7 A1).
4. Climb up the knife-edged ridge and belay on the crest (4).
5. Continue up the crest for a rope length and belay on the crest (7).
6. A long pitch leads to grassy ledges beneath the final cliff band (4).
7. A steep chimney leads to the summit ridge (7). Scramble to the top.

12 Hourglass Ridge   I Class 3 ★
This route ascends the spectacular north ridge of Mount Alice from the
Chiefs Head-Alice col. It is the classic alpine scramble in Wild Basin.
Approach via Lion Lake Trail and hike to its end at Lion Lake Number
One. Continue northwest along a faint path to Lion Lake Number Two
and onward to Snowbank Lake at 11521 feet. Follow the valley northwest to the broad col between Chiefs Head Peak and Mount Alice
(12450). Turn south and follow the ridge crest which has a very narrow
section shortly above the saddle. At about 12500 feet, the ridge broadens and an easy scramble leads to the summit. It is not unreasonable to
include in the day's outing an ascent of the *Northwest Ridge* of Chiefs
Head Peak.

Northwest Face

The northwest face lies at the head of a large cirque that drains into North Inlet. The broad and rugged face is about 1500 feet high and is ascended by two known routes. The only reasonable approach is via the Lion Lake Trail. Hike to the Chiefs Head-Alice col, and from its south side, descend a scree slope into the cirque. An abusive hike of 10.5 miles with 3 miles of bushwhacking is required to reach the bottom of the face from North Inlet.

13   Roundabout   II 6

FA: Dewitt, Goldberg, and Holsworth, 1975.

From the south side of the Chiefs Head-Alice col, descend a gully for 300 feet to a scree-covered ramp on the left, then traverse south along the ramp for another 300 feet to its end. Descend a gully for about 250 feet to two large blocks on the south side. Traverse 100 feet south to a ledge (cl4), then continue across more difficult terrain to the far side of an area of white rock and below some big flakes (6). Climb straight up over moderate terrain, then veer left and belay at the bottom of a chimney. Traverse south across the chimney and continue along a broken crack to a dihedral. Climb a short way to a ledge on the right, then traverse across to an easy gully that is followed to the summit.

14   Central Gully   IV 7 A2 AI4 ★

FA: Dakers Gowans and Mike Munger, 1974.

This remote route was first climbed during winter; however, it could provide an excellent snow climb in early summer. It ascends the long and obvious snow couloir toward the left side of the northwest face and tops out very near the summit. From the Chiefs Head-Alice col, descend the talus slope on the west for 1000 feet, then traverse south past a rib to the bottom of the couloir. Scramble up the gully as high as possible to where it bends left and presents a series of cracks and chimneys. Follow this system for several pitches and pass a short section of aid. Continue in the same system to the end of roped climbing near the summit. Seven pitches.

15   West Ridge   I Class 2 ★

Here is an alpine marathon that rivals the *West Ridge* on Isolation Peak and is an excellent peak bagger's route for those wishing to leave the car far, far behind. Set your mind for a 30-mile round trip with 8 miles off the trail. Hike the North Inlet Trail (see under "West Side") for seven miles, then take a right spur to Lake Nanita (10.5 miles). From the far end of the lake, hike southeast (cross-country) over a saddle on the northeast shoulder of Andrews Peak and descend into a cirque above an unnamed lake. Contour as high as possible and gain the col between Andrews Peak and Mount Alice (c. 13980). Turn east and follow the ridge crest for 2 miles to the summit.

MOUNT ALICE, NORTHWEST FACE
11 Northeast Ridge IV 7 A1
12 Hourglass Ridge I Class 3 ★
14 Central Gully IV 7 A2 AI4 ★
15 West Ridge I Class 2 ★

Chiefs Head-
Alice Col

The *Grey Pillar,* Longs Peak.   Photo: John Marrs Collection.

WILD BASIN ICE CLIMBS

Two good ice climbs exist up the Thunder Lake Trail. Unlike *Jaws* in Fern Canyon which faces straight into the sun, these formations are shaded and can be climbed all winter.

1 Hidden Falls   WI3+ ★

The last mile of the road is closed off during winter, so park near the gate and walk to the end of the road. Continue up the Thunder Lake Trail past Copeland Falls, then cross the stream to the left and wander through the woods to the secluded falls. This is slightly tricky but one can usually follow tracks in the snow. One good pitch with several variations leads to pin and bolt anchors in the rock. Rappel. A final pillar sometimes may be ascended to the top of the cliff.

2 Ouzel Falls   WI3

Hike the Thunder Lake Trail for about 2.7 miles and find a 50-foot column up on the left.

22

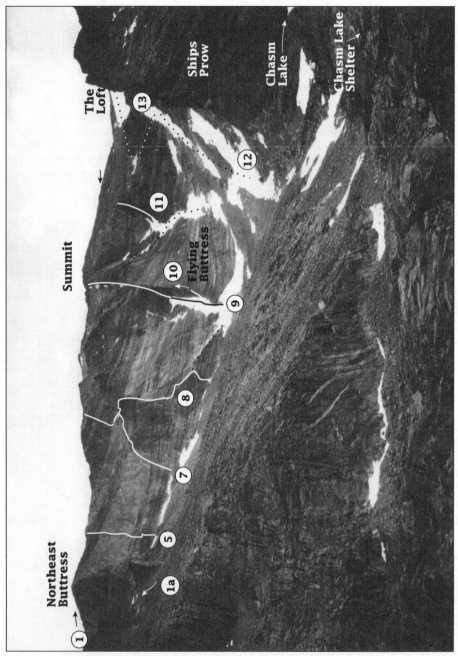

MOUNT MEEKER, NORTH FACE

1	East Ridge Class 3	9	Dream Weaver III AI3 M2+ ★
1a	Iron Gates Class 3	10	Flying Buttress III 9 to 11a ★
5	Concave III 7 A3	11	Dark Star III WI4 M3 ★
7	Sway Back II 7 ★	12	The Loft I Class 3 ★
8	East Arête III 8 ★	13	Loft Ice WI3

MOUNT MEEKER

Mount Meeker (13911) is the second highest summit in Rocky Mountain National Park. Its broad-shouldered mass rises immediately to the southeast of Longs Peak from which it is separated by a high col know as The Loft (c. 13450). Mount Meeker provides a long, easy ascent from any aspect, but its vast north face which, having been carved away by ancient glaciers, is quite steep. The most striking aspect of the north face is the Flying Buttress, a long, narrow rib that climbs directly to the summit. Several hundred feet to the east is another large buttress called the East Arête, apparently named for it relationship to the Flying Buttress. Left of the East Arête, the wall diminishes in height and forms a broad concave face bounded on the east by a prominent buttress. This buttress marks the east side of the north face and forms the right side of the Iron Gates, a passageway between two large rock columns that leads to the east ridge of the mountain.

East Longs Peak Trail. From Estes Park, drive 8.5 miles south on Highway 7 and turn west on a signed road that leads in one mile to the Longs Peak Campground and a ranger station. The trail begins just south of the ranger station and after 0.6 mile goes left at a junction with the Storm Pass Trail. At about 3.2 miles, the trail reaches a junction at Jim's Grove and goes left again. At 4.2 miles a third junction is reached below the east side of Mount Lady Washington. The left branch leads into the Chasm Lake Cirque and ends at a patrol cabin 4.9 miles from the trailhead.

Approach. To reach the north face of Mount Meeker, hike the East Longs Peak Trail to the patrol cabin below Chasm Lake, then hike south up talus or snow for a half mile. The south side may be approached from the Sandbeach Lake Trail (see Wild Basin).

Descent. From the summit, hike west to *The Loft* (see below), then northeast down snow and scree to the large basin below the north face. It also is possible to descend the *East Ridge* route.

1   East Ridge   Class 3

This long summit scramble may be approached from the basin beneath the north face of Meeker or directly from Meeker Park, the latter of which involves considerably more off-trail hiking. From the north basin, make an ascending traverse east across meadows and talus to gain the ridge crest. Hike west along the narrow, slabby ridge, passing any obstacles on the south, and continue to the summit.

1a Iron Gates   Class 3 ★

One may reach the east ridge by ascending a talus gully between two columns of dark rock at the east end of the north face. This is an excellent shortcut and gives the *East Ridge* route more character. The *Iron Gates* is also an important return route for climbs on the east side of the north face.

MOUNT MEEKER, NORTHEAST BUTTRESS, FROM THE NORTHWEST

1a   **Iron Gates Class 3**
3   **Moe Fo II 8+ ★**
4   **Main Vein III 11c ★**

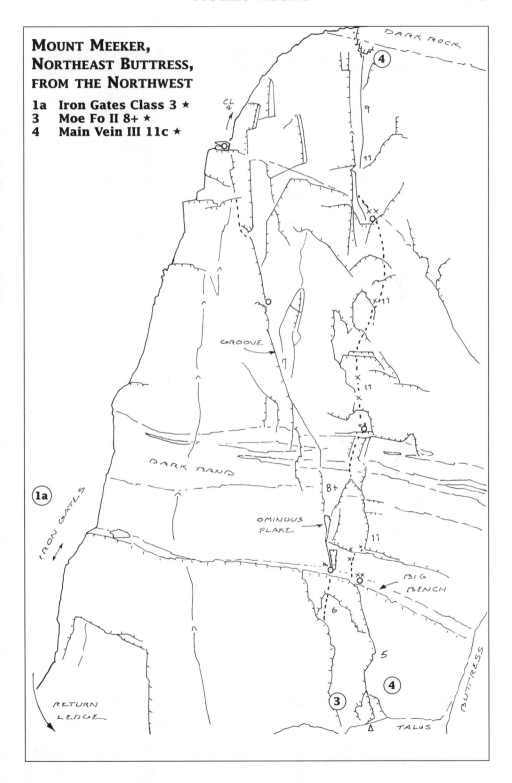

MOUNT MEEKER,
NORTHEAST BUTTRESS,
FROM THE NORTHWEST

1a **Iron Gates Class 3** ★
3   **Moe Fo II 8+** ★
4   **Main Vein III 11c** ★

DARK ROCK

CL 4

GROOVE

DARK BAND

1a

IRON GATES

OMINOUS FLAKE

BIG BENCH

BUTTRESS

8+

RETURN LEDGE

3

4

TALUS

NORTH FACE, LEFT SIDE

The following routes ascend the broad, concave wall between the Northeast Buttress (the right side of the Iron Gates) and the East Arête. Descend all routes via the East Ridge and the Iron Gates, or traverse the summit and descend *The Loft*. Note that a narrow ledge runs across the lower part of the Northeast Buttress and allows an easy return to the bottom of the wall.

2   Sunshine Column   II 9 ★

FA: Chip Salaun and W. Alexander, 1974.

This route ascends the far left side of the north face to the right of the Northeast Buttress and left of *Concave*, at an obvious right-arching flake. The relationship between *Sunshine Column* and the following two routes is not certain.

1. Climb to the top of the flake, go up and left to a ledge, then walk left and belay beside an 8-foot pillar.
2. Climb to the top of the pillar, pass a difficult section, and continue to a belay in a large crack.
3. Climb the crack, go left around a roof, and up to a stance.
4. Work up and right to the ridge crest.

3   Moe Fo   II 8+ ★

FA: Morris "Moe" Hershoff and Forrest Noble, 1994.

Begin at a right-arching, right-facing flake, 20 feet left of *Main Vein* and about 100 feet left of *Concave*.

1. Climb the flake for about 70 feet, then pass an arch and belay on a big ledge (Wall Street) beside an 8-foot pillar (6, 90 feet).
2. Climb the right side of a precarious detached flake (the Pillar of Death), then step left and climb a hand crack (8+) to a big groove. Start up the groove and belay after 150 feet.
3. Continue up the groove past overhanging blocks, then step left and climb a steep, juggy face to a pedestal on the crest of the Northeast Buttress (7, 150 feet).

Scramble to the summit ridge (cl4).

4   Main Vein   III 11c ★

FA: Hershoff, Noble, and Steve McCorkel, 1994. SR plus full set of TCUs and cams up to a #4 Camalot.

Begin about 20 feet right of the preceding route at an obvious right-arching flake and beneath a long, black roof about 120 feet up.

1. Climb to the flake, go up and left to a ledge (Wall Street), and belay at two bolts (6, 95 feet).
2. Step left and turn the big roof, clip a bolt, then traverse up and right past another bolt and gain a shallow right-facing dihedral with a seam. Climb along the seam (crux) followed by a beautiful hand crack, then work up and left to a ledge atop the higher of two dark rock bands (11c, 170 feet).
3. Face climb up and left past two bolts and into the right side of an arch, exit right past a bolt (11c), then work up and right to a ledge with a two-bolt anchor.
4. Climb shallow corners up and left to a large right-facing dihedral that leads to the top of the wall (11b, 150 feet).

5 Concave   III 7 A3
FA: Layton Kor and Larry Dalke, 1967.
This line begins about 100 feet right of the preceding routes. Scramble up talus to a deep indentation just left of a rounded prow of dark rock, and set the belay beneath a right-leaning, left-facing dihedral at right.
1. Climb to a ledge at the top of the dihedral, then make a long traverse left (poor pro) to a good ledge (7, 150 feet).
2. Climb free, then nail expanding flakes to a small ledge (A2, 90 feet).
3. Pass a 15-foot head wall by nailing a difficult crack at left, then continue on aid to a sling belay (A3, 90 feet).
4. Start out on aid and climb a series of left-facing flake/dihedrals to a small ledge, then zigzag up to a big ledge above which a scramble leads to the ridge crest (7 A2, 150 feet).

6 Cobra   III 7 A1
FA: Layton Kor, solo, early 1960s.
This little-known route climbs a long curving flake/ramp system between *Concave* and *Swayback.* Begin at the right of two small, black buttresses at the bottom of the face. Follow the arch up and right to a ledge system high on the wall, then climb straight up to the ridge crest. A bit of aid was employed on the final pitch.

7 Swayback   II 7 ★
FA: Pat Ament and Fred Pfahler, 1964.
This route follows the prominent right-arching corner and ramp between the route *Cobra* and the East Arête and gains the level section atop the buttress, or rappel from fixed anchors.
From the talus, scramble up and right for 180 feet to a giant boulder.
1. Angle up and right for 50 feet, go left over a bulge, then climb straight up for 70 feet to belay on a large flake.
2. Make a delicate traverse up and right across a smooth face, then lieback along the edge of a flake for 90 feet and belay at its top (7, 150 feet).
3. Climb straight up for a long pitch.
4. Scramble up and right over easier terrain to the level section above the East Arête.
5. Work up and slightly right on the head wall to reach the east ridge.

8   East Arête   III 8 ★
FA: Becker, Gorman, and Gustafson, 1955.
This pioneering venture ascends the prow of the left of the two great buttresses on the north face; however, no details of the pitches have been recorded. Reach the prow by hiking up and left along an obvious ramp. Climb about three pitches up the northeast corner of the buttress and gain the level section at its top. Scramble south to the head wall, then climb up and slightly right to the top of the north face.

NORTH FACE, RIGHT SIDE
The following routes are associated with the Flying Buttress or the rugged face to its right.

9 Dream Weaver   III AI3 M2+ ★
Immediately left of the *Flying Buttress* is a steep couloir that provides an excellent ascent directly to the summit. In early summer the couloir

is filled with snow; by September it is bare rock and ice with some chockstones in the mid-section. One may avoid the upper couloir by traversing right through a notch at the level section of the Flying Buttress, then scrambling down on the west side. However, the most interesting part of the route, which includes a 3-foot-wide ribbon of ice at 55 degrees, lies above this point and should not be missed.

10　Flying Buttress　　III 9 to 11a ★

FA: John Reppy, Frank Caray, and Vert Arsegl via the left-most pitches (III 5.8 A1), 1963. Pitch 2d was climbed by Moe Hershoff and George Bell, 1993. Pitch 3c was climbed by Richard and Joyce Rossiter, 1984. Variations on a Theme (pitches 1b, 2a, 3a, 4, and 5b) was pieced together by Kleker, Orey, and Alexander during 1981. There are enough variations of the *Flying Buttress* to contsitute three almost completely separate routes. Who climbed what and when is a bit sketchy.

This classic route ascends the striking, narrow rib that leads directly up the north face to the summit of Mount Meeker. Cross a snow patch at the bottom of the buttress, then scramble up easy rock on the right or left side and gain a ledge at the bottom of the steep, narrow prow.

1a. Climb a dihedral just left of the flat north face of the rib, step right and continue up a V-shaped chimney, then go right up a slab to a ledge (8, 150 feet).

1b. Climb a thin crack near the center of the rib to a stance (10), then follow a seam up the face (crux) to a pedestal at 150 feet or stretch the lead to the next ledge (10c, 165 feet).

1c. Climb a hand crack near the right side of the narrow face (8). When the crack fades, traverse up and left to a stance, then follow a seam up the steep face as for 1b (10c, 165 feet).

1d. Climb a crack system a few feet around on the west side of the rib and belay at the top of the first step (9, 165 feet).

2a. Climb a dihedral on the east side of the rib, traverse left, and climb a short corner to a long ledge with two bolts (9, 150 feet).

2b. Climb difficult thin cracks up the flat face of the rib (10a), continue in a handcrack (8), then step around onto the west side and traverse to an easy corner that leads to the bolt belay (10a, 150 feet). It may be possible to do the whole pitch on the narrow face of the rib.

2c. Traverse out onto the west side to avoid the initial 10a cracks, then cut back left to join the line after about 20 feet.

2d. Climb an overhanging groove on the west side of the rib (10d), turn a roof at two parallel cracks (11a), and continue to the regular belay.

3a. Move up and left from the bolts and jam a 1-inch crack (8), then step left and climb a left-facing dihedral until one is 15 feet below a roof (7). Traverse right past a bolt and climb around the right side of the roof past two pitons (9). Climb up and left onto the face of the rib to a stance at a horizontal crack (125 feet), or run out the rope to a long ledge with some blocks down to the right (165 feet).

3b. Turn the roof on the left in a 3-inch crack and join 3a (9).

3c. From the bolt belay, climb a steep groove on the west side of the rib to a precarious stance with rappel slings (10b, 115 feet). Move up and left and follow another corner to the ledge with blocks (9, 165 feet).

MOUNT MEEKER, FLYING BUTTRESS

9	Dream Weaver III AI3 M2+ ★
10	Flying Buttress III 9 to 11a ★
10a	Direct Finish 10a ★

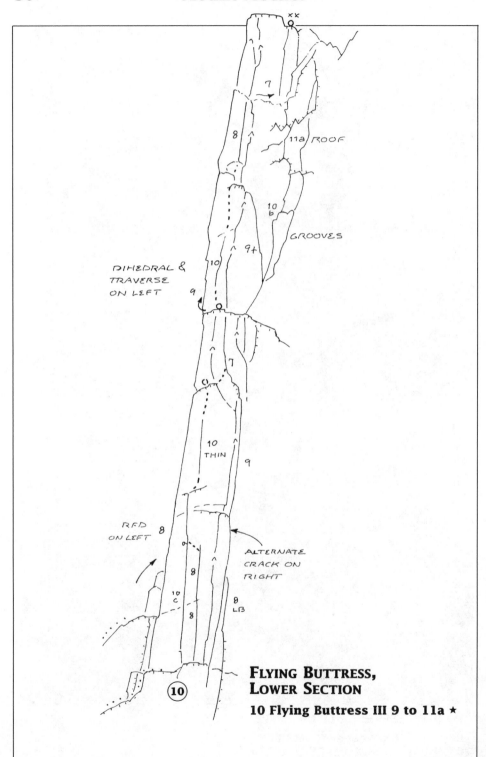

xx

7

8 ^

11a ROOF

10
b

GROOVES

9+

10

DIHEDRAL &
TRAVERSE
ON LEFT

9

7

10
THIN

9

RFD
ON LEFT

8

ALTERNATE
CRACK ON
RIGHT

8

10
c

8
LB

8

(10)

**FLYING BUTTRESS,
LOWER SECTION**

10 Flying Buttress III 9 to 11a ★

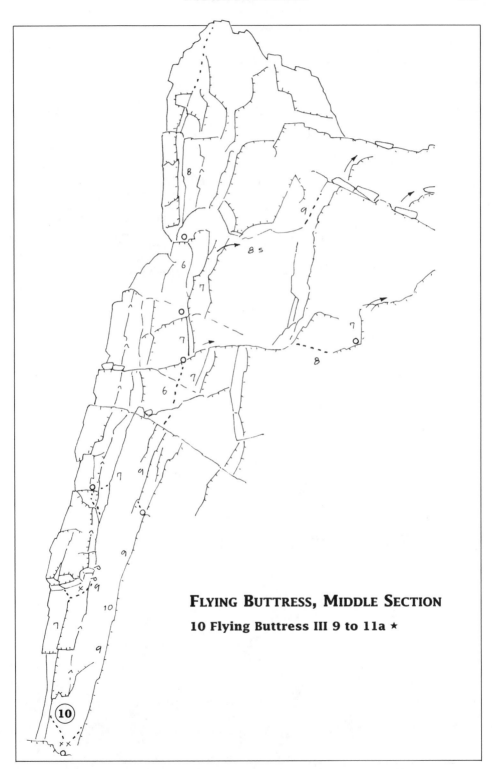

FLYING BUTTRESS, MIDDLE SECTION

10 Flying Buttress III 9 to 11a ★

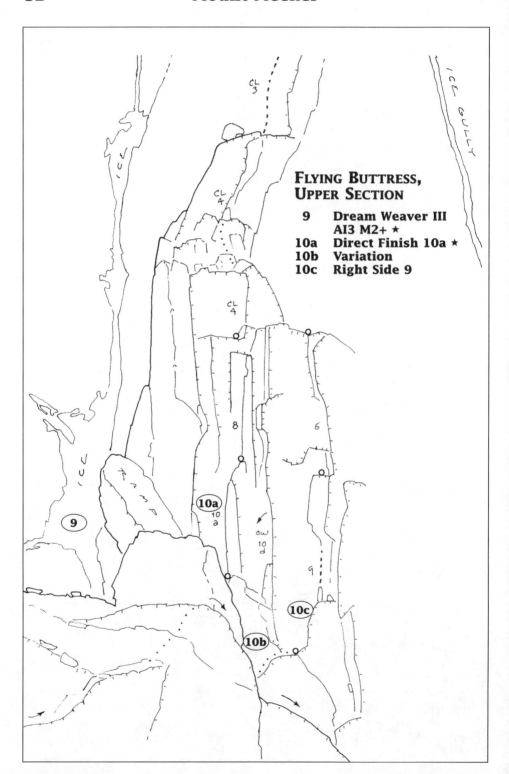

**FLYING BUTTRESS,
UPPER SECTION**

9   Dream Weaver III
      AI3 M2+ ★
10a   Direct Finish 10a ★
10b   Variation
10c   Right Side 9

4a. From the ledge with blocks, continue up a corner system just on the west side of the rib and belay beneath the final steep section (7, 80 feet). See topo for belay alternatives.

4b. Traverse right along the ledge with blocks to the base of a left-facing dihedral (easy).

5a. Follow a diagonal crack up and right to old rappel slings, then climb a vertical dihedral to the top of the rib (8, 100 feet). It is also possible to traverse right from the slings and climb a short corner (9).

5b. Climb the dihedral above the long ledge, then follow a ramp up and right to the level section in the buttress, or traverse right to another dihedral and climb it to the same fate (8, 150 feet).

One can escape the route at the level section by traversing south to a notch and descending slabs and scree to the west and north.

Upper Section. The following three lines have been established on the steep buttress above the level section.

10a Direct Finish   10a ★
FA: Tom Sciolino and Richard Rossiter, 1980.
From the notch at the south end of the level section, scramble up onto a ledge at the base of a steep, left-facing dihedral.

6. Climb the dihedral, then work up and right to a stance and belay (10a, 85 feet).

7. Climb a shallow corner and belay on a ledge (9, 80 feet).

Unrope and scramble several hundred feet up the broad arête to the summit.

10b Variation 10
The very impressive offwidth crack down to the right from the preceding line was climbed to where it bends left (sustained 10) by Jeff Lowe. Five-inch pro would be required to continue upward.

10c Right Side   9
FA: Jeff Lowe and Teri Ebel, 1990s.
Begin a short way down and right from the offwidth crack.

6. Follow discontinuous cracks to a ledge beneath a small roof (9, 85 feet).

7. Traverse right and go around a left-facing corner just below the roof, then follow a crack up and left and belay where the difficulty eases off (7, 100 feet).

11   Dark Star   III WI4 M3 ★
FA: Duncan Ferguson, Harry Kent, and Richard Page.
This route ascends the snow and ice couloir to the right of the Flying Buttress, then climbs four pitches up a chimney on the right. The chimney is behind a rock rib and is not visible until one is high in the couloir. The best conditions are from fall to spring. The steep wall to the right of the chimney sometimes may be climbed under rare conditions. The steep upper gully beside the Flying Buttress also may be climbed, but its rating is not known.

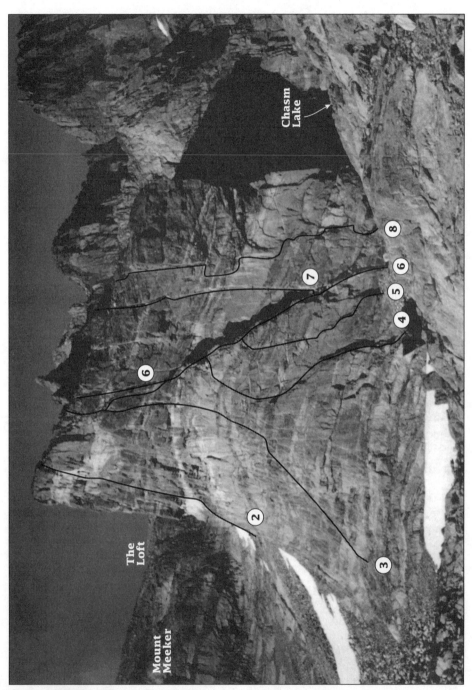

SHIPS PROW, EAST BUTTRESS

2	Nose I 9 ★	6	Stromboli II 7
3	Nexus II 9	7	Portal II 9 ★
4	Half Day's Work II 7 A1	8	Gangplank III 7 A4
5	Old Route II 7		

12 The Loft   I Class 3 ★

The Loft is the broad col between Mount Meeker and Longs Peak. It is easily reached from the shelter cabin by hiking southwest up meadows, then kicking steps up snow to a cliff band. In late summer the snow may be bypassed on the left. To pass the cliff band, scramble up and left along a prominent ramp that is marked with cairns, then work back right and up to the col. From the col, hike south and east to the summit. From The Loft, it is not difficult to reach the summit of Longs Peak via *Clark's Arrow* (page 124).

13 Loft Ice   WI3

The cliff at the top of the summer snowfield provides a nice pitch of water ice during winter.

SHIPS PROW

The Ships Prow is the long ridge between the north cirque of Mount Meeker and the Chasm Lake Cirque. Though the ridge terminates in a commanding buttress above Chasm Lake, it seldom receives more than a lingering glance from climbers due to its dwarfed status beneath the awesome faces of Mount Meeker and Longs Peak. The East Buttress is graced by several routes up to 400 feet high that are well worth the walk.

Approach. Hike the East Longs Peak Trail to the patrol cabin, then hike west up slabs and benches and gain the east shore of Chasm Lake. A short walk south leads to the foot of the east buttress.

Descent. From the top of the wall, scramble down to the west end of Chasm Lake and hike back along the north shore. Or scramble up the ridge for several hundred feet to a notch and escape via ledges that lead down to the talus on the south side.

1 Old Unnamed   II 8

Begin about 150 feet left from the left edge of the east face.
1. Follow thin cracks and corners (old pitons) to a good ledge.
2. Face climb up to the bottom of a corner/gully on the upper wall.
3. Follow the gully to a notch on the ridge crest.

2 Nose   II 9 ★

FA: Bob Kamps and Jack Laughlin, 1960.
This is the longest as well as the best route on the buttress. Begin just around to the south from the left margin of the east face. Angle up and right for three short and easy pitches to reach the east face. Follow a chimney and the broad corner system above to reach the ridge crest.

3 Nexus   II 9

FA: Stan Shepard and James Burbank, 1963.
A broad triangular area in the middle of the east face is defined by two chimney systems: The left holds the route *Nexus* and the right, *Stromboli.* Follow the chimney/couloir along the left edge of the triangle for two pitches and gain some ledges beneath the head wall (about 10 feet left of *Stromboli*). Finish with a steep left-facing dihedral.

4 Half Day's Work   II 7 A1
FA: Bob Bradley and Paul Mayrose, 1960.
Begin at a right-facing corner about 150 feet left of the *Stromboli* corner.
1. Climb moderate rock up the corner (6).
2. Continue up the system to a ledge (7, A1).
3. Work up to the right to join *Stromboli* (6).

5 Old Route   II 7
Locate a left-leaning, right-facing dihedral about 50 feet left from the *Stromboli* dihedral/chimney. Climb the dihedral and a chimney, then work up and right to join *Stromboli* (four pitches).

6 Stromboli   II 7
FA: Lamb, Jackson, and Gorman, 1954.
This early route follows the large dihedral/chimney system that slants up and left across the right side of the east face. Climb two short pitches up this system, then traverse to the left edge of the corner and do two more pitches to a ledge at the base of the head wall. Climb the left of two chimneys to reach the top of the face (7).

6a Step One   9 A4
FA: Pat Ament and Fred Pfahler, 1964.
Begin in a small dihedral about 40 feet left of *Stromboli*.
1. Climb a difficult pitch (9) that zigzags back and forth and belay on the upper of three ledges by a huge block.
2. Nail up the smooth face just left of the block (A4, 50 feet), then angle up and right for 60 feet to join *Stromboli*.

6b. Variation
From the second belay, continue straight up the chimney to a big ledge (7 A1).

6c Variation
Climb the right of the two chimneys at the top of the face (8).

6d Variation
From the ledge at the base of the head wall, traverse left and climb a right-facing dihedral. There also is an aid crack to the right of these variations.

7 Portal   II 9 ★
FA: Stan Shepard and Bob Boucher (II 5.9 A1), 1963.
This route follows the vertical, left-facing dihedral to the right of *Stromboli* and may be the best route on the Ships Prow. Begin in the *Stromboli* chimney.
1. Climb up past grassy ledges and a chockstone, then traverse right to a big ledge at the base of the dihedral (6, 130 feet).
2. Stem and jam the steep corner past some fixed pins to a sloping ledge (9, 100 feet).
3. Continue up the corner to a ledge at the base of a chimney (9, 100 feet).
4. Climb the chimney followed by an overhanging offwidth section and continue to the top of the face (9, 130 feet). It also is possible to climb the face to the left of this last section.

8 Gangplank III 7 A4
FA: Royal Robbins and Pat Ament, 1963.
This route ascends the imposing wall to the right of *Portal*. Begin just right of *Stromboli* and scramble up onto a ledge to belay.

1. Go right 6 feet, then nail a vertical crack to a sloping ledge on the right. Climb free for 15 feet, hand-traverse left, then nail another crack to belay on a narrow ledge.
2. Go left on the ledge for 35 feet, then nail a crack up and right for 75 feet until it is possible to nail left along a groove (A3). After 25 feet, move up to the next groove and belay in slings.
3. Nail straight up the easterly of three white streaks into an overhanging dihedral which is climbed for 30 feet. Exit right (hook) to a sling belay.
4. Climb an easy crack for 90 feet to a good belay at right (6).
5. Work straight up to the top of the wall (7).

9 Flying Dutchman II 4 AI3 or snow ★
This steep 1000-foot couloir splits the broad north face of the Ships Prow and is separated from Lambs Slide by Glacier Ridge. From the west side of Chasm Lake, hike south into the bottom of the couloir (see Approach A under Longs Peak). The crux is a narrow section at 55 degrees about 300 feet before the top of the couloir. By late summer the snow does connect through the crux. The couloir tops out on Lambs Slide about 150 feet southeast of The Loft.

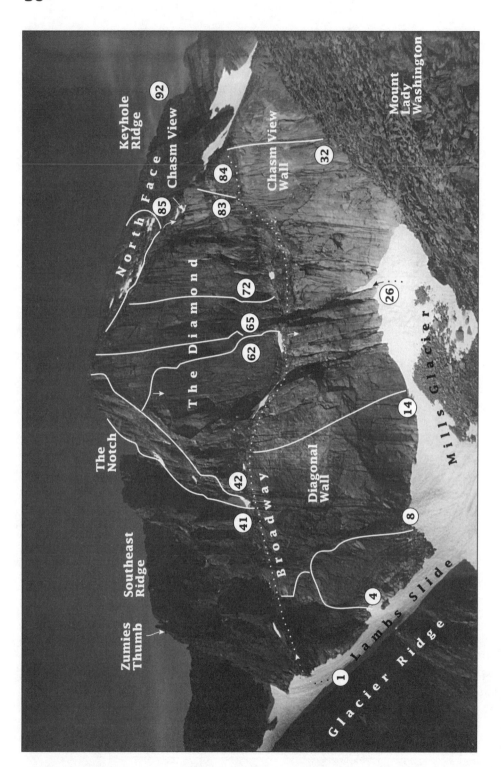

LONGS PEAK

Longs Peak (14255) is the highest summit in Rocky Mountain National Park and perhaps the most characteristic landmark in Colorado. Its broad profile and flat top are visible from points all along the Front Range, though from the southeast, only the top can be seen above Mount Meeker. The first recorded ascent of Longs Peak was made by Major Powell and party during 1868.

This large, complex mountain is impressive from any view, but its most striking aspect is the east face. More than a mile wide and reaching a height of 1900 feet, the east face is home to such legendary features as The Diamond, the Diagonal Wall, and Chasm View Wall, and is the premier arena for extreme alpine rock climbing in North America. High-standard forays such as the *Diagonal, D7,* the *Yellow Wall,* and *King of Swords* are known around the world. Yet, the east face does not lack for high-quality mid-range action, such as *Stettner's Ledges, Directissima,* and the *Casual Route.* Grand mountaineering ventures such as the *Notch Couloir* and *Kiener's* are also on site. Other facets of Longs Peak see less activity, but *The Keyhole,* which spirals around three-quarters of the mountain, is ascended by thousands of people every year.

East Longs Peak Trail. From Estes Park, drive 8.5 miles south on Highway 7 and turn west on a signed road that leads in one mile to the Longs Peak Campground and a ranger station. The trail begins just south of the ranger station and after 0.6 mile goes left at a junction with the Storm Pass Trail. At about 3.2 miles, the trail reaches a junction at Jim's Grove and goes left again. At 4.2 miles a third junction is reached below the east side of Mount Lady Washington. The left branch leads to the Chasm Lake Cirque; the right branch to the Boulderfield.

Approach A: Chasm Lake Trail. From the junction below Mount Lady Washington, follow the left branch for about 0.7 mile to its end at a patrol cabin below Chasm Lake. To reach the east face of Longs Peak, follow a vague path along the north shore of the lake and continue west to the Mills Glacier which lies directly below the great east face. Note the following features: The Diagonal Wall is at left; Chasm View Wall at right. The narrow section

LONGS PEAK, EAST FACE

1	**Lambs Slide II AI2 or snow ★**	
4	**Alexander's Chimney II 5 or M3 ★**	
8	**Stettner's Ledges II 7+ ★**	
14	**Diagonal Super Direct V- 11d ★**	
26	**North Chimney 4 or M2**	
32	**Directissima III 10b ★**	
41	**Notch Couloir III M3 ★**	
42	**Kiener's II Class 4 or M2 ★**	
62	**Casual Route IV 10a (7 s) ★**	
65	**D1 V 12a/b ★**	
72	**King of Swords V 12a (11a s) ★**	
83	**V-Notch Exit II 7 ★**	
84	**Chasm Cut-Off II 7**	
85	**North Face II 4 or M2 ★**	
92	**Keyhole Ridge II 5 ★**	

between is the North Chimney area. Towering above is The Diamond. The long, curving ledge that separates The Diamond from the lower wall is Broadway. At the far left of the basin is the snow couloir of Lambs Slide.

Approach B: Boulderfield Trail. From the junction below Mount Lady Washington, take the right branch which leads in a mile or so to Granite Pass (12090). At the pass is an intersection with the North Longs Peak Trail which begins from the Bear Lake Road. Stay left and continue to the Boulderfield at 5.9 miles. From the Boulderfield, one has access to Chasm View, the north face of Longs Peak, and The Keyhole (6.2 miles).

Descent. The easiest descent from the summit is via *The Keyhole*. Though this is the long way around, it can be done safely without a rope (see page 117). The next easiest is *Clark's Arrow* which does not require a rope, but is steeper and less easy to follow (see page 124). The most efficient descent is the North Face: From the summit of Longs Peak, scramble down the north face to the steep slab just above Chasm View (cl4). Look for a cairn and a large iron eyebolt. This may be reached in a direct line from the summit, or more easily by descending the northwest ridge (upper Keyhole Ridge) for several hundred feet, then curving around eastward to the same point. Rappel 150 feet from the eyebolt to steep snow or talus just above Chasm View. It is possible to rappel 75 feet twice using a second eyebolt halfway down. It also is possible to downclimb the 150-foot slab (4, wet). From here, one may scramble down talus to the Boulderfield or return to the Chasm Lake Cirque via *The Camel*. Note: An ice ax is recommended if the north face is covered with snow.

The Camel (Camel Slide). The Camel is a large block on the ridge crest between Longs Peak and Mount Lady Washington that, viewed from the north or south, resembles a kneeling camel. From Chasm View, hike east for a couple of hundred yards along the crest of the ridge to The Camel, then cross over to the south side of the crest. Work down and east across the south face of Mount Lady Washington to some grassy ledges at the head a scree gully, then follow the gully southwest into the Chasm Lake Cirque.

Order of Routes: Routes are catalogued left to right (counterclockwise) around the mountain beginning with the Lower East face (below Broadway), then left to right across the Upper East Face (above Broadway), followed by the North Face, West Face, Keyboard of the Winds, and the Palisades.

LOWER EAST FACE
The cliff band below Broadway spans nearly a mile and is known collectively as the Lower East face. It is bound on the left (south) by the long snow couloir of Lambs Slide and on the right by the scree gully of The Camel. Notable features from left to right are: Alexander's Chimney, a large funnel-shaped recess; Stettners Buttress, the broad, shallow rib to the right; the Diagonal Wall, the 1000-foot-high oval face below and left of the Diamond; the narrow North Chimney Area directly beneath the Diamond; and Chasm View Wall, the large reddish wall below and right of the Diamond. Note that Broadway does not continue across the top of Chasm View Wall. Use Approach A (above).

Descent. There are several ways to escape from routes ending on Broadway: A. Continue to the summit via a route on the Upper East face. B. Traverse south and descend Lambs Slide. C. Traverse north or south as needed and rappel the *Crack of Delight (*see "Descent" under The Diamond). D. Climb the *V-Notch* to Chasm View (see under The Diamond). E. For routes that top out on the ridge between Longs Peak and Mount Lady Washington, one may descend to the north and hike out via the Boulderfield, or descend *The Camel* and return to the Chasm Lake Cirque. It would be useful to have a rappel route down Stettners Buttress, but if one exists, I am not aware of it.

1   Lambs Slide   II AI2 or snow ★

Lambs Slide is the 1000-foot snow couloir that marks the southern margin of the Lower East Face. It begins from the Mills Glacier and climbs to a point just north of The Loft, the broad col between Longs Peak and Mount Meeker. The left or east side of Lambs Slide is bounded by a rock spur called Glacier Ridge. Lambs Slide is often used to reach Broadway in conjunction with ascents of the *Notch Couloir, Kiener's,* and *The Window.* To reach Broadway, exit right (north) on a broad scree ramp after about 800 feet.

Conditions on Lambs Slide vary greatly with season. In spring soft snow and avalanches are characteristic; during summer, the snow will consolidate and lend to kicking steps; during late summer and fall the couloir will usually hold very hard snow or gully ice. It is possible to climb or descend Glacier Ridge (cl4) as a means of avoiding Lambs Slide, but it is still necessary to cross some 200 feet of snow or ice to connect with Broadway.

2   Glendenning's Arête   II 4

FA: Jack Glendenning and party, 1953.
This route climbs the broken buttress to the left of Alexander's Chimney, the deep recess at the far south side of the Lower East Face. Climb Lambs Slide to the foot of the buttress.
1. Climb a steep dihedral to the left of *Bongalong* to a mossy terrace.
2. Climb the right side of a gully/chimney, cross into a narrow section, then go left below a big block and climb to its top. Work right across the head wall and belay on a ledge with blocks.
3. Climb a slot behind the block, then work up flakes and along the crest to Broadway.

3   Bongalong   II 5 A1

FA: Jerry Brown, Rod Smythe, and party, 1966.
This route begins in the first crack left of Alexander's Chimney.
1. Scramble up easy rock from Lambs Slide, traverse up and right along a big flake, then aid up a wide crack for 10 feet and continue to a belay on a large, sloping ramp.
2. Continue in the same crack system to a large mossy ledge on the prow of the buttress. Finish as for *Glendenning's Arête.*

4   Alexanders Chimney   II 5 or M3 ★

FA: J. W. Alexander, 1922; or possibly Werner Zimmerman, 1919.
Lower East Face. It begins about 500 feet up Lambs Slide and ends on Broadway. It provides an interesting climb in summer or winter and is

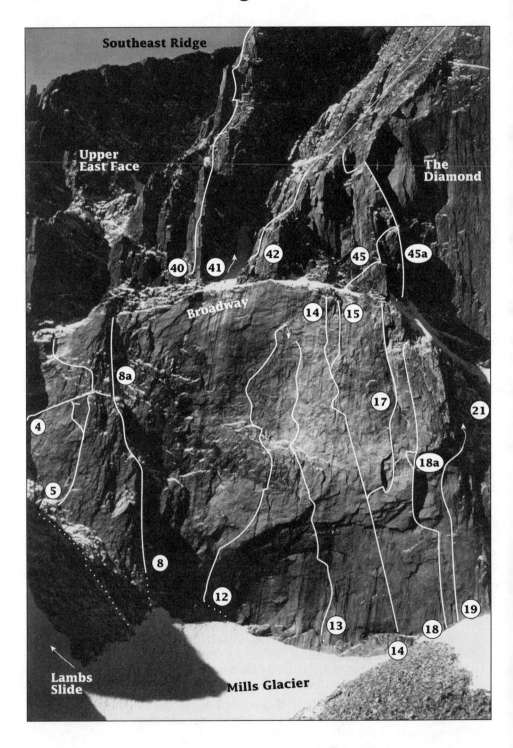

sometimes combined with an ascent of *Eighth Route, Teeter Totter Pillar,* or *The Window.*

Climb Lambs Slide for about 500 feet, then leave the snow and climb a wet gully up to the bottom of the chimney; or from the bottom of Lambs Slide, climb broken ledges along the base of the wall to reach the chimney. Belay on the highest ledge.

1. Climb a short wall through the running water at left (0) or climb a crack to the right (6) and gain a sloping ledge. Stem up the chimney (or climb ice depending on season), then work up to the right and belay about 20 feet below a huge chockstone (5, 150 feet).

2. Work out to the right and gain a prominent ledge called Alexanders Traverse. Traverse right across Stettners Buttress for 150 feet or more and belay behind the last of several flakes (Dog Ears Flake) (cl3, 130 feet).

3. Climb a right-facing dihedral for about 40 feet, then work up and left for about 80 feet and belay on a higher ledge (5).

4. Traverse left for about 75 feet (cl3) into a recessed area that has become known as the Yellow Bowl. Belay here or continue up the left side of the bowl to Broadway (4, 160 feet).

4a Left Detour 5
FA: Wickens and Sharp, 1930.
From the top of the first pitch, traverse out left around the arête and join *Glendennings Arête.*

4b Right Detour 6
FA: Bill Eubank and Brad Van Diver, 1948.
Above the initial steep wall of the first pitch, move right onto a slab and climb a dihedral to Alexanders Traverse.

4c Center 5
FA: Jack Glendenning and Bob Frauson, c. 1950.
Begin as for *Left Detour* but climb a gully in the huge left wall of Alexanders Chimney until a ledge system allows a traverse back right across the chimney, then go up and right into the Yellow Bowl.

4d Trash Patrol 7
Climb ice and snow behind the giant chockstone, then go up and left to its top. Traverse back right and climb a wet, mossy 2-inch crack to a ledge (7, 80 feet). Work up and right and gain the highest ledge above

LONGS PEAK, STETTNERS BUTTRESS AND THE DIAGONAL WALL

4	Alexander's Chimney II 5 or M3 ★	17	Directagonal V- 11c (9 vs) ★
5	Kor's Door II 9 ★	18	Grey Pillar IV 10d s
8	Stettner's Ledges II 7+ ★	18a	A Wee Earl Grey 11c s
8a	Hornsbys Direct Finish 8	19	Shining Slab III 9 ★
12	Question Mark V IIb	21	Field's Chimney I 5
13	Slippery People V 11c A0	40	Teeter Totter Pillar III 8 ★
14	Diagonal Super Direct V- 11d ★	41	Notch Couloir III M3 ★
15	Diagonal Direct V- 11c/d ★	42	Kiener's II Class 4 or M2 ★
		45	The Window III 7 or M4
		45a	Window Direct 7 ★

Stettners Buttress

1   Lambs Slide II AI2 or snow ★
2   Glendenning's Arête II 4
3   Bongalong II 5 A1
4   Alexander's Chimney II 5 or M3 ★
4c   Center 5
4e. Direct Finish 9 M4+
4f   Kuncl Direct 6
5   Kor's Door II 9 ★
6   Malander's Passage II 9 ★

7   Tight Squeeze II 7
8   Stettner's Ledges II 7+ ★
8a   Hornsby's Direct Finish 8

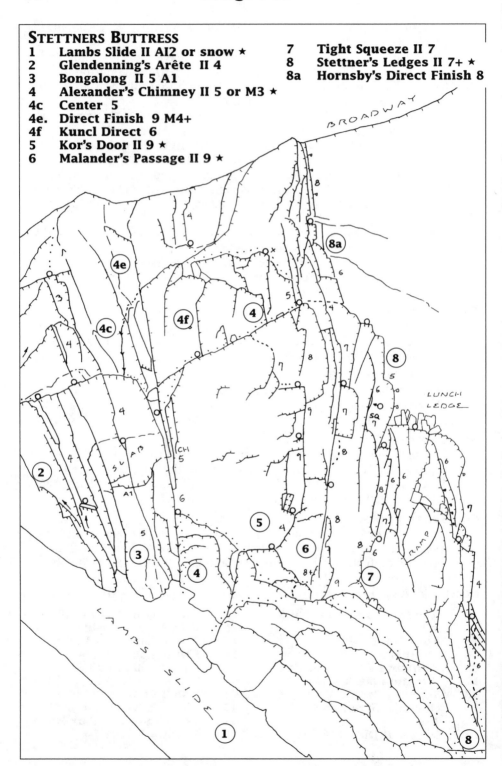

the chimney (5, 70 feet), then traverse right into the Yellow Bowl (4, 60 feet) and climb to Broadway (4). This variation has gained popularity as a winter ascent when the back of the chimney is filled with ice.

4E Direct Finish   9 M4+
FA: John Marrs, Steve Morris, and Dan Bankard, 1987. SR to a #2 Friend plus a selection of pins and ice screws.
This winter variation continues straight up to Broadway where *Trash Patrol* traverses off to the right. Climb out onto the left wall, turn the corner (8, mixed), and go straight up to a large alcove. Traverse right on a 12-inch sloping ledge for 25 feet to a large, loose flake (8, scary). Go right past the flake, then climb straight up to Broadway.

4F Kuncl Direct   6
FA: Ernie Kuncl and John Deeming, 1959.
This route is the logical continuation of *Right Detour*. From the first 30 feet of Alexanders Traverse, climb a flake and lieback along a clean left-facing dihedral to a small stance. Continue up the face to the Yellow Bowl.

STETTNERS BUTTRESS
This is the broad and shallow buttress between Alexanders Chimney and The Diagonal Wall. One must cross the Mills Glacier to reach the toe of the buttress.

5 Kor's Door   II 9 ★
FA: Layton Kor and Jonathan Hough, 1958.
This is an excellent route up the clean face between Alexanders Chimney and Stettners Ledges.
Approach as for *Stettner's Ledges* and scramble to a good ledge beneath a large rectangular inset in the lower third of the face.
1. From the right end of the ledge, climb a curving, left-facing corner and belay at the bottom of the inset (4).
2. Climb the left-facing dihedral formed by the right side of the inset, turn the roof at its top (9), and belay 10 feet higher on a 3-inch ledge.
3. Climb up to the next roof which is turned on the right, then continue up for about 20 feet to a good ledge on the left (9).
4a. From the left end of the ledge, climb right-facing corners, then angle up and left to the long traverse on *Alexander's Chimney* and finish as for that route (7, 120 feet).
4b. From the right end of the ledge, climb a right-facing dihedral, then work up and left to the end of Alexanders Traverse (8, 130 feet).
5. and 6. Finish with *Alexander's Chimney*.

6 Malander's Passage   II 9 ★
FA: John and Jim Melander, 1963.
This route follows a clean crack and dihedral system about 30 feet to the right of *Kor's Door*.
From Lambs Slide, scramble up to the next ledge down and right from *Kor's Door*.
1a. Begin about 40 feet up and left from the bottom of the crack system. Work right across a ledge, then face climb down and right (8+) to

gain a right-leaning dihedral that is climbed to gain the main crack. Jam up the crack (8) and belay at a stance just below a roof that cuts across to *Kor's Door*.

1b. Climb straight up the crack from its bottom to the same belay (9, 150 feet).

2. Jam the crack past a roof on the right and belay on a large ledge (8, 150 feet).

3. Climb a right-facing dihedral to the end of Alexanders Traverse (7, 120 feet).

4. and 5. Finish with *Alexander's Chimney*.

7 Tight Squeeze   II 7
FA: Paul Mayrose and Bob Bradley, 1962.
This route ascends a prominent right-facing dihedral system between *Malanders Passage* and *Stettner's Ledges*.

Approach as for *Stettner's Ledges* but angle up and left along the ledges until below a right-facing corner with a stepped roof.

1. Climb the face at right to get started, then work around the right side of the roof (6) and continue to a good ledge. The first ascent climbed through the roof (A1 or 8), then apparently cut back right to the ledge.

2a. Lieback up a corner for 15 feet (7), go right over a flake, then climb a shallow, right-facing dihedral for about 80 feet and traverse left to a small ledge.

2b. The first ascent took a more direct line up a steep dihedral to the same ledge (8); look for some old pitons on the upper part of the pitch.

3. Climb up and left from the belay and climb the *Tight Squeeze* chimney to a tight belay in the chimney (4, 75 feet).

4. Squeeze up the chimney for about 20 feet, then climb the face at either side. Follow the crack that continues from the chimney to the top of the fourth pitch of *Stettner's Ledges* (6, 130 feet).

5. and 6. Finish as for *Stettner's Ledges* (see below).

8 Stettner's Ledges   II 7+ ★
FA: Paul and Joe Stettner, 1927.
This famous route follows the long system of right-facing dihedrals that defines the boundary between Stettners Buttress and The Diagonal Wall. It was a visionary climb at the time of its first ascent and today is one of the most popular technical climbs on Longs Peak.

Kick steps up the Mills Glacier about 200 feet right of Lambs Slide, then scramble up broken rock to the highest ledge beneath some right-facing dihedrals.

1. Climb a corner on the left (4) or right (6) to get started, then move right into a right-facing dihedral and climb to a small ledge with a fixed pin (6, 150 feet).

2. Climb around the right side of a flake, then go up a right-facing dihedral to a big ledge with a large flake (4, 90 feet).

3a. From the alcove formed by the flake, climb a steep corner with fixed pins (crux, often

DIAGONAL WALL, LEFT SIDE
8   Stettner's Ledges II 7+ ★
9   Striped Wall IV 8 A4
10 Smear of Fear III WI6 M5
11 Anti-Nuclear Tide V 10d A4+
12 Question Mark V 2b
13 Slippery People V 2c A0

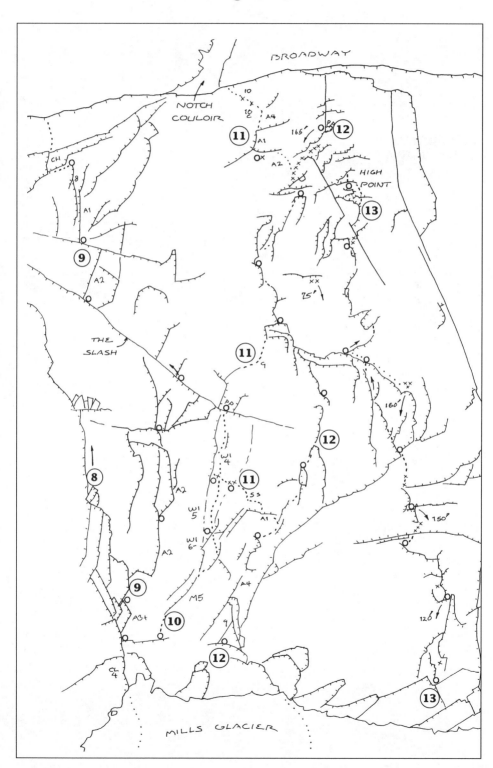

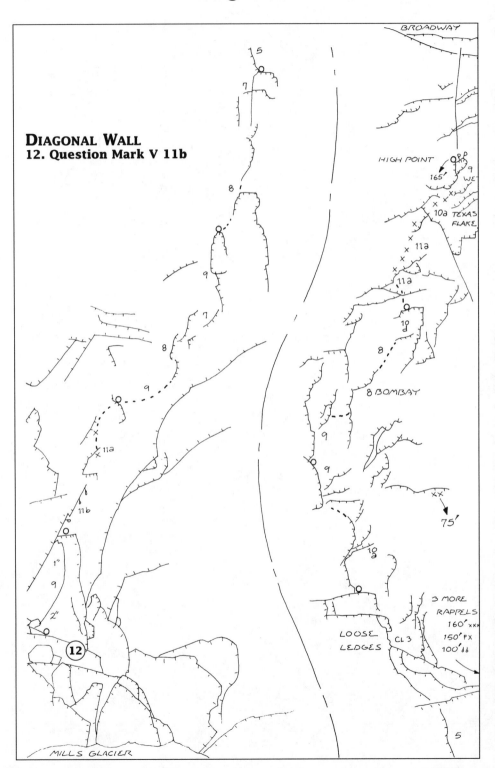

DIAGONAL WALL
12. Question Mark V 11b

wet) and continue up a shallow dihedral with a 2-inch crack. Belay on Lunch Ledge, a large terrace studded with big blocks. This lead is called the Piton Ladder (7+, 140 feet).

3b. From the right side of the big flake, climb a dihedral on the right all the way to Lunch Ledge (8).

3c. Climb the first 12 feet of the Piton Ladder, then swing left around the arête and climb ten feet to a grassy ledge (8). Continue up and left and climb to the top of a slab (6), then work right into the last 15 feet of the regular pitch.

4. Move the belay to the south end of Lunch Ledge. Climb a corner or steep flakes at left, then work up and left to belay on a ledge about 40 feet from the end of Alexanders Traverse (5). It is also possible to continue across to the end of the traverse.

5. and 6. Finish as for *Alexanders Chimney.*

8A Hornsby's Direct Finish   8
FA: Hornsby and Walton, 1949. This finish makes the climb a grade III.

5. From the top of the fourth pitch, follow shallow dihedrals up to a small ledge below a steeper section (6, 120 feet).

6. Follow a right-facing dihedral past a roof and many fixed pins to Broadway (8, 140 feet). The dihedral just to the left also may be climbed and is slightly more difficult.

DIAGONAL WALL
This is the massive oval wall between Stettners Buttress and Fields Chimney. Descend via the Crack of Delight.

9 Striped Wall   IV 8 A4
FA: Layton Kor and Wayne Goss, 1965.

This route begins in a right-facing dihedral system to the right of *Stettner's Ledges* and just left of the water streaks that run down from the Notch Couloir. It is exposed to rockfall from the couloir and is seldom climbed.

1. Scramble up into the dihedral, aid for 30 feet, and belay (A3+).

2. Work up and right beneath a roof, then climb a vertical right-facing dihedral and belay where it branches (A2).

3. Climb the right dihedral, go up and left along a ramp, then up and right to a ledge (A2).

4. Climb up and right (free and aid) and gain the Slash, a long fault that angles up and left to the Hornsby dihedral, then follow it up to the left and belay where it forms a ledge.

5. Continue up the Slash to a right-facing dihedral.

6. Climb the dihedral, then work up and left along another dike/fault and belay beneath a long, right-facing, left-leaning dihedral.

7. Start with a crack, then climb the dihedral and belay at its highest point beneath a long roof.

8. Climb down to the left for about 30 feet (7), then up and left to a chimney behind a right-facing flake which is followed to Broadway.

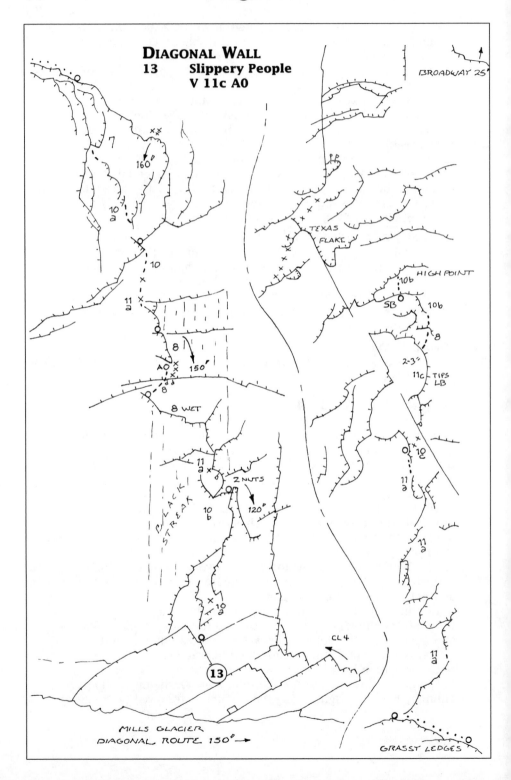

DIAGONAL WALL
13   Slippery People
V 11c A0

10 Smear of Fear III WI6 M5
FA: Jeff Lowe, Duncan Ferguson, and Malcom Daly, 1986.
Climbers have complained that this route was not in shape when they went up to do it, but not in shape *is* in shape for this route! Begin up on a ledge at the start to the *Striped Wall.*
1. Angle up and right beneath a right-leaning roof dihedral to reach the main flow. Climb very difficult ice over a bulge and belay (M5 WI6-).
2. Climb straight up and belay in a large right-facing corner (WI5).
3. Climb relatively moderate ice to a ledge at mid-face (WI4).
Make three long rappels from fixed anchors to the Mills Glacier.

11 Anti-Nuclear Tide V 10d A4+
FA: Jim Beyer, solo, 1987. SR to 4 inches plus an assortment of pins, hooks, Copperheads, et cetera.
This aid climb was established about two weeks before McGee and Kor put up the *Question Mark*, the latter of which shares the first two and a half pitches. Eight bolts are in place. Begin as for the *Question Mark*, but on the third lead, make a traverse left to a stance with two bolts. From here, the route goes up and a bit right via flakes and short corners (mixed free and aid). The last pitch begins from a sling belay (one bolt) beneath a conspicuous roof and right-facing dihedral high on the wall just right of the water streaks from the Notch Couloir.

12 Question Mark V 11b
FA: Layton Kor and Dan McGee, 1987. FFA: Greg Davis and Todd Bibler, 1990.
This is a free version of the aid route of the same name (V 10 A4). The last pitch to Broadway has not been free climbed. The rejected options were to lead up a wide crack full of alpine flowers and mosses or to climb the featureless wall at its left via a bolt ladder. To escape from the last belay, make six, long rappels back down to the Mills Glacier. A long, arching roof marks the lower third of the wall. Begin up on flake ledges just left from the left end of the arches. Eight pitches.

13 Slippery People V 11c A0
FA: Greg Davis and Todd Bibler, 1988.
This route begins from flake ledges beneath the center of the arching roofs, several hundred feet right from the *Question Mark*. The first three pitches climb up through a broad black streak that is another point of identification. Above the arches, the route trends slightly left along right-facing flakes and corners to the long, grassy ledges at mid-face. From here, continuously difficult climbing goes straight up for two more pitches to a sling belay beneath a roof. This is the high point of the route which is about a rope length down and right from the high point of the *Question Mark*. Seven pitches. Rappel as shown in the topo.

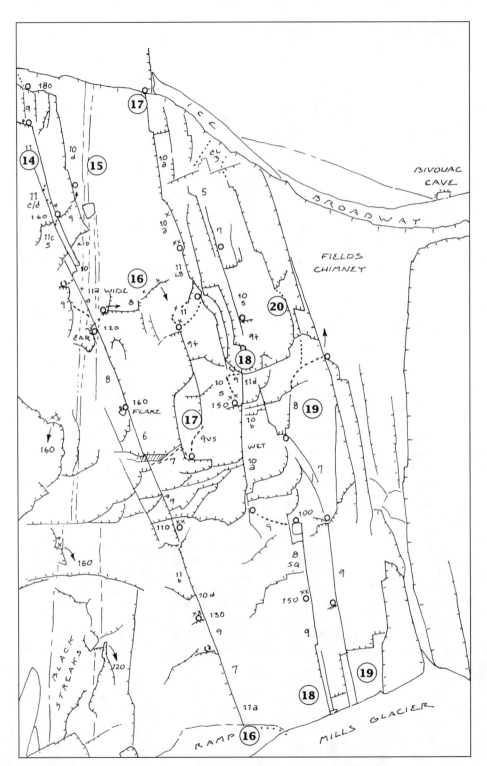

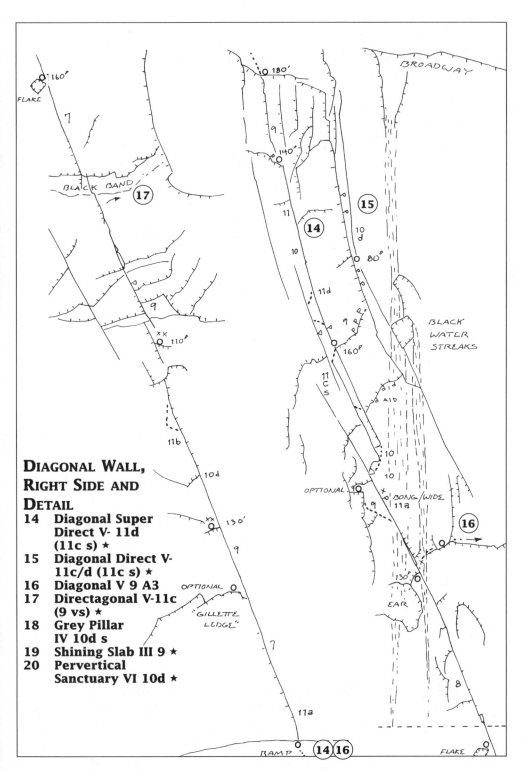

DIAGONAL WALL, RIGHT SIDE AND DETAIL

14   **Diagonal Super Direct V- 11d (11c s) ★**

15   **Diagonal Direct V-11c/d (11c s) ★**

16   **Diagonal V 9 A3**

17   **Directagonal V-11c (9 vs) ★**

18   **Grey Pillar IV 10d s**

19   **Shining Slab III 9 ★**

20   **Pervertical Sanctuary VI 10d ★**

THE DIAGONAL AREA

The following four routes ascend the long diagonal crack system and adjacent dihedrals along the right side of the Diagonal Wall. *Super Direct, Diagonal Direct,* and *Directagonal* are actually variations of the original *Diagonal,* but since any of them can be approached as complete routes in themselves, they are listed as such.

14   Diagonal Super Direct   V- 11d (11c s) ★

During the summer of 1987, Roger Briggs and Chip Chase climbed the *Diagonal* crack system without any detours all the way to Broadway. This was the last of all the variations to the original route and the only one to stay with the crack. It is in a sense the true *Diagonal* and is the recommended version of the route. Briggs and Chase speculated that this was the line Kor had followed in 1963, but this is not supported by the description in Walter Fricke's guide book. The long and beautiful final pitch, which was likely unclimbed previously, is the crux of the route. Their ascent required five and a half hours.

15   Diagonal Direct   V- 11c/d (11c s) ★

FA: Layton Kor and Tex Bossier, 1963. FFA: Jeff Achey and Charlie Fowler, 1980.

This variation to the original route follows *The Diagonal* crack system for five pitches, then makes a rightward traverse into a long, right-facing dihedral that is followed to Broadway. The traverse on the first ascent nailed right beneath an arch; the free version takes a higher line as shown in the topo.

16   Diagonal   V 9 A3

FA: Ray Northcutt and Layton Kor, 1959.

This historic route ascends the long diagonal crack system to the right of the arching roofs. It was the first major wall climb completed on the east face of Longs Peak and set the ground for the first ascent of the Diamond a year later. The original line is marked on the topo, but is rarely climbed. It follows the long diagonal crack for four pitches, then breaks right across the wall to gain a large, left-facing dihedral that is followed to Broadway. The key traverse begins at a small, diagonal roof where the crack crosses the first of two long water streaks. Look for a bolt up and right from the roof. Climb right across the water streak (9) and belay on a good ledge. Traverse right along the ledge, go up along a flake, then up and right to a bolt anchor. Rappel 50 or 60 feet and swing right to a small ledge where the line is joined by the *Directagonal.*

17   Directagonal   V- 11c (9 vs) ★

FFA/FA: Roger and Bill Briggs, 1977.

This is the first free version of The Diagonal, which breaks right lower on the wall and rejoins the original route after the rappel/pendulum. Climb the first pitch and a half of the regular line, then traverse right at a dark band (7), and proceed as shown in the topo.

18 Grey Pillar   IV 10d s
FA: Layton Kor and Tex Bossier (V 5.7 A4), 1963. FFA: John Bragg and Bill Briggs, 1978.
The funnel-shaped Fields Chimney marks the right end of The Diagonal Wall. About midway between *The Diagonal* route and the chimney, two crack systems run up the wall toward a large roof; the *Grey Pillar* takes the left of the two cracks. The crux fourth pitch is poorly protected.

18A A Wee Earl Grey   11c s
FA: Derek Hersey and Bobby Campbell, 1991.
From the bolt belay atop the third pitch, climb a thin crack straight up and join the regular line at the roof. This is the original aid line.

19 Shining Slab   III 9 ★
FA: Stan Shepard and John Burbank (IV 5.7 A2), 1963. FFA: unknown.
This route takes the clean crack system about 20 feet right of the *Grey Pillar*. There are six pitches with the last two up the left side of the Fields Chimney.

20 Pervertical Sanctuary   VI 10d ★
FA: Ron Olevsky and Bob Dobbs (original rating unknown), winter, 1974. FFA: unknown.
This is the lower section of the acclaimed Diamond route of the same name. The first ascent is thought to have begun with the first three pitches of the *Shining Slab,* then passed through a break in the right side of the big roofs and finished in the left-facing dihedrals to the right of the *Grey Pillar.*

CENTRAL CHIMNEYS
To the right of the Diagonal Wall and directly beneath The Diamond, is an area of chimneys and cracks.

21 Field's Chimney   I 5
FA: Ernie Field and Warren Gorell, 1936.
This is the large, funnel-shaped chimney to the right of the Diagonal Wall. Though the climbing is only slightly more difficult than that in the *North Chimney,* frequent rockfall makes the route dangerous and perhaps a poor choice as a means of reaching Broadway. Where the chimney branches, about 300 feet up, climb the left side.

21A Right Field's   6
Take the right branch in the chimney; some old pitons may be found.

21B Weeding's Detour   6
FA: Weeding, Auten, and Graves, 1952.
From the branch in the chimney, traverse out left onto the slabs and climb up to a crack/dihedral which is followed to the huge roof of the *Shining Slab*. Pass the roof on the right and continue to Broadway.

22 Craig's Crack   II 8
FA: Bob Craig, Roger Whitney, and Hassler Whitney, 1952.
About 50 feet right of *Field's Chimney,* two parallel crack/dihedrals run straight up to Broadway. This route ascends the left system.

Cross Mills Glacier, then scramble up onto a ledge; in early season, the snow may extend up to this ledge. Work up and right to gain the chimney and follow it for several pitches to Broadway. The chimney varies in width from 2 to 5 feet; its challenges include two chockstones qnd two roofs, and it is likely to be wet. The first ascent party climbed left out of the chimney at a point about halfway between the first and second roofs, went around the left side of a large bulge passing very near to Field's Chimney, then went back right into the upper chimney. Subsequent ascents have stayed with the chimney.

23 Overhang Dihedral   III 10c ★
FA: Layton Kor and Pat Ament (III 5.7 A3), 1964. FFA: unknown.
This route ascends the large left-facing dihedral just right of *Craig's Crack*.
Scramble up onto the ledge at the bottom *Craig's Crack* and traverse 15 feet right to the dihedral.
1. Climb the dihedral and belay in slings about 30 feet beneath the first big roof.
2. Climb up through the roof and continue up the dihedral to a sling belay beneath a small roof or "nose."
3. Turn the nose and continue up the dihedral until it is possible to move left and belay on a narrow ledge about 50 feet below the second large roof.
4. Climb the steep dihedral to the upper roof, pass it on the right, and climb another 60 feet to belay.
5. A moderate lead ends on Broadway.

24 Crack of Delight   II+ 7
FA: Layton Kor and Tex Bossier, 1963.
This route ascends a flower-filled crack and chimney system about 200 feet right of *Overhang Dihedral*.
1. Climb the initial crack (6) and continue through some wet chimneys to a belay on a grassy stance beneath a small roof (7, 140 feet).
2. Work up and left, then step right above the roof and climb a crack and chimney to a tiny stance (7, 100 feet).
3. Traverse left about 30 feet and climb a patch of vegetation; continue up a smooth, steep chimney, finish on the slab at left, and belay on a good ledge (7, 130 feet).
4. Continue up the crack/chimney and belay in a large, grassy alcove (7, 120 feet).
5. Climb out of the alcove (the left side is 3; the right side is 7) and continue over easier ground to Broadway (3 or 7, 150 feet).

25 La Dolce Vita   VI 8 A4
FA: Charlie Fowler and Renatto Casaratto, 1984.
This is the lower section of an aid climb that ascends the entire east face from the Mills Glacier. Climb the first two pitches of *Crack of Delight*, but where that route goes left, continue straight up the dihedral. Eventually veer right and climb the upper *North Chimney* to Broadway. *La Dolce Vita* has been published elsewhere as a winter climb and the first grade VI route on the east face, however, according to Charlie Fowler, the route was climbed in June. Note that The Diamond

Michael Gilbert on pitch 3 of *Eroica*.   Photo: Roger Briggs.

route *Pervertical Sanctuary* was begun from the Mills Glacier during the winter of 1974; the original rating is unknown but the ascent would have been a grade VI.

26 North Chimney   4 or M2

FA: E. H. Bruns and W. F. Ervin, 1925; according to Walter Fricke, it was soloed by Bruns, 1925.

This is the conspicuous, deep chimney beneath the center of The Diamond — the right of two large chimneys, the left being Fields. A 150-foot snow tongue protrudes up into its lower third from the Mills Glacier. The *North Chimney* offers the most direct moderate approach to routes on The Diamond but is made less attractive by the necessity of snow travel and random rockfall. It is steep and wet with loose rock and has been the scene of some nasty accidents. The chimney is often soloed to save time but conditions and experience may warrant belays.
1. When the snow is soft, climb the snow tongue for 150 feet and belay in a chimney. The buttress at left also may be climbed (cl4).
2. Climb the chimney and a wet face to a big block that is passed on the left, then go up a broader face to a loose bench (cl4, 130 feet).
3. From the top of the bench climb about 60 feet to a higher bench, then climb the head wall (straight ahead or on the left) to Broadway (4, 130 feet).
One also may climb the steeper wall farther to the left where the rock is solid, but this may be as hard as 9.

CHASM VIEW WALL

Chasm View Wall is the broad reddish face to the right of the North Chimney. The top of the 600-foot wall forms the connecting ridge between Longs Peak and Mount Lady Washington.

Approach. Hike in via the East Longs Peak Trail and take the left branch into the Chasm Lake Cirque. Hike over boulders along the north shore of the lake, then contour around to the far north side of the Mills Glacier. Scramble up talus or snow to the bottom of the wall. Most of the routes begin from a long ramp that angles up and right into the middle of the face.

Descent. For routes that finish on Broadway, the easiest return to the bottom of the wall is to rappel the *Crack of Delight* (see under The Diamond). For routes that finish on the ridge crest, return to Chasm Lake Cirque via *The Camel* (see under Longs Peak). See also the *V-Notch Exit* under The Diamond.

27 Eclipse   II 10a ★

FA: Pat Ament and Bob Boucher (III 9 A1), 1963. FFA: Beyer and Casey, 1991.

This route ascends the smooth striped slab to the right of the North Chimney. Begin about 150 feet right of the North Chimney; scramble up onto a ledge and belay at its right end beneath a shallow left-facing, left-arching dihedral.

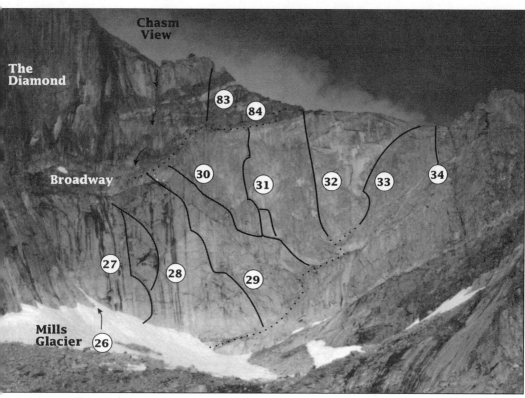

CHASM VIEW WALL

26	North Chimney 4 or M2	31	Red Wall III 10a ★
27	Eclipse II 10a ★	32	Directissima III 10b ★
28	Zigzag II 8 A2	33	Indirectissima II 9
29	Invisible Wall IV 7 A4	34	Van Divers Fantasy I 6
30	Tip Toe III 7	83	V-Notch Exit II 7 ★
		84	Chasm Cut-Off II 7

28   Zigzag   II 8 A2

FA: Layton Kor and Tex Bossier, 1963.

This route begins with the fist pitch of *Eclipse* but breaks right and passes the big roofs on the right.

29   Invisible Wall   IV 7 A4

FA: Layton Kor and Larry Dalke, 1965. SR plus a selection of pins and hooks.

Identify a distinct fault/dike that angles up and left to the north end of Broadway. This route goes up and left across the lower left side of Chasm View Wall and finishes along this fault.

Start up the long ramp that leads into the middle of the face and belay at the bottom of a reddish, left-facing dihedral that curves up and left toward a square-cut roof and dihedral.

1. Climb an orange left-facing dihedral and belay at its top (8, 140 feet).

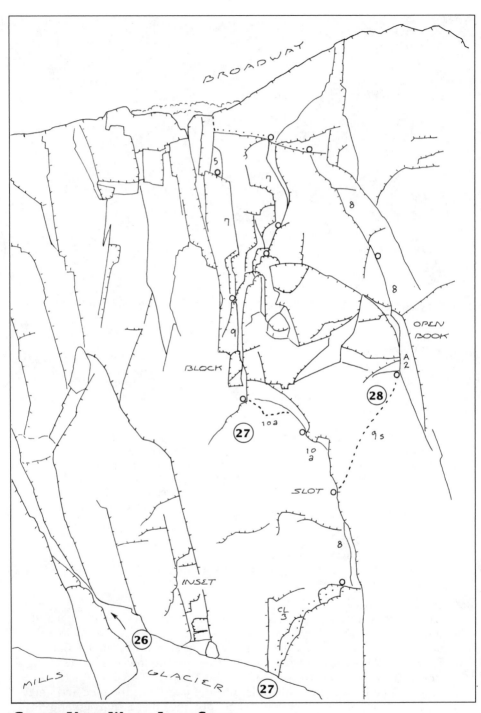

CHASM VIEW WALL, LEFT SIDE
26   **North Chimney 4 or M3**
27   **Eclipse II 10a ★**
28   **Zigzag II 8 A2**

2. Continue up and left and belay on a slab beneath the big square-cut roof (7, 120 feet).

3. Climb up to the roof and traverse left around it to a clean 90 dihedral at the top of a slab.

4. Climb the dihedral, first free then on aid and belay near its top (A1, 60 feet).

5. Continue up the corner (A3), then tension traverse left and nail an arch to the bottom of a dihedral (A3). Aid up the corner until an adequate anchor allows a belay (A3, 150 feet). This can be done as two pitches.

6. Continue up the dihedral past a small roof, then follow a good crack up and right to a grassy alcove.

7. Traverse left around a corner, then climb 20 feet (A4; rurps and hooks) to gain the diagonal fault.

8. Hand traverse left, then walk to Broadway.

AA Royal Flush   IV 11c ★

FA: Bernard Gillett, Jerry Hill, and Scott Ahlgren, 1993.

This route begins as for *Invisible Wall,* crosses *Tip Toe,* then finishes with beautiful right-facing dihedrals in the upper wall.

1. Climb the first pitch of *Invisible Wall,* an orange, left-arching left-facing dihedral, and belay at its top (8).

2. Follow cracks up and left to a roof as for *Invisible Wall,* but jam a hand crack through the right side of the roof (8), and belay at the bottom of a slot.

3. Squeeze up the slot and a strenuous finger/hand crack (10b), then traverse right via knobs (9s) and belay at a flake.

4. Climb a dihedral to a diagonal roof. Climb up and left beneath the roof (8) to a fault line on *Tip Toe,* go up a broken dihedral system, and belay on any of several ledges.

5. Scramble up and left along the big ramp on *Tip Toe,* then climb up to a stance at the bottom of a long right-facing dihedral (6).

6. Stem up the beautiful dihedral (10a), exit left, climb 15 feet, then traverse left 20 feet to the right end of a small roof (#2 Friend to protect second). Move down and left ten feet and belay.

7. Climb around the left side of the roof and follow a thin crack (11c with good stopper placements) to a ramp. Go up and left along the ramp, then straight up to a big grassy ledge that is the right end of Broadway.

Reach the crest of Chasm View Wall via the *V-Notch* or *Chasm Cutoff.* One may also traverse south along Broadway (beyond the North Chimney) and rappel the *Crack of Delight.*

30 Tip Toe   III 7

FA: Cecil Oulette and Dick Woodford, 1956.

This unusual route takes a slowly rising traverse from the grassy benches below the middle of the wall to the north end of Broadway. The first pitch is the same as for the *Red Wall.*

From the Mills Glacier, scramble up the big ramp for about 600 feet to some grassy benches from which a smooth grey ramp angles up to the left. Walk up the ramp 30 or 40 feet to set the first belay.

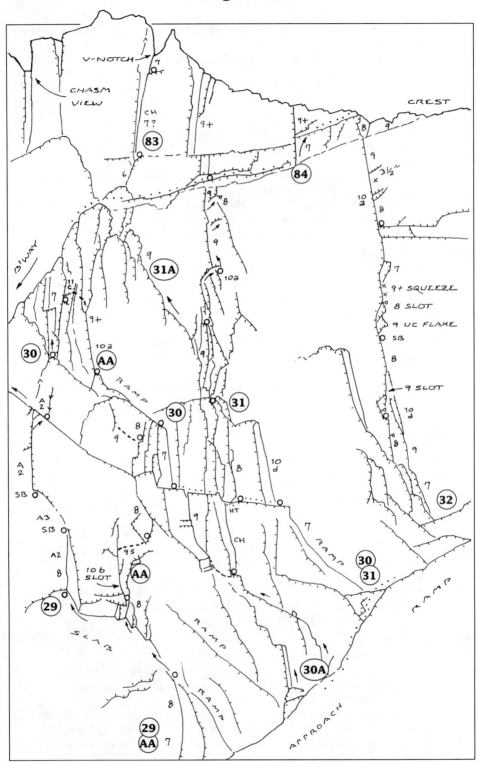

1. Climb the steepening ramp to a big ledge, then walk left 50 feet to an undercut right-facing dihedral (7, 150). The second pitch of the *Red Wall* starts here.
2. Hand traverse around the bottom of the arête, go up a ramp, then continue left via another hand traverse to a spacious, grassy ledge (100 feet).
3. Go around the corner to the left, then climb short corners up and left to a higher ledge system.
4. Follow this system up and left and belay on a sloping ledge.
5. Go easily up and left beneath some steep corners and belay at the bottom of a large right-facing dihedral with two wide cracks.
6. Climb the right handcrack for 25 feet, then change to the left crack and climb to its top (7). An easy ramp leads down and left to Broadway.

30a Big Toe   9
FA: Harvey Carter and John Auld, 1959.
Begin about 50 feet up and right from *Invisible Wall* at a big flake along the base of the wall. Traverse left along an easy ramp and belay beneath a chimney in a right-facing dihedral. Go up a slab around to the left, climb a short vertical wall, then work up a large right-facing dihedral to a spacious ledge at the end of the second pitch of *Tip Toe.* Harvey Carter's description suggests that the route finishes in a shallow, right-facing dihedral above and right of the fifth pitch of the regular route.

31 Red Wall   III 10a ★
FA: Layton Kor and Tex Bossier, 1963. FFA: unknown.
This route is very steep and continuously interesting. Identify a series of right-facing flake-dihedrals to the left of the more obvious *Directissima* in the center of the wall (below).
From the north side of Mills Glacier, scramble up a ramp to the grassy ledges in the middle of the wall (cl4). A smooth grey ramp slants up to the left. Hike about 40 feet up the ramp and belay.
1. Climb to the top of the ramp, then traverse 50 feet left and belay at the bottom of an undercut right-facing dihedral (7, 150 feet).
2a. Climb a handcrack up the dihedral and a wide section to a grassy ledge, then scramble up and left to the bottom of a prominent flake/dihedral (8, 120 feet).
2b. Climb the very clean right-facing dihedral from the big ledge at the top of the ramp (10d).

Chasm View Wall
AA Royal Flush   IV 11c ★
29 Invisible Wall   IV 7 A4
30 Tip Toe   III 7
30a Big Toe   9
31 Red Wall   III 10a ★
31a Allan-Pennings   9 (?)
32 Directissima III 10b ★
83 V-Notch Exit II 7 ★
84 Chasm Cut-Off II 7

3. Climb a crack up and left along the left side of a flake; go up a wide inset for 30 feet, then step right and belay on top of the flake (9, 80 feet).

4. Climb a right-facing dihedral for about 15 feet to a bolt and a pin, step right into the next corner, and continue to an overhang. Make a difficult stem/lieback to gain the slab beneath the roof, then work right and down along flakes for 20 feet to a right-facing dihedral. Climb up 10 feet to a semi-sling belay below the right edge of the roof (10a, 100 feet).

5. Climb around the right end of the roof and follow a right-facing dihedral past a couple of pins toward a roof (9). At a third piton, work right across a slab to a semi-sling belay in a groove (9, 100 feet).

6. Climb a V-shaped chimney to a huge ledge in the black schist at the top of the face (8, 50 feet).

7. Finish with *Chasm Cut-Off* (7) or climb the giant right-facing dihedral above the belay (9+, loose).

31a Allan-Pennings   9 (?)

Gain the top of the big flake on the *Red Wall,* then traverse left into the first of three, shallow right-facing dihedrals (*Royal Flush*), and follow it to the top of the wall (?).

32   Directissima III 10b ★

FA: Layton Kor and Bob LaGrange (III 5.8 A2), 1960. FFA: Roger Briggs and Chris Reveley, 1974. SR plus an extra 3.5 and 4 Friend.

This classic is imperative for the wide crack enthusiast. Identify a vertical, right-facing flake-dihedral system that tops out at the right end of the dark rock at the top of the wall. The crux is at a roof on the fourth pitch but the squeeze chimney on the third will burn more calories.

Scramble up the ramp as for the *Red Wall* but continue up and right to the highest ledges at the bottom of the *Directissima* crack system.

1a. Climb an obvious, flower-filled right-facing dihedral that leads to a ramp beneath a small roof (8, 100 feet). Belay from slings around a horn with an old bolt.

1b. Climb the large dihedral at left past pin scars, then step down and right to the belay (9).

1c. Climb a right-facing flake just right of the dihedral (9).

2a. Climb straight up past the right end of the roof, pass through a slot, and join the dihedral on the right. Continue up the dihedral to a semi-sling belay at on old bolt beneath a flake-roof (9, 100 feet).

2b. Move right and climb a grassy right-facing dihedral to the same belay (10d).

3. Undercling around the flake and continue up a short slot (9). Work straight up into a chimney with two old bolts and a ringed piton. The chimney tapers into a squeeze and then a wide crack, which leads to a rest stance below an overhanging flake. Undercling the flake (or pull around to the right) and continue more easily for another 50 feet to a small ledge (9, 140 feet).

4. Climb a dihedral to a roof and make a committing move to a good jam (crux), then follow a wide crack to the top of the wall (10b, 130 feet).

33   Indirectissima   II 9

FA: Walter Fricke and Jock Glidden (II 5.7 A2), 1967.

This route ascends a distinct hollow flake system on the right side of the wall.

Begin from highest grassy ledge about 50 feet up and right from the start to *Directissima*.

1. Work up and right along an easy ramp and corner system to a horizontal break, then hand traverse left to a grassy ledge (7, 90 feet).
2. Climb the chimney at right to a good ledge at its top (4, 70 feet).
3a. Traverse down and right for 20 feet (7) to a dihedral which is climbed for 50 feet (A2); just below a 4-inch section, traverse right and climb the face for 20 feet to a big ledge (100 feet).
3b. Instead of traversing down to the right, climb up and left around a huge flake and reach the big ledge from the left (9, 100 feet).
4. Scramble up to the highest ledge, then follow a ramp up and right to the crest of the ridge (cl4, 150 feet).

34   Van Diver's Fantasy   I 6

FA: Brad Van Diver, 1948.

Follow the big central ramp to the far upper right section of Chasm View Wall (cl4) and belay at a flake that stands out 4 feet from the wall and is about 75 feet left of a right-facing dihedral. Climb the flake, then step across to the wall and climb to the ridge crest. The original route may have climbed directly up to the flake from the Mills Glacier.

35   Rollyco Stair   II 6

FA: Pat Ament and Larry Dalke, 1964.

This route climbs the slab to the left (west) of *The Camel* gully to the upper bench of Mills Glacier. Begin on a sloping ledge just above the snow at the base of a small, overhaning corner.

1. Climb the corner, then work up the slab to a belay stance near a grassy area (130 feet).
2. Climb straight up the slab past a tricky step to a good belay stance (150 feet). Walk off to the left.

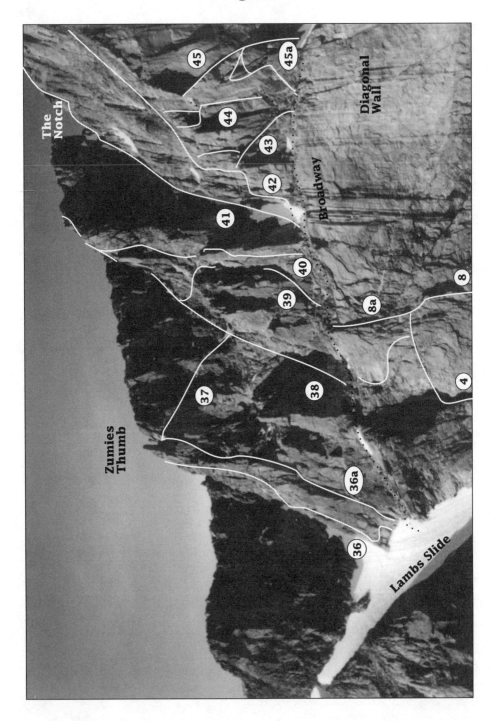

UPPER EAST FACE

The entire wall above Broadway is known as the Upper East Face. This is roughly divided in two by the Notch Couloir, the deep snow and ice gully that descends from the prominent skyline notch southeast of the summit (The Notch). The large broken face to the left of the Notch Couloir does not have a name but is characterized by a series of buttresses, pinnacles, and gullies. To the right of the Notch Couloir are Kiener's Chimneys and a sloping head wall that is the small-but-true east face of Longs Peak. Further right is The Diamond, the very impressive flat (northeast) face directly below the summit.

Approach. Routes to the left of The Diamond (south of *Pervertical Sanctuary*) are usually approached via *Lambs Slide* or a route on the Lower East Face such as *Alexande'rs Chimney* or *Stettner's Ledges*. It is reasonable to reach routes to the right of the Notch Couloir via the *North Chimney,* however, this is steeper and more dangerous than Lambs Slide.

Descent. For routes south of the Notch Couloir that finish on the crest of the southeast ridge, hike down the broad south side of the ridge to The Loft, then descend snow or talus to the east, bear north to the shelter cabin, and pick up the East Longs Peak Trail (see *The Loft* under Mount Meeker).

To continue to the summit of Longs Peak from the top of the ridge (south of The Notch), rappel 50 meters into The Notch; scramble up a bit, then traverse 150 feet north along the east side of the ridge to an east-facing chimney that is climbed to the ridge crest (4. 100 feet). Scramble northwest to the summit. Or descend the gully on the west side of The Notch and join Keplinger's Couloir.

Zumies Thumb is the narrow pinnacle atop a 600-foot buttress that rises above the south end of Broadway. The ascent (and descent) of the Thumb would be fairly simple via The Loft except that the final pinnacle is separated from the main ridge by a deep gap. The first ascent party hiked up the

UPPER EAST FACE, LEFT OF DIAMOND

4	Alexanders Chimney II 5 or M3 ★
8	Stettners Ledges II 7+ ★
8a	Hornsbys Direct Finish 8
36	Zumies Thumb III 9 ★
36a	Zumies Couloir (rating unknown)
37	Thumb Route II Class 4, AI2+
38	Eighth Route II6
39	Joe's Solo II to AI3
40	Teeter Totter Pillar III 8 ★
41	Notch Couloir III M3 ★
42	Kieners II Class 4 or M2 ★
43	Broadway Cut-Off II 5
44	Schobinger's Cracks II 8
45	TheWindow III 7 or M4*
45a	The Window Direct 7 ★

southeast ridge from The Loft, rappelled into the gap, climbed the Thumb, rappelled back to the gap, then jugged to the ridge crest on a rope that had been left in place (Tyrolean traverse would work here). The difficulty of reaching the ridge crest without a fixed line is not known. To descend the east side of the ridge from the gap, make three long rappels southward and descend the west arm of Lambs Slide back to the main couloir.

36 Zumie's Thumb　　III 9 ★

FA: (of Thumb) Tom Hornbein, Dexter Brinker, and Harry Waldrup, 1951; of entire buttress, Charles Schobinger and John Amato, 1959.

This route ascends the buttress above Broadway and finishes with the original route on The Thumb. The climbing on the buttress is moderate and does not exceed 6. Bolts and fixed pins will be found atop the Thumb for the rappel back to the notch. Bring double ropes.

Begin from the snow about 70 feet up and left from Broadway. Scramble up and right, then back left and gain a grassy ledge near the left edge of the east face.

1. Climb a grassy crack to a sloping stance beneath an obvious grassy gully (125 feet).
2. Climb the gully to bottom of two chimneys. Climb the right wall of the left chimney to a ledge at its top.

Scramble (unroped) up and right for about 300 feet to a col.

3. Climb the right wall of the buttress and belay behind a large flake (150 feet).
4. Traverse up and left to the top of a pointed flake, then continue to a big ledge that is about 100 feet below the left corner of the Thumb.
5. Climb a prominent crack for about 25 feet, traverse left to another crack, and climb to a large platform beneath the south side of the Thumb (60 feet).
6. Work up the wall and gain an obvious crack that is followed to a large sloping ledge (9 or aid off a pin). An easy crack leads to the narrow summit.

36a Zumie's Couloir　　(rating unknown)

This route (which may be hypothetical) ascends the chimney/gully system immediately right of Zumies Buttress; the final pitch to the notch looks fairly difficult.

36b Northwest Corner　　A2

FA: Harvey Carter and Clifford Smith, 1953.

From the notch, aid up the northwest corner of the Thumb, traverse seven feet left and continue to the summit.

37 Thumb Route　　II Class 4, AI2+

FA: Grant and Jones, 1946.

The fault line that apparently created the notch between the Thumb and main ridge continues as a steep gully down and right across the cliff to a bowl about 500 feet above Broadway. The *Thumb Route* ascends this gully, which is usually filled with snow or alpine ice.

Climb *Eighth Route* (see below) to the top of the bowl, then break left and follow the distinct fault/gully to the notch behind Zumies Thumb. It is unknown where the first ascent went from here. One could climb the Thumb and/or make three long rappels to the south and descend the west arm of Lambs Slide. It may be possible, however, to climb to the ridge crest and descend *The Loft*. A large chimney extends from the notch to the ridge crest, but its difficulty is not known.

38 Eighth Route   II 6

FA: Ernie Field, Warren Gorrell, and Hauk, 1940.

This old route ascends the large right-trending couloir above Alexander's Chimney. In early summer the couloir will contain considerable snow; later in the season some ice climbing may be required. Sometimes the ascent can be made over wet, grassy ledges and bare slabs.

Begin from Broadway between two large ribs or flatirons (the left of these is a real beauty). Scramble up the center of the couloir (cl4) to a bowl about 500 feet up and above the tops of the ribs (*Thumb Route* goes left here). From the top of the bowl, continue up the couloir toward the head wall and two steep chimneys 80 feet high and 20 feet apart (cl3). When about 25 feet from the chimneys, climb up and right to a good ledge at the base of a slab (0). Climb the slab for 130 feet and belay in a two-foot slot (2). Climb 20 feet, traverse left and up a block to a ledge, diagonal up and right, then go straight up to the crest of the ridge (6, 70 feet). Continue up the ridge to the highest point above The Notch.

38a Variation

One or both of the chimneys at the top of the couloir may have been climbed: A grade of WI4 has been suggested for the left chimney. It also is possible to climb straight up the slab to the very exposed crest of the ridge high above Teeter Totter Pillar, then westward to the top.

39 Joe's Solo   II 6 AI3

FA: Joe Stettner, 1936.

The large buttress that forms the left side of the Notch Couloir begins from Broadway as three narrow, flat-faced ribs. *Joe's Solo* climbs the steep gully between the middle and right of the ribs, then continues up the northeast edge of the upper buttress. The exact line of the upper pitches is not known. The initial gully may contain snow or alpine ice. It is possible to traverse left on a bench above the flatirons and join *Eighth Route* at the big bowl halfway up.

40 Teeter Totter Pillar   III 8 ★

FA: Michael Covington and Duncan Ferguson, 1977. Rack up to a #4 Friend.

This route climbs the east face of the narrow rib (the right of three) immediately left of the *Notch Couloir,* then continues up the northeast corner of the upper buttress as for *Joe's Solo*. The difficulty and exact line of the upper pitches are not known.

Scramble up to the bottom of a wide crack that splits the right side of the east face.

1. Climb the crack and belay on a good ledge at right (8, 100 feet).
2. Continue up the crack system for about 90 feet to a ledge, step around to the right and climb a shallow corner with a flake to another ledge (8, 160 feet).

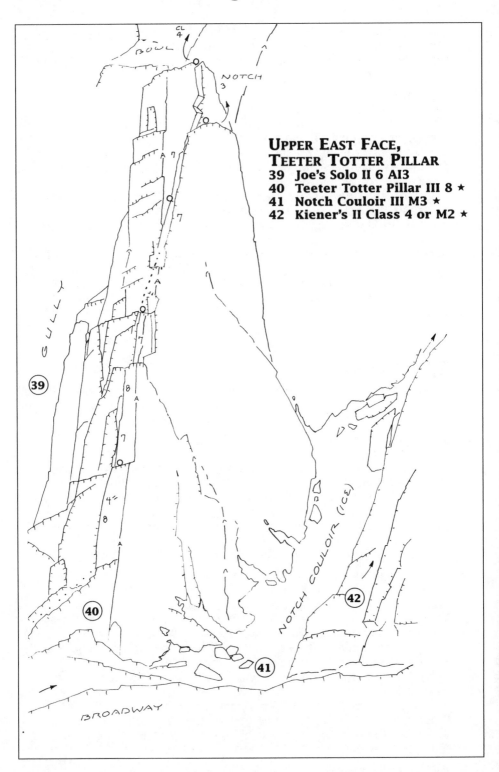

**UPPER EAST FACE,
TEETER TOTTER PILLAR**
39 Joe's Solo II 6 AI3
40 Teeter Totter Pillar III 8 ★
41 Notch Couloir III M3 ★
42 Kiener's II Class 4 or M2 ★

3. Climb the face just left of the arête and gain a long, left-facing, right-leaning dihedral/ramp on the north face. Climb about halfway up the dihedral and belay on a small ledge (7, 120 feet).

4. Continue up the dihedral to a ledge on the north face (7, 90 feet).

5. Traverse west along the ledge to a notch that separates Teeter Totter Pillar from the main buttress. Go through the notch and traverse south into a bowl (3).

Scramble up the right side of the bowl to where the terrain steepens and climb directly up the northeast corner of the buttress.

40a Variation

From the notch behind Teeter Totter Pillar (pitch 5), climb up and right onto a rib, then traverse west across the north face of the buttress on broken ledges to the middle of the wall above the Notch Couloir. Climb steep cracks and corners straight up to the crest of the ridge. Rating unknown. FA: Gary Neptune.

41 Notch Couloir   III M3 ★

FA: Elkanah Lamb may have descended the route in 1871, but J.W. Alexander is credited with the first ascent in 1922. Light SR plus a few ice screws and a handful of pitons.

This classic alpine route ascends the prominent snow and ice gully between Teeter Totter Pillar and the *Kiener's* buttress and gains the distinct notch (The Notch) in the southeast ridge of Longs Peak. The conditions in the couloir vary greatly depending on season. During spring and early summer, a predisposition for snow avalanches makes an ascent inadvisable. The best snow ascent is usually in July or August. Autumn and early winter can yield an excellent ice climb.

Climb *Lambs Slide* and hike north along Broadway for a thousand feet or so until at the bottom of the large couloir. Climb several pitches up snow or ice and pass through a steep, narrow section, then continue more easily to The Notch at the top of the couloir. Scramble north out of The Notch and traverse 150 feet to an east-facing chimney (The Stepladder) in the summit ridge. Climb the chimney (4, 100 feet), then scramble to the summit.

41a Variation

It is possible to leave the couloir above the steep narrow section and traverse right to finish with *Kiener's*. Another possibility is to descend the couloir below the west side of The Notch. From here, one may continue to the summit via *Keplinger's Couloir* or descend via *Clark's Arrow* and *The Loft.*

THE WINDOW AREA

The following routes ascend an area of chimneys and ramps between the Notch Couloir and the pillar of The Obelisk on The Diamond.

42 Kiener's   II Class 4 or M2 ★

FA: Walter Kiener, 1924. An ice ax, mountain boots, and crampons are needed as well as a light rock-climbing rack.

Also known as the *Mountaineer's Route, Kieners* is the easiest line on the east face of Longs Peak. The route follows a series of chimneys and

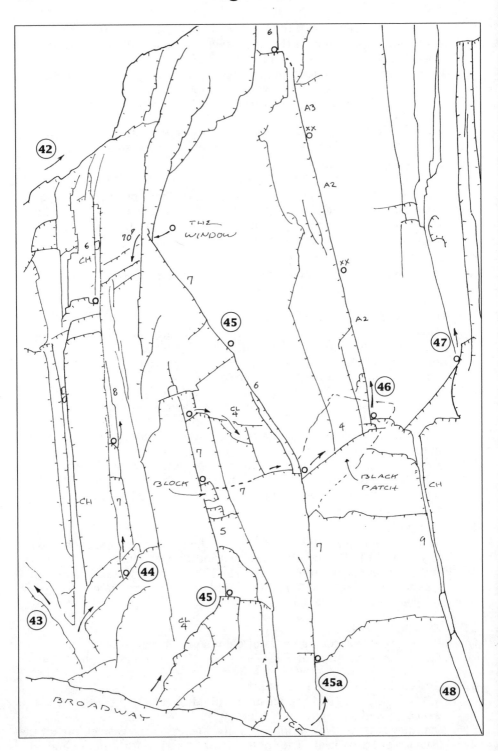

ramps that delineate the upper left margin of The Diamond. During spring and early summer, the route can hold a lot of deep, loose snow that makes it difficult to climb and subject to avalanche.

From the Mills Glacier, kick steps (or use crampons) up *Lambs Slide*. About 200 feet before reaching the top of the couloir, exit right and scramble up onto Broadway. Traverse Broadway to the north (right) for about 1000 feet to reach the bottom of the Notch Couloir. This traverse is fairly easy except for an exposed step-around above the top of the *Hornsby's Direct* dihedral. From fall to midsummer, Broadway is usually covered with snow.

Make an ascending traverse across the snow or scree of the Notch Couloir and gain an alcove in the rock on the far side (about 50 feet above Broadway). Traverse 20 feet right along a ledge and belay at the base of a short wall. Climb the wall, then go up a ramp/dihedral which becomes a chimney. Continue to the top of the chimney and belay on a ledge at right (cl4, 150 feet). Climb a second long pitch up corners and chimneys to a scree (or snow) bench at the bottom of a large slabby face. The section between Broadway and the bench is called Kiener's Chimneys.

Scramble up the right margin of the face toward a reddish buttress on the upper right skyline above The Diamond. After about 600 feet, the slope narrows into a gully. Climb up and right in the gully, mantle over some ledges, and traverse right around the red buttress on a good ledge (the Step-Around). Turn west and scramble 200 feet up talus to the summit.

43 Broadway Cut-Off II 5
FA: Ernie Field and Warren Gorrell, 1936.
This route begins from a grassy, broken area about 200 feet right of Kiener's Chimneys. Climb a conspicuous ramp that angles up to the left to the bottom of a chimney. Climb the chimney past a chockstone and join the upper ramp of *Kiener's*. It may be possible to continue up and left along the ramp to intersect Kiener's Chimneys.

44 Schobinger's Cracks II 8
FA: Chuck Schobinger and John Amato, 1958.
From the bottom of the Broadway Cut-Off ramp, angle up and right past the bottom a long, deep, and very impressive chimney to a crack and chimney system on the right. Climb a wide crack until it seems appropriate to change to a wide crack on the right and continue to some big

ledges on the left. Climb the chimney with a large chockstone halfway up (Eubank's Chimney) and join upper *Kiener's.*

45 The Window   III 7 or M4 ★
FA: Bill Eubank and Brad Van Diver, 1950.
Midway between Kiener's Chimneys and the pillar of The Obelisk, is a large K-shaped buttress, the waist of which is separated from the main wall by a long narrow slot called The Window. This classic route ascends the right leg of the K (a steep 280-foot ramp), then passes through The Window and climbs a chimney to join *Kiener's.* The ramp is at least partly covered with snow or ice until late summer when a crack may be exposed that offers a line of protection. It is, however, feasible to climb directly up the ice and protect the two pitches with ice screws. Begin from Broadway about 400 feet right of the Notch Couloir.
1. Angle up and right along moderate rock to a large pedestal (cl4, 90 feet).
2. Climb up a right-facing corner and gain the top of a large block (5, 90 feet).
3a. Traverse right along the block, climb down and right to another dihedral, then up the corner until a thin traverse leads right to the Window Ramp (7, 80 feet).
3b. Climb the dihedral and the face at left and gain a rubble-covered ledge (7, 80 feet; optional belay). Work down and right along the ledge and do a short hand-traverse to the Window Ramp (cl4).
4. Climb the slab/ramp past a narrow section and belay (6, 50 feet).
5. Continue up the steep ramp on ice or rock (depending on season) and belay in The Window, which is about 6 inches deep and 18 feet high (7, 150 feet).
Rappel 70 feet out the south side of The Window to a large, sloping ramp and set the next belay at the south side of the ramp beside a chimney.
6. Climb south across the first chimney into a second with a large chockstone (Eubank's Chimney).
7. Climb the chimney (often wet) and pass the chockstone on the left (6, 120 feet).
Follow *Kiener's* to the summit.

45a Window Direct   7 ★
FA: Dale Johnson and Cary Huston, 1960.
It is possible to climb directly up to the bottom of the ramp. Begin about 200 feet right of the regular start and around the corner of a buttress. Cross the top of the icefield at the bottom left side of the Diamond, then scramble up broken rock to steeper terrain. One pitch up cracks and corners along the right side of a small buttress leads directly to the Window Ramp (7, 120 feet).

46 Hypotenuse   III 8 A3
FA: George Hurley and John Hough, 1966.
This route ascends the steep left-leaning, right-facing dihedral to the right of *The Window*. The corner is mossy and sometimes wet.
Begin with *The Window* and gain a ledge system in black rock at the bottom of The Window Ramp.

2. Climb up and right through a patch of black rock to the bottom of the *Hypotenuse* dihedral (4, 75 feet).

3. and 4. Climb two pitches (mixed free and aid) to the near the top of the dihedral and belay from bolts.

5. Follow a thin crack system up and left to a 6-inch ledge and belay (A3), then climb free to the top of the wall (6 A3, 120 feet).

47 Baknn's A.P   III 7 A1
FA: Tryda and McCallister, 1977.
This route ascends the crack system to the right of the *Hypotenuse* and a short way left of The Obelisk column. Five pitches. Approach as for *The Hypotenuse*.

48 Black Death   III 9
Begin as for Pervertical Sanctuary, near the lower end of the ice patch below the Window Ramp. Climb in from the left and follow a conspicuous crack and chimney system for one or two pitches to a ledge on the right. From the right end of the ledge, climb a shallow left-facing dihedral and crack to a ramp beneath the Obelisk dihedral.

Roger Briggs on the King of Swords   Photo: Michael Gilbert.

THE DIAMOND

The Diamond is the most famous alpine wall in the United States. Its imposing plane towers above Chasm Lake like a giant drive-in movie screen — one million square feet of rock hanging in the sky upon which one might project his dreams and aspirations. The northeast-facing wall lies between 13000 and 14000 feet, its top a mere 200 feet from the summit of Longs Peak. It is dead vertical to overhanging, remote, bloody cold, and blind to storms approaching from the west. Just peering up at the looming face from broadway stimulates the imagination, if not second thoughts. To climb any route on The Diamond is a formidable challenge and should not be taken lightly. The sun leaves the face at about 11:00 AM, after which the temperature plummets. Storm gear must be carried, and speed of ascent is essential.

The Diamond is host to 34 major routes, of which only 18 have been climbed free. All are associated with the long vertical crack systems that characterize Diamond climbing. The rock on the left side of the wall is generally very good, and most of the routes are free climbs; the rock on the right side is steeper and somewhat rotten, and most of the routes are aid climbs. Some ascents can be completed car-to-car in a long arduous day, but because of the approach distance, altitude, and severity of the routes, most parties will want to bivouac. Standard sites are in the boulders below the Mills Glacier, on Broadway, and at Chasm View. The park service limits the number of people who can stay overnight at these locations. All routes begin from Broadway, the long ledge that runs across the bottom of the wall.

Approach A: Chasm Lake Cirque. This approach requires an ascent of Mills Glacier and a route on the Lower East Face to reach Broadway. The *North Chimney* provides the most expedient passage. Any of the longer routes such as *The Diagonal* or the *Grey Pillar* will turn the ascent into a grade VI. It is possible to climb *Lambs Slide* and traverse back north along Broadway, but this involves considerable snow travel and is seldom done. See Approach A under Longs Peak.

Approach B: Chasm View. The least dangerous but more roundabout way to reach Broadway is to rappel from Chasm View. From the Boulderfield, hike up talus to Chasm View (13529), the notch at the far right corner of The Diamond, and make three, 150-foot rappels to the north end of Broadway. See Approach B under Longs Peak.

THE DIAMOND

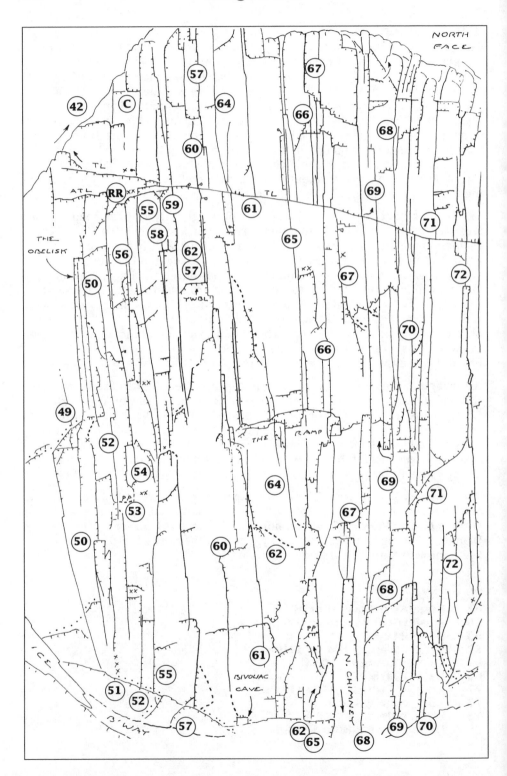

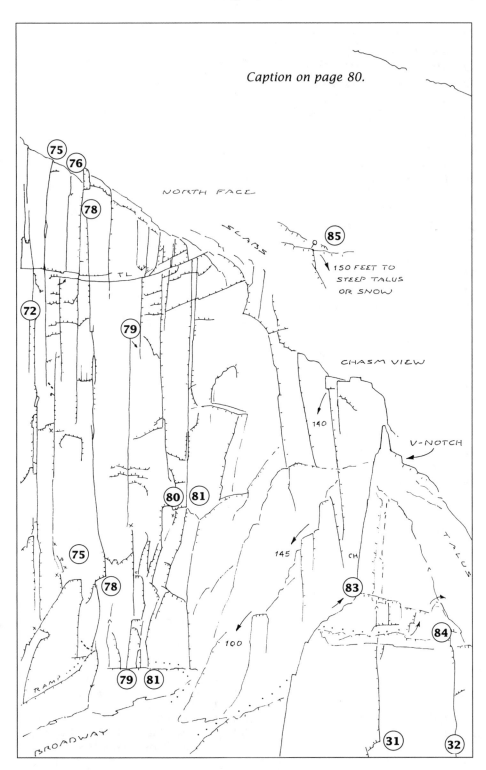

Caption on page 80.

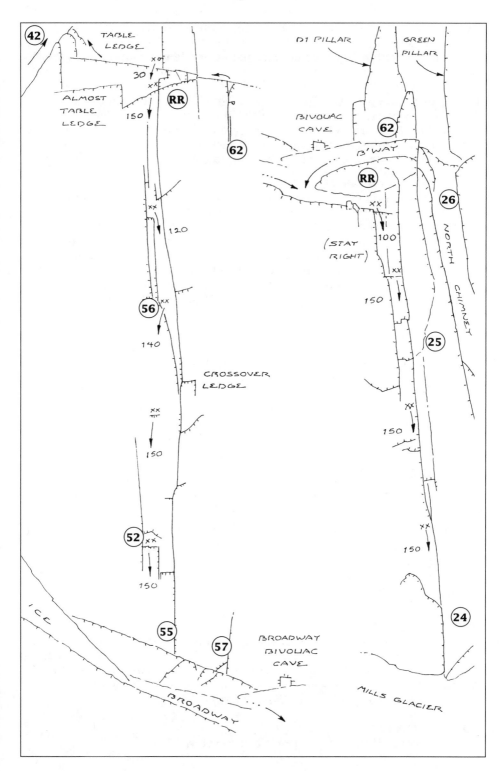

Descent. From the summit, scramble down the north face as described under Longs Peak (above). Note that from the top of The Diamond, it is not necessary to continue to the summit, just scramble north into the big bowl of the north face and descend northeast to the rappel above Chasm View. If taken by storm on The Diamond and forced to rappel back to Broadway, rappel the *Crack of Delight* and kick steps down Mills Glacier; but this is really a drag if gear was stashed at Chasm View. To return to Chasm View, scramble up *The Camel* (see above) and hike west along the north side of the ridge. A much shorter option for reaching Chasm View from Broadway is to climb the *V-Notch Exit* (Route 83), but this will be of no use in a storm or in the dark.

RR. The Diamond Rappel Route. From the top of *D7* (Almost Table Ledge), make five long rappels from fixed anchors to Broadway. The second and third anchors are on the route *Soma* to the left of *D7*. The fourth anchor is not on any route but has two bolts at a good stance. The fifth anchor is at the top of the first pitch of *Curving Vine,* from which a final rappel places one on Broadway. Walk north and down a bit to a bolt anchor with a chain at the top of the *Crack of Delight* (directly below the start to the *Casual Route*). Make four more long rappels from bolt anchors to the Mills Glacier. None of the rappels exceed 150 feet, but it is a good idea to knot the ends of the ropes.

TABLE LEDGE

Table Ledge is a long, horizontal crack system that runs across the upper part of The Diamond. Every route ends at this crack or crosses it. The far south end of the crack forms a grassy bench where one can exit left to *Kiener's.* The remainder of the crack is not a ledge. About 30 feet below the left end of Table Ledge is another narrow bench called Almost Table Ledge. There are three ways to finish a climb from the bench at the south end of Table Ledge crack:

Finish A. Traverse left on Table Ledge and join *Kiener's* (Route 42).

Finish B. From the middle of Table Ledge, climb either of two cracks to the top of the face and join *Kiener's* (7, 120 feet).

Finish C. Over Thirty Hang   7 A2   FA: George Hurley and Jonathan Hough, 1967. From the pin belay on Table Ledge, climb a left-facing dihedral and belay beneath a large overhang (130 feet). Aid left beneath the roof for 20 feet, then climb 30 feet straight up to the top of the face. The 6-inch crack through the roof may have been free climbed.

THE OBELISK AREA

The Obelisk is a 210-foot pillar at the upper left side of The Diamond. Three excellent routes ascend this narrow column and converge at Obelisk Ledge at its top. A final pitch, the original last pitch of *Curving Vine* (9), leads to Almost Table Ledge from which one may continue to Table Ledge and *Kieners,* or traverse right to the *Diamond Rappel Route.*

49   The Obelisk   IV+ 11b/c ★
FA: George Hurley, 1974. FFA: Chris Reveley, 1977.

This route climbs the great white left-facing dihedral along the left side of the Obelisk pillar. The final pitch ascends a slightly overhanging 5- to 6-inch slot. SR plus some offwidth gear.

Begin with the *Window Direct* and traverse up and right to a sloping ledge at the base of the dihedral, or climb the first three pitches of *Pervertical Sanctuary* and traverse left to the same ledge.

1. Climb a long handcrack and belay at a stance with two bolts (11, 100 feet).
2. Continue up the corner and belay at the base of the final offwidth (10a, 35 feet).
3. Climb the awesome slot, which may be partly protected by small nuts on the inside, and belay on Obelisk Ledge (11, 75 feet).
4. From the right side of the pillar, follow a steep crack to Table Ledge (9, 130 feet).

50 Pervertical Sanctuary   IV+ 11a ★

FA: This is The Diamond section of a long aid route by Ron Olevsky and Bob Dodds that began from the Mills Glacier with *Shining Slab* and *Grey Pillar*, 1974. FFA: Bruce Adams and Tobin Sorensen, 1975. SR plus extra gear from 1 to 4 inches.

This popular tour ascends a crack system up the far left side of The Diamond and finishes with two excellent pitches (fingers to hands) up the right side of The Obelisk. A point of identification is the Mitten Flake, a large flake about 100 feet above Broadway that is reminiscent of a mitten with the thumb on the right.

Begin near the bottom of an icefield at the lower left side of The Diamond.

1. Work in from the left and climb the left side of the Mitten Flake to a belay at its top (8, 130 feet).
2. Climb the crack above the Mitten and belay on a ledge at right (9, 100 feet).
3. Climb the crack and left-facing corner to where it veers left, then work up and right past a bolt and gain the ledge at the bottom right side of The Obelisk (9, 100 feet).
4. Jam a difficult handcrack and belay on a wedged block (11a, 130 feet).
5. Jam up the 4-inch crack in the right-facing corner along the right side of The Obelisk and belay at the top of the pillar (10a, 80 feet).
6. From the right side of the pillar, follow a steep crack to Table Ledge (9, 130 feet).

51 Ariana   V- 12a ★

FA: George Hurley, 1975. FFA: of entire free line, Roger Briggs, 1985.

This route ascends a long, thin crack up the middle of The Obelisk. The fourth pitch is the crux and is well-protected. Rack: SR with extra stoppers and small cams.

Begin up on a ledge below three bolts, to the right of the start to *Pervertical Sanctuary*.

1. Climb past the bolts and gain a crack that is followed to a belay on the "thumb" of the Mitten Flake (11, 165 feet).

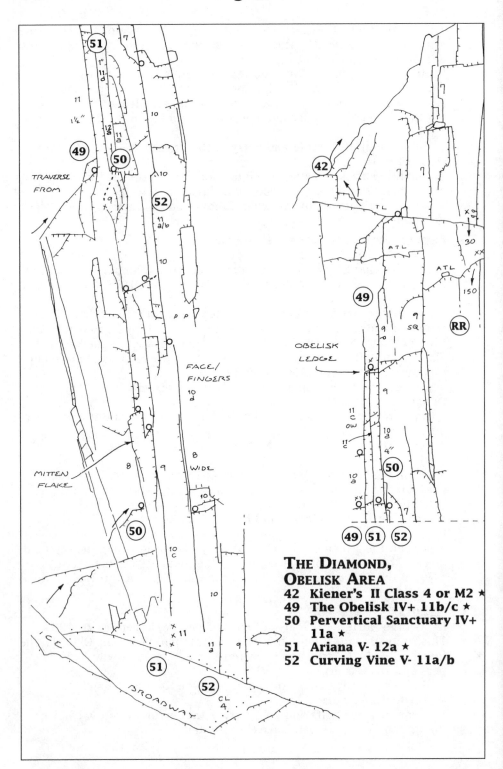

THE DIAMOND, OBELISK AREA

42 Kiener's II Class 4 or M2 ★
49 The Obelisk IV+ 11b/c ★
50 Pervertical Sanctuary IV+ 11a ★
51 Ariana V- 12a ★
52 Curving Vine V- 11a/b

2 and 3. Follow *Pervertical Sanctuary* to the ledge at the bottom of The Obelisk.

4. Climb a steep and unrelenting 1-inch crack up the middle of The Obelisk to a semi-sling belay at two bolts (12a, 115 feet).

5. Continue up the crack to Obelisk Ledge (11c, 95 feet).

6. From the right side of the ledge, follow a steep crack to Table Ledge (9, 130 feet).

YELLOW WALL AREA

This section of The Diamond lies between The Obelisk (at left) and the dihedral of the *Grand Traverse.* The very flat wall is characterized by long, thin cracks, an abundance of face holds, and small ledges. At the bottom right of this area, directly beneath the Grand Traverse Dihedral, is a small, square-cut inset called the Broadway Bivouac Cave. If not the Longs Peak Hyatt, it is at least a good point of reference.

52   Curving Vine   V- 11a/b

FA: Michael Covington and Pete Robinson (V 5.6 A3), 1966 . FFA: unknown. Slightly enhanced SR.

The route shown in the topo is the free version. The original line made a pendulum on the first pitch to gain the long crack that is the main feature of the route. About 200 feet below Table Ledge, the crack fades and a second pendulum was made into the crack that is now the fifth pitch of *Ariana.* The free version goes left well below this pendulum and finishes with the fifth pitch of *Pervertical Sanctuary.*

Begin in the first crack system to the right of the bolt ladder on *Ariana*, about 20 feet left of the start to *D7*. It is possible to climb the first 90 feet of *D7* and traverse left on a ledge to join the route (9).

1. Climb a shallow left-facing dihedral and the chimney/crack above, then traverse left on a ledge and belay at the *Curving Vine* crack (10c, 160 feet).

2. Climb a wide crack in a right-facing dihedral (8) and continue to the end of the crack. Move up and left and climb a small right-facing dihedral, then go left and again and reach a good ledge near the end of the rope (10d, 160 feet).

3. Move 5 feet to the right and follow a crack past an offset to a stance (11a/b, 155 feet).

4. Follow a flake/ramp up and left to the belay on a wedged block in the dihedral of *Pervertical Sanctuary* (8, 70 feet).

5. Climb the wide crack in the dihedral to the top of The Obelisk (10a, 80 feet).

6. From the right side of the pillar, follow a steep crack to Table Ledge (9, 130 feet).

53   Hidden Diamond   V- 11d ★

FA: Ed Webster and Robert Anderson, 1985. FFA: Ed Webster and Pete Athens, 1985. Rack up to 4 inches with extra RPs or equivalent.

This difficult route begins with the first two pitches of *Curving Vine,* traverses right to join *D Minor 7* for two pitches, then continues straight up where the latter veers off to the right. The crux fourth pitch includes a fist crack followed by a strenuous knifeblade crack.

1 and 2. Climb *Curving Vine.*

3. Climb a right-facing dihedral for 20 feet, then traverse right past two pins (10a) to the next crack system, which is *D Minor 7.* Climb the crack past a slot and along the right side of a long, white inset; pass a small roof and belay at a stance in a right-facing dihedral (10, 150 feet).

4. Climb an easy chimney that tapers to a hand-and-fist crack (10d), then climb a shallow dihedral past two pins (crux) and belay on a ledge at left (11d, 130 feet).

5. Continue up the crack past a large, precarious flake (may be gone) and belay on a ledge at right (10a, 120 feet).

The following pitches can be avoided by traversing right to *Soma.*

6. Climb a crack to a loose chimney and follow it to the upper right end of Obelisk Ledge (9, 150 feet).

7. Climb a crack through an awkward bulge and continue more easily to Table Ledge (9, 115 feet).

54   D Minor 7   V- 11d

FA: Bob Bradley and Rick Petrillo (V 5.7 A3), 1967. The section of the climb between *D7* and *Hidden Diamond* as well as the final pitch were climbed free during 1994 by Roger Briggs.

This is an early aid route that has been confused with the *D7 Variation* above Crossover Ledge. Fortunately, Bob Bradley contributed a large marked photograph of The Diamond that clearly shows this route — it is also described correctly in Walter Fricke's old guide. It begins with the first 130 feet of *Curving Vine,* jogs right to follow *D7* for 200 feet, then angles up and left for 120 feet into a crack system that is now shared with the third and fourth pitches of *Hidden Diamond.* At a point slightly lower than the Yellow Wall Bivouac Ledge, *D Minor 7* again jogs right into the next crack system *(Soma)* and continues to Almost Table Ledge.

CROSSOVER LEDGE

This ledge spans 25 feet between D7 and the Yellow Wall about 320 feet above Broadway. It provides a belay for Soma, D7, the Black Dagger, the Forrest Finish, and the Yellow Wall. It can be reached in two long leads via D7, which allows a very rapid start to any of these routes.

55   D7   V- 11c ★

FA: Larry Dalke, Wayne Goss, and George Hurley, 1966. FFA: John Bachar, 1977. Rack up to 4 inches with extra mid-range gear.

D7 features beautiful, solid rock and good cracks all the way up; it is one of the best routes on Longs Peak. As an aid climb, it was the easiest and most popular route on the wall (V 5.6 A2), and was generally considered the best candidate for the first free ascent of The Diamond, however, the final smooth head wall below Table Ledge rebuffed all attempts. In 1975, Wayne Goss and Jim Logan made the first free ascent of The Diamond by climbing the first four pitches, then traversing right into the *Forrest Finish,* and on to Table Ledge via the last pitch of the *Black Dagger.* Two years later, John Bachar climbed *D7* all the way to Table Ledge and unveiled one of the finest free climbs in the park.

Derek Hersey free solo on the *Yellow Wall*.   Photo: Steve Bartlett.

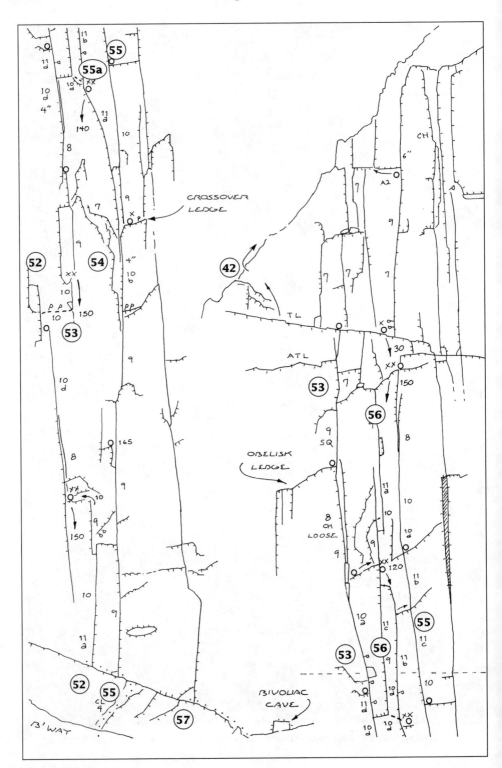

Begin at the second left-facing dihedral left of the Broadway Bivouac
Cave and scramble through a broken rock band to a ledge at its base.
1. and 2. Follow a continuous crack for two long pitches of ascending
difficulty and belay on Crossover Ledge (9 to 10b, 320 feet).
Traditionally, this section is climbed in three pitches.
3. The prominent right-facing dihedral that proceeds from the left end
of the ledge is not the standard line and leads into the *D7 Variation* (see
below). Climb the smaller right-facing corner and crack a few feet right
of this and gain a sloping ledge (10d, 115 feet).
4. Climb three parallel cracks to another small ledge (11c, 115 feet).
5. Climb a thin crack that widens to about 10 inches and continue more
easily to Almost Table Ledge (11a, 130 feet).
6. Climb a short pitch up and right to reach Table Ledge, then traverse
left about 20 feet to belay (8, 50 feet).

55a D7 Variation   11b ★
Also known as the Headwall Bypass, this provides a slightly easier finish to D7.
4. From Crossover Ledge, climb the left of two right-facing dihedrals or
climb 50 feet of *D7* and step left into the line. Follow a thin crack as it
veers left and belay at a stance with two bolts (11a, 110 feet).
5. Climb the crack (which now goes straight up) for 75 feet, then traverse right on a sloping ledge, and continue with the fifth pitch of *D7*
just above the crux (11b, 150 feet). It may be possible to move up and
left from the end of this pitch and finish with *Soma.*

56 Soma   V- 11 ★
FA: Roger Briggs and Michael Gilbert, 1994.
This hybrid route begins with the *D7 Variation,* explores a previously
unclimbed dihedral, and finishes with the final pitch of *D Minor 7.* Part
of the crack on the fifth pitch is filled with beautiful alpine flowers.
These fragile plants can be spared by face climbing around them.
4. From Crossover Ledge, climb the first pitch of the *D7 Variation* (see
above).
5. From the bolt belay, traverse 6 feet left to the bottom of a hanging
right-facing dihedral (10d). Climb the dihedral and subsequent crack,
which starts out thin (10d), goes offwidth (9), then turns fingers (11b/c)
and belay from bolts in a small right-facing dihedral (11, 130 feet).
6. Step left out of the dihedral and climb a right-facing flake that leads
back into the crack system. Climb the crack for 10 feet, then move right
to another crack that is climbed to Almost Table Ledge (11a, 155 feet).

THE DIAMOND, D7 AREA

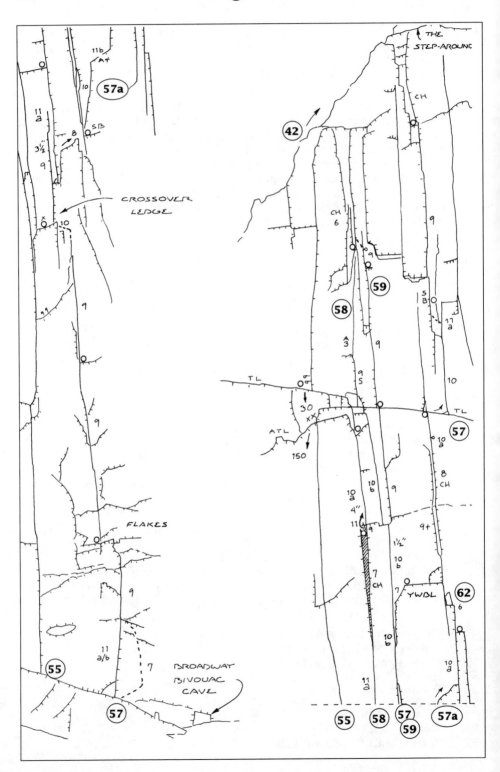

57   Yellow Wall   V- 10d or 11b ★

FA: Layton Kor and Charlie Roskoz (V 5.8 A4), 1962. FFA: of dihedral on first pitch, Roger Briggs, 1976; of *A4 Traverse* on fifth pitch, Charlie Fowler and Dan Stone, 1978; of *Briggs-Candelaria Version*, Roger Briggs and Rob Candelaria, 1976. SR plus an extra #2.5 through #4 Friend.

This magnificent line was the second route completed on The Diamond and is among the most coveted alpine rock climbs in North America. It has two high-standard variations, of which the *Briggs-Candelaria* is the most frequented and is described here as the standard line of the route. From the Broadway Bivouac Cave, scramble up and left along a ramp for about 75 feet to the bottom of a shallow left-facing dihedral.

1a. Work up and right across the face, then up and left to gain the crack above the dihedral (7). Continue to the top of the crack, then work up and left to belay at the base of another crack (9, 120 feet).

1b. Climb the left-facing dihedral to the same fate (11a/b, 120 feet).

2. Climb the crack to a stance on the right (9, 130 feet).

3. Continue up the crack and shallow left-facing dihedral (often wet), then make a difficult move left to Crossover Ledge (10d, 120 feet).

4. Climb a left-facing dihedral above the right end of the ledge, then move right into the *Black Dagger* crack system. Climb a few feet, then move right again into the *Forrest Finish* crack and climb to a semi-sling belay beneath an offwidth section (9, 100 feet).

5. Climb the wide section (8, up to 12 inches) and continue up the crack of varying width, then break right along a ramp and belay on the Yellow Wall Bivouac Ledge (10b, 160 feet).

6. From the right side of the ledge, climb an inset (9+) followed by a narrow chimney (8), then pass a bulge with a fixed pin (crux) and belay at Table Ledge (10a, 130 feet).

From here it is possible to traverse left to Table Ledge (8) and exit to *Kiener's,* however, the route continues above.

7. Traverse right 15 feet, then climb a steep and exposed crack system to a sling belay below the right corner of a roof (11a, 100 feet).

8. Climb a right-facing dihedral to the top of the wall (9, 130 feet).

57a A4 Traverse   11b s

From the fourth belay, climb a shallow, right-leaning, left-facing corner, then make a desperate traverse right with marginal pro to another shallow corner. Follow this up and right to a vertical crack that leads to a ledge in the Grand Traverse Dihedral. Belay here or climb to the Yellow Wall Bivouac Ledge (180 feet).

58   Black Dagger   V- 11a ★

FA: Wayne Goss and Roger Dalke (V 5.7 A3), 1966. FFA: Duncan
Ferguson, 1980. SR plus many pieces from a 0.5 inch to 1 inch.

This unique route takes *D7* or the *Yellow Wall* to Crossover Ledge, then
continues straight up into the long, tapered chimney for which the
route is named.

4. From the right side of Crossover Ledge, climb up for 40 feet and gain
the bottom of a left-facing dihedral. Bypass a wide crack via the face on
the left, then jam a difficult handcrack to a sloping ledge on the left
(11a, 120 feet).

5. Climb the shallow left-facing dihedral above the ledge via a wide
crack that tapers to hands and gain the Black Dagger Chimney. Climb
the chimney to near its top (7) and belay on the right (11a, 150 feet).

6a. Climb out the right side of the roof (10a) and traverse 6 feet right
on a narrow ledge, then climb a steep crack to Almost Table Ledge (10b,
90 feet).

6b. Climb out the left side of the roof (11a) and gain a wide crack that
goes straight up to Almost Table Ledge (11a, 90 feet).

7 and 8. The original finish to the *Black Dagger* goes straight up a crack
system (A3) that leads to a chimney that is climbed free (6) to the top of
the face. The more common finish is to exit left to *Kiener's* via Table
Ledge (8) or to join the *Forrest Finish* about 10 feet to the right.

59   Forrest Finish   V- 10

FA: Bill Forrest, solo (V 5.7 A3), 1970.

This direct route, which parallels the *Black Dagger* on the right, was the
first solo ascent of The Diamond. It ascends the first four pitches of the
Yellow Wall, then follows an independent crack system straight to the
top of the face.

5. From the belay where the *A4 Traverse* of the *Yellow Wall* goes up and
right, climb straight up the crack, which varies from a 12-inch chimney
to fingers and belay just down and left from The Yellow Wall Bivouac
Ledge (10b, 150 feet).

6. Continue up the same crack, which begins wide then tapers to a
beautiful handcrack, and gain the top of a smooth wall. Easier climbing
leads to Table Ledge and a belay at the base of a right-facing dihedral
(10b, 150 feet).

7. Climb the dihedral and belay on a small ledge (9, 120 feet).

8. Work up and left past a fixed pin and climb a moderate chimney to
the top of the face (9, 110 feet).

60   Bright Star   V 10a A3 ★

FA: Ed Webster, solo, 1984. FFA of first four pitches: Charlie Fowler and
Scott Cosgrove, 1987. Rack: KBs to 4 inches with many small stoppers
and two sets of Friends.

This route is dedicated to the memory of Lauren Husted. It ascends five
original pitches above the left side of the Broadway Bivouac Cave, follows a pitch each of the *Grand Traverse* and the *Yellow Wall* (the *Casual
Route*), then continues straight up the head wall above Table Ledge for

two more difficult and dramatic pitches. The first ascent took three days.

1. From the left side of the Broadway Bivouac Cave, work up and left to the bottom of a crack and follow it to a narrow ledge (11 or A2+, 130 feet).

2. Continue in the same crack system and belay on a flake at right (11 or 9 A2+, 110 feet).

3. Work up and right via flakes and gain another crack that leads to a stance in a right-facing dihedral (11s or A2, 90 feet).

4. Climb the dihedral for about 50 feet, then break left into another right-facing dihedral and climb to its top (the free version joins the *Casual Route* at this point by moving right into the Grand Traverse Dihedral). *Bright Star* goes up and left to belay atop a pedestal (11 or 7 A1, 130 feet).

5. Climb a hand crack followed by a chimney that merges with the Grand Traverse Dihedral and belay on a small ledge (9 A1, 100 feet).

6. Climb the dihedral to the Yellow Wall Bivouac Ledge (8, 140 feet).

7. Climb an inset followed by a chimney and a bulge and belay just below Table Ledge (10a, 130 feet). This is the crux pitch of the *Casual Route*.

8. Climb a scary crack to a square roof, pass it on the left, and belay in slings in a left-facing dihedral above the roof (A3, 100 feet).

9. Climb the dihedral to a second roof which is passed on the right, then follow a steep and very exposed crack to a ledge on the left (8 A2, 150 feet).

Scramble up and left for 50 feet (cl4) and join *Kiener's* about 75 feet below the Step-Around.

61 Grand Traverse   V 8 A4

FA: Bob Boucher and Pat Ament, 1964. The two long pitches above Table Ledge may have been climbed free at 11b each. SR to a #4 Friend plus aid gear from RURPS and KBs.

This classic aid route is rarely climbed but for its central pitches which are overlapped by the *Casual Route*. The name is derived from a 90-foot A4 traverse along Table Ledge.

Begin just right of the Broadway Bivouac Cave.

1. Nail straight up a vertical head wall, turn a roof, and gain a stance on the right. Traverse right on aid for 12 feet to a crack that is climbed to a belay ledge (A4 at first, then easier, 100 feet). It may be possible to nail directly up the crack from Broadway.

2. Continue up the crack system to a sling belay (A2, 100 feet).

3. Continue in the same system to a tapering slot (A2, 90 feet).

4 through 7. Follow the *Casual Route* to Table Ledge.

8. Traverse right for about 90 feet (easy at first, then A4) to the bottom of a prominent crack that splits the steep head wall.

9. Nail up the crack to small but beautiful ledge (A3, 150 feet).

10. Run the rope out to a sling belay near the top of the head wall (A2, 150 feet).

11. A short pitch brings one to the top of the wall (A2, 30 feet).

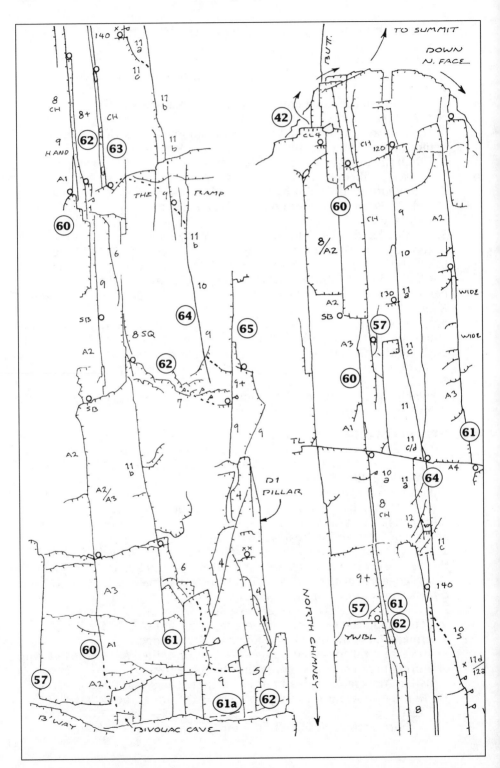

61a Free Start   11b ★
FFA: Bernard and Robert Gillett, 1992.
1. Begin in a short left-facing dihedral near the center of the D1 Pillar, turn a small roof, then angle up and left along flakes (*Grand Traverse*) to a small ledge (9, 150 feet).
2. Climb a shallow, left-leaning, left-facing dihedral and crack to a belay at the end of the traverse on the *Casual Route* (11b, 150 feet).

D1 PILLAR
The following five routes begin from a 180-foot, cone-shaped pillar just left of the North Chimney. Though there are at least three ways to climb the pillar, the usual method begins about 20 feet left of the North Chimney: Climb up and right along a left-facing corner, then go up and left to a belay ledge with a fixed anchor (5, 140 feet). There is another good ledge about 15 feet higher. A short easy pitch leads to the top.

THE RAMP
About 200 feet above the top of the D1 Pillar, the wall curves back to form a large sloping ledge called The Ramp, which is intersected by the Casual Route, Diamond Lil, Eroica, D1, and Jack of Diamonds.

62   Casual Route   IV 10a (7 s) ★
FA: Duncan Ferguson and Chris Reveley, 1978.
This climb was known as the *Integral Route* until it was free-soloed by Charlie Fowler about 1984. When asked what it was like to solo The Diamond, Charlie said, "Casual." The *Casual Route* is the easiest line on The Diamond. It is always interesting and sustained in difficulty but at an easier level than the other free climbs. The route follows the right margin of the Yellow Wall area with the last pitch up to Table Ledge the crux. Note: There are several options for the arrangement of belays other than that shown in the topo.
Begin at the D1 Pillar about 150 feet right of the Bivouac Cave and about 20 feet left of the North Chimney.
1. Climb a short left-facing corner, then work up and left to ledge with a fixed anchor (5, 140 feet).
2. Work up and left to the bottom of the D1 crack, then climb the crack for about 40 feet to a belay stance (9, 100 feet).
3. Traverse straight left, then angle up and left along flakes and small ledges to a stance at the bottom of a squeeze chimney (7, 100 feet). There are several fixed pins along this traverse. Do not start the traverse from the top of the D1 pillar: This is 10c with poor pro.

THE DIAMOND, D1 PILLAR AREA

42	Kiener's II Class 4 or M2 ★		62	Casual Route IV 10a (7 s) ★
57	Yellow Wall V- 10d or 11b ★		63	Diamond Lil V 9 A3
60	Bright Star V 10a A3 ★		64	Eroica V+ 12b (10 s) ★
61	Grand Traverse V 8 A4		65	D1 V 12a/b ★
61a	Free Start 11b ★			

4. Climb the squeeze chimney, then continue up and slightly left to a belay in a big right-facing dihedral at the left end of The Ramp (8, 160 feet).

5. Climb the dihedral to a large grassy ledge (8+, 155 feet) or belay at a stance halfway up the corner.

6. A short (or long) pitch leads to the Yellow Wall Bivouac Ledge (6, 50 feet).

7. From the right side of the ledge, climb an inset (9+) followed by a narrow chimney (8), then pass a bulge with a fixed pin (crux) and belay at Table Ledge (10a, 130feet).

8. Traverse left past fixed pins, then down a bit to Almost Table Ledge. Climb up and right past fixed pins to Table Ledge and traverse left to a left-facing dihedral with a fixed anchor and belay (8, 140 feet).

Exit left and finish with *Kiener's,* or do the *Diamond Rappel Route* from Almost Table Ledge.

63   Diamond Lil   V 9 A3

FA: Michael Covington, Doug Scott, and Dennis Henneck, 1976. The entire route except for the long chimney and dihedral above the left side of The Ramp has been climbed free as *Eroica.*

64   Eroica   V+ 12b (10 s) ★

FA: Roger Briggs and Eric Doub, 1987. SR with double RPs, Stoppers, and TCUs.

Eroica is the name given to Beethoven's Third Symphony, though the route is named in memory of the late Eric Goukas. It is one of the best routes on The Diamond, generally safe but very challenging. It free climbs all of *Diamond Lil* but the long chimney and dihedral above the left side of The Ramp.

1 and 2. Climb the first two pitches of *D1.*

3. Traverse out left, then follow a steep crack for about 140 feet. Work up and left past another crack and belay in a third (11b, 150 feet).

4. Climb to the top of The Ramp (9), then follow a crack for 50 feet, break left into another crack system and belay at a stance with a bolt and fixed pin (11c, 140 feet).

5. Follow the crack up and left past fixed pins and a bolt, then make a scary traverse up and left (10 s), and belay in a right-facing dihedral (11d/12a, 150 feet).

6. Climb the corner for 40 feet, then traverse right 12 feet to another crack and climb straight up to a small ledge (11c). From the left end of the ledge, climb a difficult crack to Table Ledge, then traverse right 10 feet and belay in an alcove beneath a left-leaning crack (12b, 110 feet).

7. Climb the very sustained crack and belay on a stance at left (11d, 130 feet).

8. Continue in the same crack (a left-facing dihedral) to easier terrain at the top of The Diamond (11a, 120 feet).

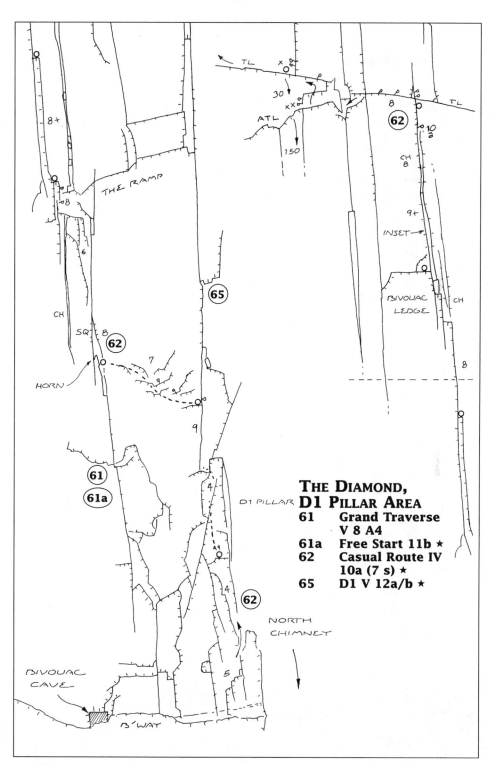

THE DIAMOND,
D1 PILLAR AREA
61 **Grand Traverse**
V 8 A4
61a **Free Start 11b ★**
62 **Casual Route IV**
10a (7 s) ★
65 **D1 V 12a/b ★**

65 D1   V 12a/b ★

FA: Dave Rearick and Bob Kamps (V 5.7 A4), 1960. FFA: John Bachar and
Billy Westbay, 1976 (via the wet chimney above Table Ledge). FFA of
dihedral above Table Ledge: Roger Briggs and Jeff Achey, 1980. SR plus
extra pieces up to 3.5 inches.

Also known as the *Ace of Diamonds, D1* was the first route on The
Diamond. It was one of the more difficult aid routes and is no piece of
cake as a free climb. From the D1 Pillar, it follows a continuous crack
system straight up the middle of the wall to the top.The crux and cleanest pitch is a shallow left-facing corner above Table Ledge.

1. Climb to the fixed belay on the D1 Pillar (5, 140 feet).
2. Continue to the top of the pillar, then follow a right-facing dihedral
up and right and back left to a ledge (9, 150). The ledge also may be
reached via the finger crack on the second pitch of the *Casual Route
(9+).*
3. Climb a right-facing dihedral and turn the roof at its top, then follow
a crack to the top of The Ramp (10d, 150 feet). It is advantageous to
belay on the next ledge above: This can be done with an additional
short pitch (10a, 30 feet) or in one long lead with a 60-meter rope.
4. From the ledge above The Ramp, climb straight up the crack to a
ledge on the right with two bolts (11a, 150 feet).
5. Continue up the crack system to an alcove at Table Ledge (10d, 100
feet).
6a. Step left and climb a difficult crack to a left-facing dihedral that is
followed to a pedestal with a two-pin anchor (12a/b, 120 feet).
6b. Climb the wet and nasty chimney straight up from the alcove to the
same stance (11, wet, 120 feet).
7. Climb the upper chimney to the top of the wall (9, wet or icy, 140
feet).

66 Jack of Diamonds   V 9 A4

FA: Layton Kor and Royal Robbins, 1963.
This early aid line is rarely climbed and has not received a complete
free ascent. The route runs parallel to *D1,* about 50 to the right. It is
very steep with a somewhat rotten midsection. The big right-facing
dihedral below Table Ledge may have been climbed free at 10c.
Begin at the top of the North Chimney in the corner that forms the right
margin of the D1 Pillar.

1. Climb the corner along the right side of the pillar and belay on a narrow ledge (8, 150 feet).
2. Continue to the top of the pillar and follow *D1* for 50 feet (9). Veer
right in a crack system and belay on a ledge slightly higher than the
corresponding ledge of D1.
3. Follow the crack up a steep wall, turn a roof, and gain the right end
of The Ramp.

THE DIAMOND, D1 PILLAR AREA

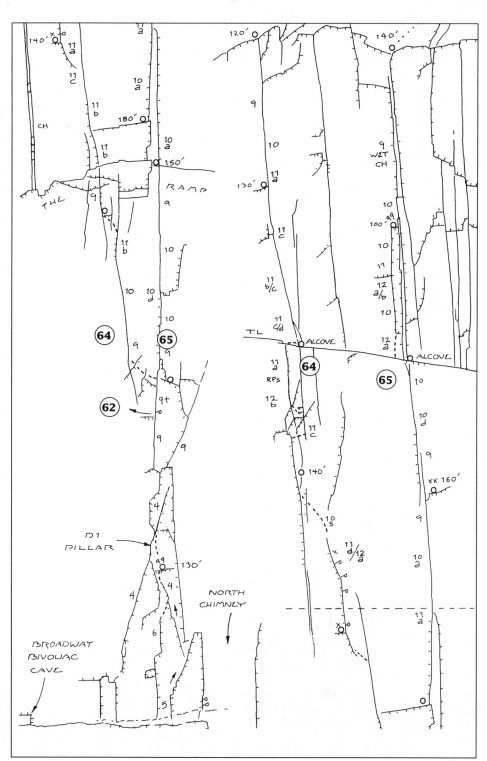

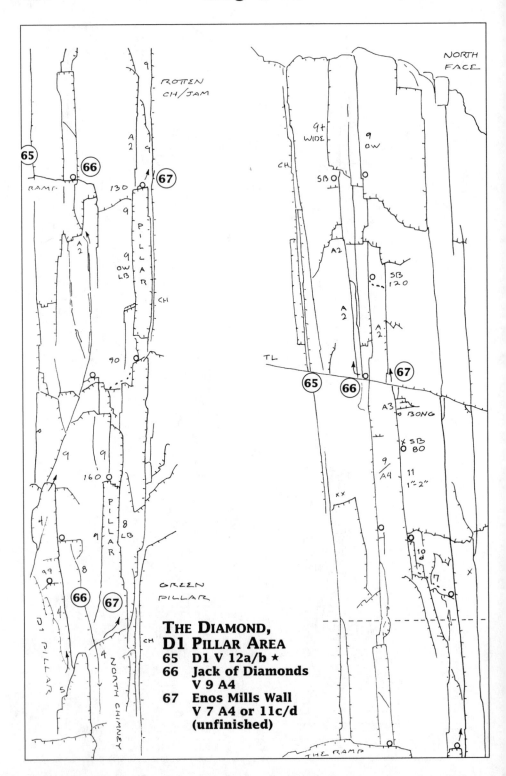

**THE DIAMOND,
D1 PILLAR AREA**
65 D1 V 12a/b ★
66 Jack of Diamonds
V 9 A4
67 Enos Mills Wall
V 7 A4 or 11c/d
(unfinished)

4. Climb the right of two cracks past a small ledge and continue to a stance in a large right-facing dihedral (160 feet).

5. Climb the dihedral and the crack above to Table Ledge (10c? or 9 A4, 100 feet).

6. Traverse 8 feet left along Table Ledge, then climb the left of two cracks to a sling belay beneath a large roof (A2, 150 feet).

7. Climb around the left end of the roof and jam a wide crack up a left-facing dihedral, then veer right in an easy right-facing corner that leads to the broken rock of the north face (9+, 120 feet).

67 Enos Mills Wall   V 7 A4 or 11c/d (unfinished)

FA: Layton Kor and Wayne Goss, 1967. FFA through fifth pitch: Jeff Achey and Leonard Coyne, 1980. Rack up to 4 inches.

The first ascent of this route was also the first winter ascent of The Diamond (climbed in early March). Now a classic aid route, it has repelled all free climbing attempts, however, the pitches up to the sling belay 30 feet below Table Ledge have been climbed free. The line follows a series of steep dihedrals about 75 feet right of *D1*.

1 and 2. This route originally began in the North Chimney along the right side of the D1 Pillar as shown in the topo; however, it is much easier and faster to climb the first two pitches of *D1* and belay on a ledge up to the right.

3. Climb the dihedral and belay on top of the pillar (9, 80 feet).

4. From the right side of the pillar, climb a large left-facing dihedral and chimney for about 60 feet, then angle up and left to a crack and continue until it is possible to climb up and left to a ledge at the base of a huge right-facing dihedral (10, 150 feet). The aid version nails the crack above the left side of the pillar (A2).

5. Climb the strenuous and awkward overhanging dihedral (1.5- to 2-inch crack) to a sling belay under a 3-foot roof (11c/d or A4, 140 feet). Rappel or continue on aid.

6. Turn the roof and nail 30 feet to Table Ledge (the first ascent belayed here). Continue up a crack in rotten rock for about 120 feet until a 10-foot traverse left leads to another sling belay (A2, 160 feet).

7. Climb 50 feet and turn a large, stepped roof, then aid and jam up a crack of varying width (up to 5 inches) to the top of the wall (A2, 150 feet).

67a Variation

Begin from the right side of the North Chimney at Broadway. Climb (mixed free and aid) up the left side of the Green Pillar for 180 feet. Where a chimney/ramp system veers off to the right, move left and climb to the top of a thin expanding flake. Mixed free and aid climbing leads to the bottom of the long flat pillar mentioned above. Climb a right-facing dihedral and chimney along the right side of the pillar (mostly free) and belay on top. Aid up a vertical wall for 80 feet, then pendulum left to a good crack that is climbed to a ledge on the regular route.

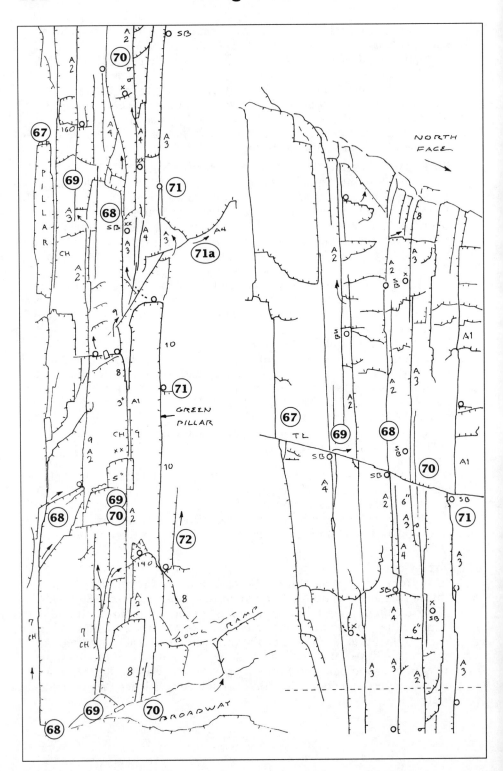

GREEN PILLAR

This 300-foot-high buttress sits across the North Chimney from the D1 Pillar, and is the left and larger of three such features on the north side of the wall. The following four aid climbs begin from this pillar.

68   La Dolce Vita   VI 8 A4

FA: Charlie Fowler and Renato Casaratto, 1984. SR up to 4 inches plus Hooks, RURPs, KBs, and many small angles.

This is The Diamond section of an aid route that begins from the Mills Glacier. It ascends the buttress just left of the North Chimney to reach Broadway, then continues up The Diamond directly above the Green Pillar. The lower section is described under the Lower East Face.

Begin in a chimney along the left side of the Green Pillar.

1. Climb the chimney for 100 feet, then exit right along a ramp and gain a ledge at the bottom of a steep crack (7, 160 feet). This crack also may be reached by climbing up and left from the chimney on *Queen of Hearts*.
2. Climb the crack to the left end of a big ledge (9 A2, 100 feet).
3. Climb a crack and ramp up and right to a higher ledge at the top of the Green Pillar that is suitable for a bivouac (9, 60 feet).
4. Go up and left into a right-facing dihedral and climb to a sling belay beneath an A-shaped roof (A3, 80 feet).
5. Climb through the apex of the roof and work up a wide crack (4 to 6 inches) along the right side of a larger A-shaped formation. Follow this overhanging, left-facing dihedral and belay above the apex where the corner becomes vertical (A4, 150 feet).
6. Continue up the left-facing system and a crack of varying width to a narrow stance below a right-facing dihedral (A4, 100 feet).
7. Climb the dihedral to a niche at Table Ledge (A2, 90 feet).
8. Aid the same crack system straight up the head wall to another sling belay (A2, 150 feet).
9. A final short pitch leads to the top of the head wall. Twenty feet short of the top, break right at a ledge and free climb (8) to the edge of the north face (A2, 100 feet).

69   Queen of Spades   V 8 A4

FA: Mark Hesse and Doug Snively, 1974.

This is one of several aid lines on the right side of The Diamond that has received little attention from free climbers. Rack up to 5 inches; mostly nuts with a few pitons.

Begin at the bottom of a chimney that splits the lower part of the Green Pillar.

THE DIAMOND, GREEN PILLAR AREA

67   Enos Mills Wall V 7 A4 or 11c/d (unfinished)
68   La Dolce Vita VI 8 A4
69   Queen of Spades V 8 A4
70   Gear and Clothing V 9 A4
71   Dunn-Westbay V 8 A3
71a Tail of the Tiger A4
72   King of Swords V 12a (11a s) ★

1. Climb to the top of the chimney, then work up and right along mossy ledges to the base of a steep crack and dihedral (7, 130 feet).
2. Climb the crack and right-facing dihedral, followed by a roof and chimney to a good ledge on the left. This is about 50 feet down and left from the top of the pillar and is suitable for a bivouac (9 A2, 150 feet).
3. From the left end of the ledge, climb a right-facing dihedral to a roof and climb through its left side (A2), then continue to a small stance after 70 feet. Aid left under a flake (A3) to an adjacent crack that is climbed for 60 feet to a belay (160 feet).
4. Aid the crack to a large flake, drop down and gain the left side of the flake, then climb past a bolt to a belay (A3, 150 feet).
5. Traverse left into a prominent crack that splits the smooth, overhanging head wall above. Climb the crack past a very thin section and belay at Table Ledge (A4, 150 feet).
6. Aid 20 feet right along Table Ledge to a shallow left-facing dihedral that is climbed to a sling belay (A2, 120 feet).
7. Continue up the corner to a small roof, then traverse left to the next crack that is climbed to a big ledge 30 feet from the top of the wall (A2, 150 feet).
8. Climb a wide crack above the left end of the ledge, or scramble up and left from the right end of the ledge to reach the broken rock of the north face.

70 Gear and Clothing   V 9 A4
FA: Kyle Copeland and Marc Hirt, 1985. Rack: 5 KB, 10 LA, angles up to 1.25 inches, 15 wired stoppers, 3 sets of Friends, a 6-inch piece, 50 carabiners, and 40 hero loops.
This route gains the top of the Green Pillar, then goes straight up the wall just right of *La Dolce Vita*.
Begin toward the right side of the Green Pillar.
1. Climb a slot to a ledge, then move left and climb a thin crack to a belay on a ledge with a good horn (8 A2, 120 feet).
2. Climb the crack and right-facing dihedral, followed by a roof and chimney to a good ledge on the left. This ledge is about 50 feet down and left from another ledge at the top of the pillar; either is suitable for a bivouac (9 A2, 150 feet).
3. Move up and right along a big ramp to a thin and rotten crack that is climbed to a sling belay from two bolts next to a big roof (8 A4, 140 feet).

THE DIAMOND, BLACK FLAKE PILLAR AREA
71a   Tail of the Tiger A4
72   King of Swords V 12a (11a s) ★
73   Smash the State V 8 A5
74   Its Welx V 9 A4
75   The Joker V 12c ★
76   Christopher Robin V 9 A3
77   Steep Is Flat V 10 A4+
78   Waterhole #3 V 5 A2

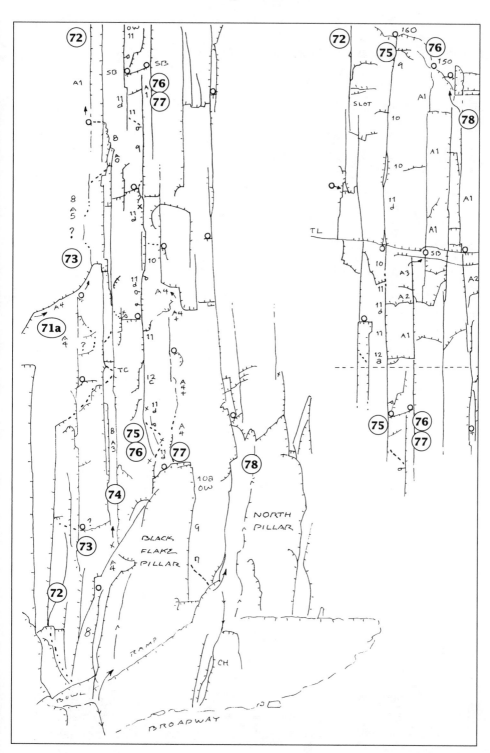

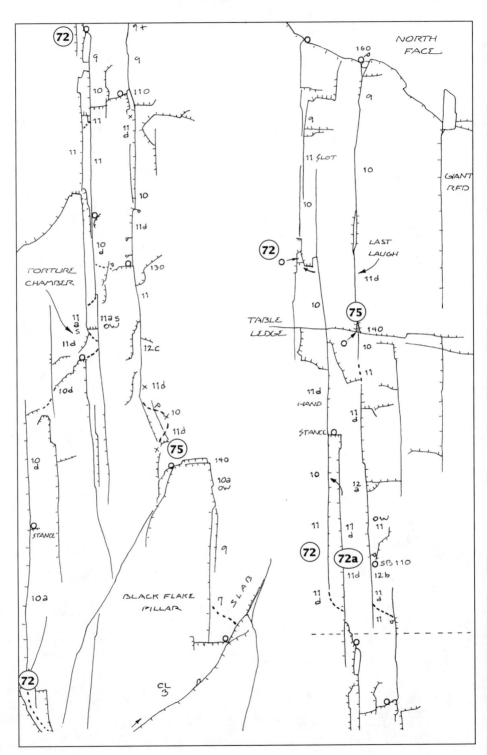

4. Climb a steep right-facing dihedral (A4), then move left and climb a left-facing dihedral to a stance with a bolt (A4, 75 feet).
5. Continue up the dihedral which is thin at first but wide higher up (6 inches) and belay at a bolt after the corner fades (A2, 140 feet).
6. Climb a shallow, overhanging slot (KB) to a double crack system. Climb the right crack until it gets wide, then switch left and turn a 5-foot roof at Table Ledge. Climb another 20 feet and belay in slings from #3 and #4 Friends (A3, 130 feet).
7. Continue in the same parallel cracks, switching sides to avoid wide sections, and belay at a bolt (A3, 140 feet).
8. Aid up the crack system for 75 feet, then climb free to the end of the rope and belay on slabs at the top of the wall (A3, 140 feet).

71 Dunn-Westbay   V 8 A3
FA: Jimmy Dunn and Billy Westbay, 1972. SR to 3 inches plus KBs, hooks, and 0.25-inch bolt hangers.
This route ascends the gigantic right-facing dihedral along the right side of the Green Pillar, then continues straight up the wall.
Begin on the right side of the Green Pillar.
1. Free climb up to a grassy ledge in the huge dihedral (8, 140 feet).
2. and 3. A short pitch followed by a long pitch, or vice versa, brings one to the top of the pillar where a bivouac can be made (8 A2 or 10, 160 feet).
4. Aid up a thin crack, move right on a hook, then work up and left along a flake and belay at its top (A3, 90 feet).
5. Nail a rotten crack and belay in slings (A3, 140 feet).
6 and 7. Continue up the steep crack for two pitches to Table Ledge (A3, 140 and 75 feet).
9. Move 5 feet right and nail a good crack to a stance on the right (A1, 70 feet).
10. More easy aid leads to the top of the wall (A1, 150 feet).

71a Tail of the Tiger   A4
FA: Kris Walker and Walt Walker, 1973.
From the top of the Green Pillar, start the fourth pitch of the *Dunn-Westbay*, then aid up and right along a crack and curvilinear roof to *King of Swords*.

72 King of Swords   V 12a (11a s) ★
FA of first two pitches and FFA of pitches three through seven: Roger Briggs and Dan Stone, 1985. Double SR with three #1 to 2.5 Friends.
Except for the first two pitches, which are original, this is the free version of the aid climb *Its Welx*. It is one of the finest routes on The Diamond. Be prepared for continuously difficult climbing, phenomenal exposure, and a bit of poor rock.
Begin at the right side of the Green Pillar, beneath the first major crack system right of the *Dunn-Westbay* dihedral.

THE DIAMOND, BLACK FLAKE PILLAR AREA, DETAIL
72   King of Swords V 12a (11a s) ★
72a   Gilbert Variation 11d ★
75   The Joker V 12c ★

1. Climb 90 feet up to a vertical right-facing dihedral and follow it to a stance (10a, 120 feet).
2. Follow the corner for another 60 feet, then work up and right for 50 feet to a pedestal above a right-facing dihedral (10d, 150 feet).
3. This pitch navigates a rotten recess called the Torture Chamber and is one of the most intimidating of the climb. Step right into the main crack (*Its Welx*) and climb to where it goes offwidth. Move left (11d) and climb a crack for 25 feet (11a s), then work back into the main crack and climb to a tiny stance (11d, 100 feet).
4. Climb straight up a fist crack past a roof to a stance (11, 150 feet).
5. Work straight up until it is possible to move left on flakes and gain a clean finger crack that forms the left side of a long pillar. Climb the crack and belay atop the pillar (11c/d, 100 feet).
6. Climb a hand crack to Table Ledge and continue for about 40 feet, then traverse left and belay (11d, 140 feet).
7. Climb a steep crack with a difficult slot, then shoot straight for the top of the wall passing some small roofs along the way (11, 140 feet).

72a　Gilbert Variation　　11d ★
3. Step right into the main crack but continue up the gaping offwidth section (11a s).
5. Climb the super-clean dihedral along the right side of the pillar until it is possible to move left and continue to the top of the pillar (11d, 100 feet). FA: Michael Gilbert.

73　Smash the State　　V 8 A5
FA: Jim Beyer, solo, 1989.
It takes your money without your consent, spends it on things you don't want, then tells you what you can and cannot do. Now why would anyone want to *Smash the State?*
Though I have a rough topo of this route, apparently drawn by Jim Beyer, it is difficult tell exactly where it goes. It begins in the recess between the Green Pillar and the Black Flake Pillar, then wanders back and forth between *King of Swords* and *The Joker*. It appears to take the left-hand version on the fifth pitch of *King of Swords* and then continues with that route to the top of the wall.

BLACK FLAKE PILLAR
This small buttress sits across a gap to the north from the Green Pillar and has a flat and narrow black face. It is 150 feet high and is accessed by a ramp that angles up and right along its base. The following four routes begin from this feature.

74　Its Welx　　V 9 A4
FA: Dan McClure and Mark Hesse, 1973.
This very difficult aid route begins in the recess between the Green Pillar and the Black Flake Pillar. Except for the first two pitches, the route has been climbed free under the name *King of Swords* (above).
1. Climb a chimney along the left side of the Black Flake Pillar and belay beneath a thin crack that arches up and right (8, 75 feet).
2. Aid up the thin crack (A4) to a bolt, then climb straight up a rotten crack system to a narrow ledge beneath a gaping recess now known as the Torture Chamber (8 A3, 150 feet).
Continue as for *King of Swords.*

75   The Joker   V 12c ★

FA/FFA: Roger Briggs and Steve Levin (with the addition of several bolts, fixed pins, and nuts) took several falls on three pitches and used two points of aid passing the Last Laugh above Table Ledge, 1993. The first complete free ascent was made by Roger Briggs and Pat Adams, 1994. Rack: medium RPs to large stoppers, two sets #0.5 to 3 Friends, plus a #3.5 and 4 Friend. Pitches two and three have many fixed nuts and require only a #0.5 to 3 Friend with two #2 Friends on the second pitch, plus many QDs.

This route free climbs the first three and a half pitches of *Christopher Robin,* then switches to a previously unclimbed crack on the left and continues straight to the top of wall. It is at time of writing the hardest free climb on The Diamond. Begin at the alcove below *King of Swords* and scramble up and right along a ramp to the bottom of a big right-facing dihedral that forms the right side of the Black Flake Pillar.

1. Climb the dihedral and belay at the south end of the ledge on top of the pillar (10a, 140 feet).
2. Start with a small right-facing dihedral, follow cracks up and right past two bolts, then work back left into the main crack system and continue to a stance on the left (12c, 130 feet).
3. Follow the crack system straight up and gain a good ledge on the left (11d, 110 feet).
4. Climb straight up the crack to a fixed pin, work up and left to another crack, and continue for 30 feet to a sling belay at a fixed pin (12b, 110 feet).
5. Climb a flip-flop right-to-left-facing dihedral and belay in a niche at Table Ledge (12a, 140 feet).
6. Climb the difficult crack above the niche past a wide (and wet) section called the Last Laugh, then continue in the same crack to the top of the wall (11d, 160 feet).

76   Christopher Robin   V 9 A3

FA: Kris Walker, solo, 1972. Rack up to a #4 Friend with an assortment of thin pitons.

This spectacular aid route ascends the overhanging wall about 30 feet right of *King of Swords.* It was assumed that *The Joker* free climbed the entire line of *Christopher Robin,* but after reviewing the routes with Kris Walker, it became apparent that they diverge halfway up the fourth pitch. Begin as for *The Joker.*

4. From the right end of the bivouac ledge, climb a shallow left-facing dihedral straight up to a tiny stance on the right (9 A1, 100 feet).
5. Climb the left-facing dihedral on the right to the highest of several small roofs at an offset section of the Table Ledge crack (A3 near the top). Traverse about 10 feet right (still on aid) to a sling belay at the bottom of a beautiful crack that leads straight up the head wall (A3, 150 feet).
6. Aid the flower-filled crack to the top of the wall (A1, 150 feet).

77   Steep Is Flat   V 10 A4+

FA: Jim Beyer and Pat McInerney, 1990. SR to 4 inches plus 20 copperheads, 10 KB, 6 LA, 2 angles each up to 0.75 inch, 7 beaks, and a double set of hooks.

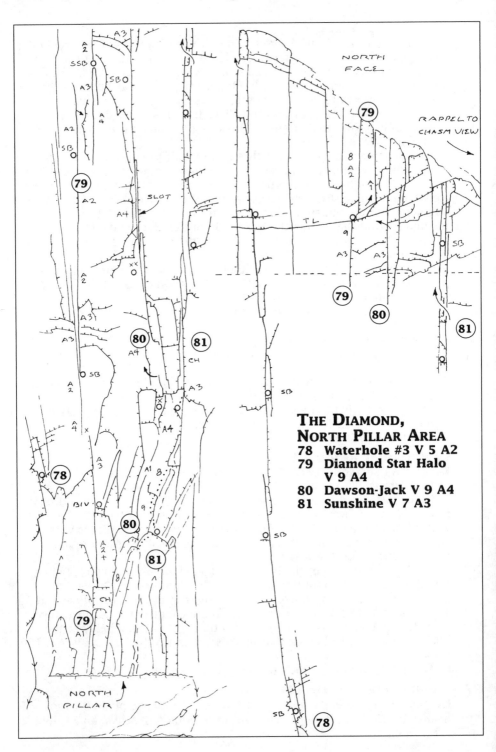

**THE DIAMOND,
NORTH PILLAR AREA**
78 Waterhole #3 V 5 A2
79 Diamond Star Halo
    V 9 A4
80 Dawson-Jack V 9 A4
81 Sunshine V 7 A3

This route climbs the steep wall between *Christopher Robin* and *Waterhole #3* to arrive at the bivouac ledge for *Christopher Robin*. The upper part of the route appears to be largely the same as *Christopher Robin* except that Beyer switched to a crack on the right about 30 feet from the top. The line of the route shown in the topo is based on Beyer's sketch and is approximate.

NORTH PILLAR

This is the farthest right of three buttresses to the right of the North Chimney. It is shaped somewhat like an owl and is higher than the Black Flake Pillar. About 200 feet above the North Pillar, two curvilinear streaks of dark rock known as The Horsetails sweep up to the right and aid in locating features on the following routes.

78   Waterhole #3   V 5 A2

FA: Kris Walker, solo, 1971. SR plus an assortment of pitons (mostly thin).

This aid route ascends the left side of the North Pillar, then sweeps up and left in a continuous crack system that leads to an enormous roof at the top of the wall. It was the first route on the right side of The Diamond and the first solo ascent of a completely new route. Bill Forrest made the first solo ascent of The Diamond in 1970, but the first two-thirds of his route followed *The Yellow Wall.*

Scramble up a ramp to gain the recess between the Black Flake Pillar and the North Pillar. The route described utilizes the fewest possible belays; the first ascent took three days and required 10 pitches due to an inadequate rack.

1. Climb a steep crack along the left side of the North Pillar and belay at a stance above an A-shaped roof (150 feet).
2. Follow a good crack up and left and belay in slings above the The Horsetails (160 feet).
3. Follow the crack system past a wide section and a roof, and belay at a stance in the bottom of a chimney (130 feet).
4. Climb 60 feet and change to a crack on the left, continue past Table Ledge (a roof at this point), and belay 10 feet higher (140 feet).
5. Follow a crack up a right-facing dihedral to a big roof that is passed on the left, and continue a very short way to the top of the wall (150 feet).

79   Diamond Star Halo   V 9 A4

FA: Charlie Fowler, Kyle Copeland, and Joe Burke, 1986. Rack: 12 KB, 12 LA, five each angles up to 1 inch, four each 1.25- and 1.5-inch angles, two 2-inch angles, two 3-inch angles, assorted hooks, 15 bashies, a few RURPs, many wired nuts, several Tricams up to #7, and three complete sets of Friends.

This spectacular aid route ascends the North Pillar, then goes straight up the overhanging wall through the right side of The Horsetails. The wall leans out so far that water dripping from the top falls 15 feet free of the lower face. When the cracks fizzle out, a double pendulum affords access to a left-facing dihedral system that leads to the top of the wall.

Scramble onto a ledge at the bottom of the North Pillar and set the initial belay at a left-facing dihedral.
1. Climb the dihedral to a small ledge (optional belay), then aid a thin crack to a recess in the top of the pillar (9 A2+, 130 feet). Bivouac site.
2. Climb the right-facing dihedral above the left side of the recess until the crack fades, move left past a bolt, and aid up a very difficult crack/seam to a sling belay (A4, 100 feet).
3. Follow parallel cracks up the wall past some roofs and belay in slings (A3, 150 feet).
4. Continue up the crack system for about 40 feet (A2), then tension traverse right to a thin, left-facing flake and place a pin. Traverse right again to a rotten seam and climb 60 feet to a stance (A4, 120 feet).
5. Climb straight up into an overhanging left-facing dihedral with a short wide section and follow it to a small, grassy platform at Table Ledge (9 A3, 150 feet).
6. Climb a short left-facing corner past a roof and follow a crack to the top of the wall (8 A2, 75 feet).

80   Dawson-Jack   V 9 A4

FA: Lou Dawson and Richard Jack, 1975. SR to 3 inches plus RURPs, hooks, and many pitons.
This very difficult route ascends the long, left-facing dihedral at the far right side of The Diamond. Begin up on a ledge at the right side of the North Pillar and beneath a right-leaning chimney about 30 feet right of *Diamond Star Halo.*
1. Climb the chimney (8 wet) and continue up a crack to a ledge (8, 140 feet).
2. Face climb up and right (9) to a crack that is aided to a bolt beneath the huge roof (A1 to A4, 90 feet).
3. Nail right to pass the roof, then tension traverse left to a crack that leads to an overhanging left-facing dihedral, and climb the dihedral to a bolt belay (A4, 130 feet).
4. Climb thin cracks beside a rotten slot, then follow an easier crack past a hollow flake and continue to a sling belay beneath a series of roofs (A4, 150 feet).
5. Climb through the roofs (A3) to Table Ledge, then traverse left to a good stance (likely the last belay for *Diamond Star Halo* (A3, 120 feet).
6. Climb up and right into a left-facing dihedral that leads to the top of the wall (5 A1, 80 feet).

81   Sunshine   V 7 A3

FA: Jim Beyer, solo, 1973. Augmented SR plus hooks, and pins from KBs to 4 inches.
Fifty feet right of the long left-facing dihedral of *Dawson-Jack*, a long right-facing dihedral leads to a gigantic roof. *Sunshine* follows the latter dihedral and climbs out the left side of the roof.
Begin toward the right side of the long grassy ledge that runs beneath the North Pillar, a short way right of the wet chimney of the preceding route.
1. Climb broken cracks to a grassy ledge beneath a large flake.

2. Climb the flake and the wall above to a grassy ledge, then go up and right in a trough to a right-facing corner that is climbed to another ledge.

3. Work up and right to a rotten left-facing dihedral that leads up and left to a big roof. Aid around the right end of the roof (A3) and gain a chimney that is climbed to another roof. Pass this on the right and continue to a good ledge.

4. Climb up past a flake and belay on a square-cut ledge between parallel cracks.

5. Climb the crack on the right and go left around a roof. Continue up through a break between a small roof on the left and a big roof on the right, and belay in slings.

6. Follow a crack to the top of the wall.

Keyboard of the Winds, South Tower.   Photo: Robert Cassady

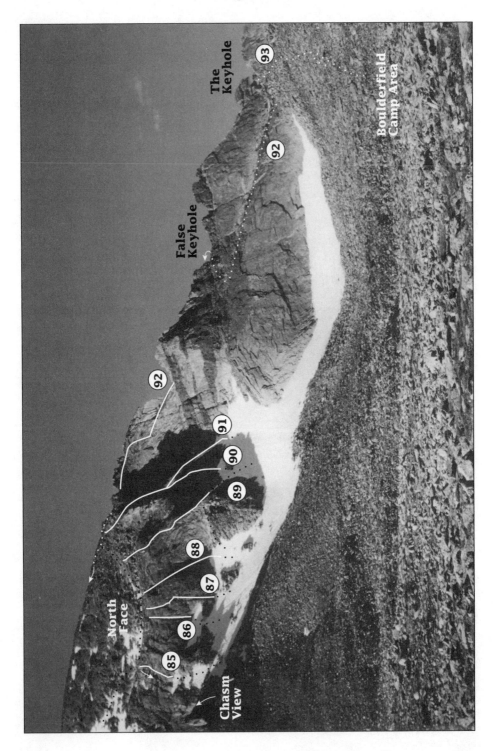

Upper Chasm View Wall
The following three routes begin from the north end of Broadway and ascend the banded wall just right of The Diamond.

82 Hornbein Crack   II 8+
FA: Tom Hornbein and Cary Huston, 1953. Rack up to six inches.
This climb begins from the north end of Broadway and ends at Chasm View. There are four pitches each harder than the preceding; the last pitch features a 50-foot lieback up a vertical offwidth crack. The crack about 10 feet east of the offwidth has been climbed on aid.

83 V-Notch Exit   II 7 ★
FA: Roger Briggs.
This is the easiest way to reach Chasm View from Broadway. Traverse north along Broadway and identify a distinct V-notch on the skyline about 200 feet right of Chasm View. Continue past the Chasm View rappels and scramble up ramps and ledges until directly beneath a steep chimney. Climb the chimney and crack system that lead to the notch in a single pitch, then walk through to the talus slope on the north side. Other parties have reported this route to be more difficult (9) and the chimney somewhat loose.

84 Chasm Cut-Off   II 7
FA: Bill Eubank, Tom Hornbein, and Brad Van Diver, 1950.
This ancient route follows a ledge system along the lowest band of schist that runs across the top of Chasm View Wall and provides an escape from Broadway that does not involve the North Chimney or Lambs Slide. From the north end of Broadway, follow a narrowing, grassy ledge system that traverses out over Chasm View Wall. Pass a small corner and an undercut area. Eventually the ledge fades and one is confronted with a small overhang; climb this directly by pulling on a fixed pin. Traverse right a ways, climb a small flake, and step around onto the ridge crest.

North Face
The north face of Longs Peak lies between the north edge of The Diamond and the Keyhole Ridge (the northwest ridge). There are several routes on the north face, most of which were established by guides during the 1930s when there was a small hotel in the Boulderfield. Except for the *North Face* route (aka *The Cables*) and the *Keyhole Ridge*, the others are seldom climbed. The popular route called *The Keyhole* passes through a large notch of the same

North Face, View from the Boulderfield
85   North Face II 4 or M2 ★
86   Evs Chimney 2
87   Webbs Walk-Up 4
88   Zumies Chimney 2
89   Marys Ledges 3
90   Left Dovetail I 4 AI3
91   RightDovetail I 4 AI3
92   Keyhole Ridge II 5 ★
93   The Keyhole Class 2 ★

name at a low point in northwest ridge, then continues around the west and south sides of the peak. Use Approach B for Longs Peak and hike to the Boulderfield (5.9 miles). The north face is directly above the Boulderfield.

85   North Face   II 4 or M2 ★
FA: probably Enos Mills, early twentieth century.
Of all the moderate routes on Longs Peak, this one is the most direct. It is a good snow climb during winter and spring and an excellent scramble during the summer. In 1925 and 1926, steel cables were installed on the slab above Chasm View, which eliminated the need for a rope. The *North Face* (thereafter known as *The Cables*) became the most popular route on the mountain. The cables, and most of the eyebolts to which they were secured, were removed in 1973. One bolt at the top of the slab and one halfway up were left in place for belays and rappels. *The Keyhole,* which is easier but considerably longer, quickly became the most popular route on the mountain.
From the Boulderfield, hike over boulders and scree toward the far north corner of The Diamond and gain the notch at Chasm View. Here one can gaze out across The Diamond and into the void of the Chasm Lake Cirque. Climb a moderate slab and right-facing dihedral to the right of The Diamond for 150 feet to an eyebolt and easier ground. Cracks and corners to the right are of equal difficulty. Scramble south to the summit.

86   Ev's Chimney   2
FA: Ev Long and Melvin Wickens, 1931.
Climb a couple of easy pitches up the wet chimney at the right edge of the *North Face* slabs.

87   Webb's Walk-Up   4
FA: Peter Webb and John Koch, 1963.
Begin a short way right of *Evs Chimney* and follow a crack system up and left for about three pitches.

88   Zumie's Chimney   2
FA: Clerin Zumwalt and Ev Long, 1932.
This route ascends the chimney at the left side of the buttress that runs up the middle of the wall. Three pitches.

89   Mary's Ledges   3
Wickins and Gilman, 1930.
This route ascends the right side of the prominent buttress in the middle of the north face.

90   Left Dovetail   I 4 AI3
FA: Warren Gorrell, Alene Wharton, and Dr. Watson, 1935.
To the right of the previous route is a smaller buttress. Climb a shallow gully up and right across this buttress to a snow patch in a gully at the far right side of the north face, then climb the face above the left side of the snow patch to easier ground.

91   Right Dovetail   I 4 AI3
FA: Melvin Wickins, 1930.

At the far right side of the north face, a snow couloir climbs to a notch in the northwest ridge of Longs Peak. A forked snow patch that resembles a bird's tail (the Dovetail) occupies the lower part of the couloir. This route climbs the couloir for about 300 feet to a higher snow patch, then follows a ramp and gully up and right to the notch on the Keyhole Ridge.

92 Keyhole Ridge   II 5 ★
FA: J.W. Alexander and Smith, 1924.
This is an excellent route up the exposed and spectacular northwest ridge of Longs Peak. From the Boulderfield, hike to the Keyhole Shelter, then traverse south along a ledge system on the east side of the ridge to a notch called the False Keyhole (cl2). This point also can be reached from the west side and places one above the first tower on the ridge. Scramble up the ridge crest to the steeper part of the second tower (cl4), then follow an easy ramp on the east side (cl4). From the end of the ramp, climb straight up to the top of the tower (4). Descend 10 feet to a ledge on the west side and follow it to the notch on the south side of the second tower. This notch may also be reached by traversing the west side of the second tower: From the False Keyhole, make an ascending traverse around a small buttress and belay out on a spectacular gendarme with a flat top (4). Climb straight up the west side of the second tower until it is possible to traverse a narrow ramp up and right to the notch (4).
Scramble up a wide ramp to the east side of a dramatic buttress and set a belay. Work up and left along a narrow ramp for about 75 feet, then climb straight up perfect rock to the ridge crest (5). It also is possible to climb up and left directly from the belay (6). Scramble along the crest just on its east side, and pass through a small notch to the west side. Regain the crest and continue up solid rock to the summit plateau.

93 The Keyhole   Class 2 ★
FA: Brown, 1870.
This unlikely route is the easiest, longest, and most popular on Longs Peak. It is traveled by thousands of people every year. From the Boulderfield (12750), hike southwest over large talus to a curious notch (like a fallen arch) called The Keyhole (13150). A beehive-shaped stone shelter stands just southeast of the notch and can provide some protection in stormy weather. Cross to the west side of The Keyhole where the slope drops for 2000 feet into Glacier Gorge. Head south (left) along a faint path that is marked periodically by red spots with yellow centers painted on the rocks. The route climbs slightly at first along an area called The Ledges, then descends to pass the northwest rib of the summit block.
Continue following the painted dots as they lead gradually back up to intersect a long gully called The Trough at 13300 feet (c. 0.3 mile from The Keyhole). Hike up The Trough, which holds snow until late summer, and gain a platform on the crest of the southwest ridge at 13850 feet. This spired ridge that extends to Pagoda Mountain is called the Keyboard of the Winds. Follow a ledge called The Narrows for about 700 feet across the south face. When the ledge fades, scramble up and left

to a break in the steep summit block called The Homestretch. Follow parallel cracks up slabs to the northeast and gain the summit plateau. The summit is marked by a large cairn.

93a Direct Trough   Class 3 or AI2
The Trough also may be reached from Glacier Gorge. From Black Lake, follow the trail into the Spearhead Cirque. Climb snow or rocky slopes into the bottom of The Trough and join *The Keyhole* route at 13300 feet.

93b West Chimney   4
FA: Long and Zumwalt, 1932.
Climb the left of two chimneys between The Narrows and The Homestretch.

93c East Chimney   2
Climb the right of two chimneys between The Narrows and The Homestretch.

West Face
The west face of Longs Peak would bask in etenal obscurity were it not directly above The Trough of *The Keyhole* route. Yet, for the thousands of people who pass beneath this massive wall every year, it is very seldom climbed. From the Spearhead Cirque, the wall appears steep and difficult, but upon closer inspection, it proves less imposing. The west face is about 600 feet high and, being entirely above 13000 feet, provides some of the most spectacular moderate climbing in Colorado. Reach the west face via *The Keyhole* or by hiking up the *Direct Trough* from Glacier Gorge (q.v.).

94 Northwest Couloir   II Class 4
FA: Enos Mills climbed this route in 1896 but found evidence of a prior ascent. About midway between The Keyhole and the left edge of the west face (the northwest rib), a steep rocky gully climbs to the ridge crest. Work up the left side of the gully and pass through a hole. Above, easier terrain leads to the crest of the northwest ridge, which is followed without difficulty to the summit. Beware of loose rock.

95 Northwest Rib   II 5 ★
To the right of the Northwest Couloir, a distinct rib or buttress climbs to the crest of the northwest ridge and provides an excellent route. Begin on the left side of the rib, then work up and right to the prow, which is followed for three pitches to the ridge crest.

96 Dialogue on Zen   II 7 ★
FA: Tim Hogan and Richard Rossiter, 1986.
"Things are not what they appear—nor are they otherwise." A short way right of the northwest rib, a trough climbs to the crest of the Keyhole Ridge. The left side of the trough is formed by two right-facing dihedrals. This route ascends the left of the two dihedrals.
Begin among slabs and ledges to the right of the northwest rib.
1. Climb a 4-inch crack and belay on the upper of two ledges (4, 90 feet).
2. Climb a thin crack in a clean slab and gain a right-facing dihedral that is followed to a stance above an offset in the dihedral (6, 150 feet).

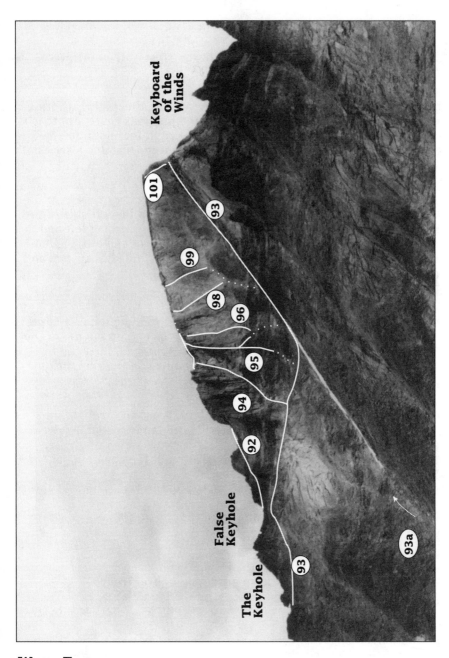

Keyboard of the Winds

False Keyhole

The Keyhole

WEST FACE

92	**Keyhole Ridge II 5** ★
93	**The Keyhole Class 2** ★
93a	**Direct Trough Class 3 or AI2**
94	**Northwest Couloir II Class 4**
95	**Northwest Rib II 5** ★
96	**Dialogue on Zen II 7** ★
98	**Van Divers West Wall II 2**
99	**West Wall II 5** ★
101	**Southwest Ridge II 4** ★

3. Climb the dihedral to where it fades, then move right and belay at a stance in the next corner to the right (7, 150 feet).
4. Climb a chimney and the face above to the crest of the northwest ridge (5, 100 feet).

97 Far Left   II 6

This route passes to the right of a large left-facing dihedral that forms the right side of the trough mentioned in the previous route. Approach as for the previous route, but angle up to the right for about 200 feet before engaging the steeper part of the face. Ascend slabs to a series of cracks that are followed to the top of the wall.

98 Van Diver's West Wall   II 2

FA: Brad Van Diver and Bob Working, 1956.
This route follows a right-facing dihedral/trough up the left side of the wall. Follow *The Keyhole* all the way to The Trough, then cut left and climb to the top of a gully that runs along the left side of a triangular buttress. Work up and left into a long, right-facing dihedral system and follow it up and left to the top of the Keyhole Ridge.

99 West Wall   II 5 ★

FA: Bill Eubanks and Brad Van Diver, 1950.
This route ascends the middle of the west wall from the top of a large, triangular buttress at the bottom center of the face. Gain the top of the triangular buttress via the gully on its left or right side, then climb straight up on solid rock and pass through a break in the summit rim.

100 Fourth of July   II 4

FA: Kenyon King and Clarence Gusthurst, 1963.
The exact location of this route is not known. From The Trough, traverse left to "an obvious open book crack" with "an excellent belay flake."
1. Climb 50 feet up and left to a large platform at the beginning of the open book.
2. Lieback and jam up a steep flake/crack (piton in vertical crack) and belay on a big ledge.
3. Work up the face, traverse a short way right, then follow a crack to the top of the wall.

101 Southwest Ridge   II 4 ★

FA: J. W. Alexander and partner, 1924.
This line begins from the platform at the top of The Trough.
Scramble up about 40 feet and belay behind a large flake.
1. Traverse left and up ledges until a steep gully leads back to a belay on the crest of the ridge.
2. Pass an overhang, then work up to an exposed belay.
3. Scramble over ledges, then pass the final blocks on the right.

KEYBOARD OF THE WINDS

The sweeping, serrated southwest ridge of Longs Peak presents a very dramatic skyline from the Spearhead Cirque. There are at least seven towers, all above 13000 feet, several of which are quite impressive. Despite their high visisbility, only one route has been recorded. Approach via Glacier Gorge.

102 Music for the Fingers   II 10a

FA: Greg Sievers and Rob Cassidy, 1994.

This route ascends the south face of the first tower north of the Longs-Pagoda col. From Green Lake, scramble up slabs and scree (or snow) to the col, and begin the climb 30 feet right of the southwest corner of the tower.

1. Climb small, broken dihedrals up and right and belay on a small platform split by a four-inch crack (8, 150 feet).
2. Climb a four-foot-wide inset followed by thin cracks in an orange band, then lieback up a right-facing edge (crux). Angle left for 10 feet, then work up and right to white rock near the summit. Good cracks (8) lead to the top (10a, 120 feet).

103 Keplinger's Couloir   II Class 3

FA: Major Powell and party, 1868.

This is the route by which the mountain was first ascended. It is most easily reached from Sandbeach Lake in Wild Basin, however, the route was originally approached from Grand Lake. This route is an arduous but not difficult alternative to *The Keyhole*.

Park at Copeland Lake (8350) and hike the Sandbeach Lake Trail to Sandbeach Lake (10283). From the lake, head north, then west and follow Hunters Creek to an unnamed lake at 11180 feet. Directly north of the lake is the narrow southeast spur of Pagoda Mountain. Hike north up the valley just east of the spur to about 11800 feet, then veer right and climb the left and most obvious of several gullies (*Keplinger's Couloir*) to the basin below The Notch on the southeast ridge of Longs Peak. Make an ascending traverse northwest along ramps and ledges and intersect *The Keyhole* just below The Homestretch. Climb the final slab of *The Keyhole* to the summit. See also *Clark's Arrow*.

THE PALISADES

The Palisades are a series of very impressive towers and buttresses south of The Notch, on the west side of the southeast ridge of Longs Peak. The most prominent features are two large towers, each about 400 feet high. The Great White Tower is nearest The Notch and features the earliest known route, the *Great Chimney*, on its north side. Wysteria Tower rises some 300 feet to the south and is among the most beautiful features in Rocky Mountain National Park. If these towers were at Lumpy Ridge, their routes would be renowned classics with every nook and cranny explored, but being seven hard miles from the nearest trailhead, only the most striking lines have been climbed.

The Palisades are most easily viewed from the Narrows of *The Keyhole*, but most easily approached via *The Loft* and *Clark's Arrow*. The shortest return to the bottom of the Palisades is via Gorrells Traverse or by a 50-meter rappel into the Notch. It also is easy to hike down the southeast ridge of Longs Peak to The Loft and return via *Clark's Arrow*. Another option is to leave nothing at the bottom of the climb and hike home from the top; but once on location, it may be worthwhile to do more than one route.

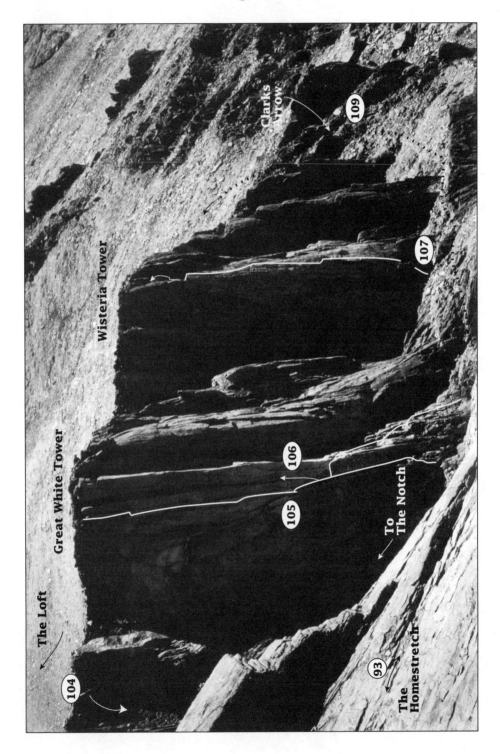

104 Gorrells Traverse   II Class 4

FA: probably Werner Zimmerman, 1919, but made known by Ernie Gorrell.

This unlikely route connects the top of the ridge south of The Notch with the final section of *Keplinger's Couloir*, and hence, the summit of Longs Peak. Though it is described here as a summit route, it is more useful as a means of return to the base of the The Palisades. Use Approach A and climb *The Loft* route as described under Mount Meeker. From The Loft, hike northwest to the high point of the southeast ridge above The Notch. Descend to the west and locate two cairns that mark the tops of two chimneys. Downclimb the north chimney for about 200 feet to a broken platform that is about 100 feet above the gully leading up to The Notch. Rappel into the gully from the north end of the platform or (better) traverse up and left toward The Notch until it is possible to scramble down into the gully. Cross the gully and merge with the last section of *Keplinger's Couloir*, or turn south to reach the bottom of The Palisades and *Clark's Arrow*.

105 Cold Turkey Waltz   II 10 ★

FA: Salaun and Alexander, 1977. SR to 4 inches.

The Great Chimney splits the north face of the Great White Tower, just left of the northwest arête. This route climbs the second crack left of the Great Chimney.

1. Climb up and right to a stance at the bottom of the crack.
2. Jam the crack past two small roofs, a short crux, and belay at a stance in a right-facing dihedral.
3. Climb to the top of the dihedral and change to the crack on the right. After a short way, move back to the original crack and continue to the top.

106 Great Chimney   II 6 ★

FA: Camp Hale outing, 1957.

This route ascends the prominent chimney just left of the northwest arête of the Great White Tower. Begin in the huge chimney to the right of the arête that is capped by a large overhang.

1. Scramble up broken rock for about 100 feet, then traverse up and left around the northwest arête to a pedestal. Move down and left into a right-facing dihedral and belay. It may be possible to climb directly up to this belay.
2. Climb to near the top of the dihedral, then pull up and right into a crack that widens into the main chimney higher up. Belay on a flake after it is possible to squeeze into the chimney.
3. Climb up and around the right side of a chockstone and continue to the top of the tower.

THE PALISADES, FROM THE NORTHWEST

107 Autumn Sonata   III 10c ★

FA: Alexander and Salaun,1981. SR to 5 inches.

This fantastic route follows a prominent crack system up the west face of Wysteria Tower. Begin at the north side of a huge block that has separated from the wall.

1. Climb the block for 25 feet, then stem across to the main wall and crank into the bottom of a prominet left-facing dihedral that is followed to the highest of several stances (10a, 130 feet).
2. Continue up the dihedral past a roof (10c), then follow an easier crack up and right to the top of a flake (120 feet).
3. From the left side of the flake, climb to the top of a right-facing dihedral with a wide crack and step left on a ledge to belay (9, 100 feet).
4. Climb past the right end of a roof to some flakes, then go right and up a crack to the top (7, 75 feet).

108 Alexander and the Hawk   II 10 ★

FA: Salaun and Alexander, 1977. SR to 5 inches.

This route climbs a big open-book dihedral on the southwest side of the second buttress south of Wysteria Tower, which is the first major buttress north of the block upon which Clark painted his arrow. Lieback up a big flake to a stance (8), then jam a wide crack to a bench (10). Rappel or climb a chimney to the top of the cliff.

109 Clark's Arrow   II Class 3 or AI2 ★

Clark's Arrow is an excellent and seldom traveled route to the summit of Longs Peak, being shorter than *The Keyhole* and only slightly more difficult. Use Approach A and climb *The Loft* route as described under Mount Meeker. From the far west aspect of The Loft, contour northwest and locate some cairns. Scramble down a gully for about 150 feet to a small buttress on the right (north) that has a white arrow in a circle (Clark's Arrow) painted on its west face. Hike north along a faint path that passes beneath the towers of The Palisades and gain the scree-filled basin below The Notch (13600). Make an ascending traverse northwest along ramps and ledges and join *The Keyhole* just below the Homestretch. Follow cracks up the Homestretch to the summit.

LONGS PEAK SPEED RECORDS.

High-speed ascents of Longs Peak have been logged by some of Colorado's best endurance athletes, and some very challenging events have been created along the way. Following are examples of known events and times.

1. Timed ascents (one-way) from the East Longs Peak Trailhead via the *North Face*:

Roger Briggs — 1:24, 1975.

Chris Reveley — 1:23, 1979.

Mike Sullivan — 1:18:31, 1984.

2. Round trip (trailhead to summit to trailhead):

Chris Reveley — 2:04 (which includes the record descent time of 0:42 minutes).

3. Longs Peak Triathlon via *Kiener's* (bicycle from north Boulder city limits to East Longs Peak Trailhead; up trail and *Kiener's* to summit, then reverse to Boulder):

Bill Briggs — 15 hours, 9 October 1974.

4. Longs Peak Triathlon via The Diamond with rope solo of the *Casual Route* (climbing gear supplied on location):

Bill Briggs — no time given, 25 August 1986.

5. Longs Peak Triathlon (one-way) via free solo of the *Casual Route*; no support team:

Roger Briggs — 5:45, 8 August 1991 (timed by second party).

GLACIER GORGE, FROM THE NORTH

GLACIER GORGE

The west slope of Longs Peak drops 3000 feet into a rugged basin at the head of Glacier Gorge known as the Spearhead Cirque. Here, some of the most impressive walls and spires in Rocky Mountain National Park tower above fields of wildflowers, ice-scoured slabs, and jewel-like lakes, comprising an alpine paradise of exceptional beauty. For nearly a century, climbers have made their way up the long U-shaped valley of Glacier Gorge, to this place above tree line where the trail fades and the earth rises up, to explore the great faces and carouse in the mystic wildness.

The Spearhead Cirque, also known as the Black Lake Cirque, is 2 miles wide and is formed by Longs Peak (on the east), Pagoda Mountain, Chiefs Head Peak, McHenrys Peak, and the Arrowhead. In the middle of the cirque, profiled against the broad north face of Chiefs Head, is a spectacular island peak called Spearhead. Below, surrounded by steep cliffs and waterfalls is Black Lake, from which Glacier Creek cascades northward to join the Big Thompson River.

Glacier Gorge Trail. To reach Glacier Gorge and the Spearhead Cirque (as well as Loch Vale and Sky Pond), take the Bear Lake Road and park at a lot inside a hairpin turn one mile before the end of the road. The Glacier Gorge Trailhead is across the road to the south. If this lot is full (and it often is), continue up to the Bear Lake parking area at the end of the road. On summer weekends, this lot also will be full by about 9:00 AM. To reach the trailhead from the Bear Lake area, walk west as though going to Bear Lake with the tourists, but go left at a trail junction and hike downhill for a half mile to the Glacier Gorge Trailhead.

Hike the Glacier Gorge Trail to the Loch Vale Junction at 1.9 miles. Take the left branch and continue to Mills Lake at 2.5 miles and Black Lake at 4.7 miles. Hop boulders up the inlet to Black Lake, then follow the trail along the east side of the lake and up a drainage to the southeast. Take a right branch and continue to where the trail fades in the tundra about a half mile northeast of Spearhead. Cairns mark two similar routes that lead across glacier slabs to a pond below Spearhead. Bivouac permits are available for this area, but any of the routes can be completed car-to-car in a long day by an athletic team.

Note: A useful shortcut to the Glacier Gorge Trail branches right after about 0.25 mile and saves perhaps 20 minutes of hiking. This well-developed footpath begins at an inobvious point just beyond the third stream crossing and regains the main trail a short way east of the Loch Vale Junction.

Solitude Lake Trail. Hike the Glacier Gorge Trail for about 4 miles to where the trail passes through a second boggy area on split logs and re-enters the trees. This primitive trail breaks right from the trees and crosses a grassy meadow to Glacier Creek. Ford the creek by jumping from boulders, then labor up the steep hillside to Shelf Lake and Solitude Lake. This trail accesses routes on the Arrowhead, the east face of Powell Peak, and McHenrys Notch.

HALF MOUNTAIN

Half Mountain (11482) forms the terminus of the extensive north ridge of Longs Peak. Its steep west face rises 1600 feet above Mills Lake and, with Longs Peak, forms the eastern slope of Glacier Gorge. The summit of Half Mountain is seldom visited but the steep buttresses just below and to the south are of interest to climbers. There are five distinct features, the northern three being the most impressive. The two more southerly buttresses are lower angle and nothing is known of them. The farthest north is actually the southwest buttress of Half Mountain. The second buttress may be identified by a horizontal block protruding from the upper south face. The third and largest is the Astro Tower, which apparently has the only two routes recorded in this area.

Approach. The easiest approach to any of these features probably is to hike directly up to them from the vicinity of Mills Lake. They also may be reached from above by taking a contour west from some logical point along the North Longs Peak Trail. It is easy to scramble off the back side of any of the buttresses.

Astro Tower (11402). Astro Tower is characterized by a large roof across the upper west face and a series of large dihedrals on the south side. The relationship between the following two routes is not known. It is possible that they start in the same place; then again, they may not even be on the same buttress.

1 **Central Buttress　　II 11**
   FA: Billy Westbay and Doug Snively, 1983.
   Begin near the center of the face and climb cracks to a ledge (9). Jam a hand crack to a roof (11). Turn the roof and follow thin cracks to the top (11).

2 **Space Walk　　II 11a ★**
   FA: Richard and Joyce Rossiter, 1983. SR to a #4 Friend.
   This steep route ascends cracks and dihedrals up the southwest corner of the buttress. Begin about 100 feet right of a large, right-facing dihedral and beneath a small roof that arches up and left.
   1. Climb around the left end of the roof and follow a crack to a ledge (9, 75 feet). It is also possible to start down to the left and traverse back right into the line.
   2. Climb a smooth left-facing dihedral and belay on a pedestal at right (7, 100 feet).
   3. Climb a clean one-inch crack in the right wall of a dihedral and belay on a small ledge (9, 70 feet).
   4. Climb a steep corner with a thin crack (crux), traverse up and left to a sloping stance (optional belay), and jam a difficult flared crack to a roof (10c). Traverse left beneath the roof (9) until it is possible to exit straight up (11a, 150 feet).

ASTRO TOWER FROM THE SOUTHWEST
2   Space Walk II 11a ★

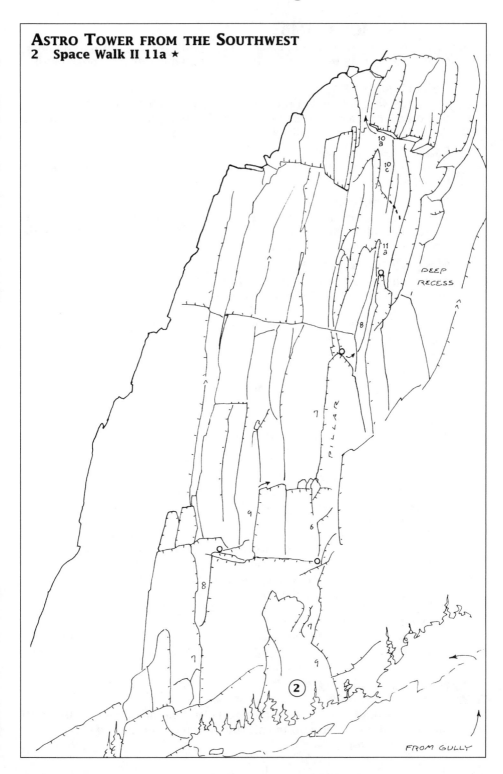

DEEP
RECESS

10
a

10
c

11
a

8

P
I
L
L
A
R

7

9

6

8

7

9

7

2

FROM GULLY

BLACK LAKE ICE CLIMBS

The cliffs and slabs surrounding Black Lake provide some good ice climbing. Skis or snowshoes may be useful on the hike in, depending on snow depth.

1   Reflections   WI3

This is a two pitch route on the left (east) just before the final steep section of the trail up to Black Lake. A slab is followed by a pitch up a tiered section. Other small formations are nearby.

2   South Slabs   WI2-3

Climb any of several short cliffs and ramps above the southeast side of the lake.

3   Tears of a Clown   9

This is not an ice climb. To the right of *South Slabs*, the cliff forms a big dihedral 120 feet high. Climb a crack just left of the inside corner. Walk off or do a second, easier pitch.

4   West Gully   II WI4 ★

This is an excellent three- or four- pitch route up a frozen waterfall on the cliff above the west side of Black Lake. The first pitch is moderate; the second pitch is the crux; the last pitch (or two) ascends a 200-foot slab to the big shelf above the lake and below McHenrys Peak. Descend the steep slope to the north of the falls or traverse around the basin to the east side of Black Lake.

5   Stone Man   WI5

This is a transitory pillar that forms in the ice curtain to the right of *West Gully*.

6   Yellow Tears   WI5

This is the next formation to the right of *Stone Man*.

PAGODA MOUNTAIN

Pagoda Mountain (13497) is the first major summit on the long ridge that runs southwest from Longs Peak toward the Continental Divide, and stands between the Keyboard of the Winds and Chiefs Head Peak. The east and west ridges of Pagoda are fairly gentle and provide excellent scrambles. The 1000-foot north face is steep and slabby with a prominent buttress at its center. Approach via the Glacier Gorge Trail and gain the tundra benches below Spearhead, then continue south to Green Lake beneath the north face. Descend from the summit via the *East Ridge* route.

1   East Ridge   I Class 2 ★

From Green Lake, scramble southeast to the col east of the summit, then hike easily up the long ridge to the top. Be prepared for moderate snow travel until late summer.

2   Northeast Face   II 5

FA: J. Johnson, 1975.

Begin this route as for the *East Ridge*. From a point well left of the north buttress, climb directly up the slabby face and join the *North Buttress* route near its top.

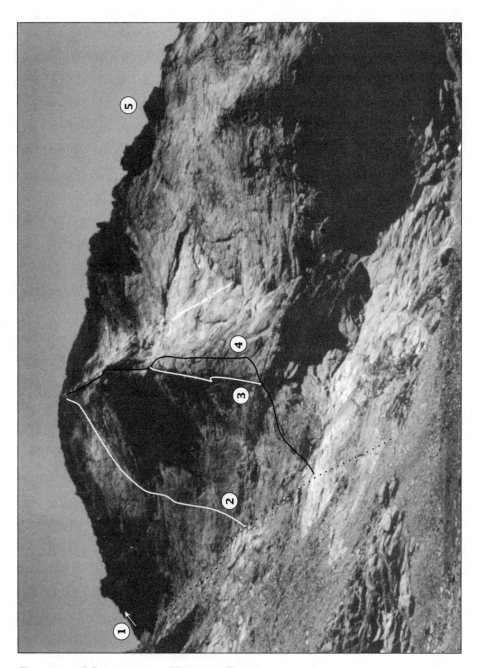

PAGODA MOUNTAIN, NORTH FACE
1   East Ridge   I Class 2 ★
2   Northeast Face   II 5
3   North Buttress   II 6 ★
4   Direct North Buttress   III 8 ★
5   West Ridge   II 7, moderate snow

3 North Buttress   II 6 ★
FA: Buckingham, Brook, Catwood, and Cox, 1958.
This route ascends the north buttress from the ledges above the initial cliffband. Scramble in from the left and follow dihedrals along the left side of the buttress for five pitches above which the crest of the ridge is followed to the summit.

4 Direct North Buttress   III 8 ★
FA: Dan Hare and Jeff Bevan, 1974.
Reach the bottom of the north buttress as for the preceding route or take a slightly more direct line. Follow a right-facing dihedral system along the right side of the buttress for about five pitches, above which the regular route is followed up the crest of the ridge.

5 West Ridge   II 7, moderate snow
From Green Lake, climb the snow couloir that leads to the col between Pagoda and Chiefs Head, then head east to the summit. There are several cliffy steps and gendarmes along the way.

6 Southwest Face   II 5
From Green Lake, climb the snow couloir that leads to the col between Pagoda and Chiefs Head. Hike to the south side of the col, then traverse east along a big grassy ledge for 1000 feet. Climb 20 feet of easy cracks (3) and gain a ramp that goes up and left for about 1000 feet to a point about 300 feet below the summit (cl3). Climb a left-facing dihedral for 200 feet (5) just right of a wet, grey chimney, then follow easy slabs to the summit (2).

CHIEFS HEAD PEAK
Chiefs Head Peak (13579) is located between Pagoda Mountain and Stone Man Pass, the col east of McHenrys Peak. The Continental Divide reaches eastward to the summit of Chiefs Head but does not continue to Pagoda or Longs. The broad north face of Chiefs Head spans more than a mile and rivals in size the east face of Longs Peak. This great wall is divided by a rib that descends northward to a col, and rises up again to terminate in the island spire of Spearhead. The steep wall to the east of the rib is known as the Northeast Face, the wall to the west as the Northwest Face; however, both walls actually face north-northeast. All north face routes are steep and serious and should be attempted only by expert climbers. The gentle east and west ridges provide fine scrambles.

NORTHEAST FACE
The broad and bulging wall between Pagoda Mountain and the Central Rib is called the Northeast Face. It is very steep, receives little direct sunlight, and may remain wet or icy through most of the summer. A dormant glacier rests along the base of the wall. Points of identification are the deeply cut dihedrals and roofs in the middle of the face and the large ledge and cave up and right from these. A distinct lack of crack systems, a characteristic of Chiefs Head, has kept climbing activity to a minimum; however, a few very good routes have been established. Approach as for Spearhead, but continue south past Green Lake to the bottom of the great wall. The easiest descesnt from any route is the *East Couloir*.

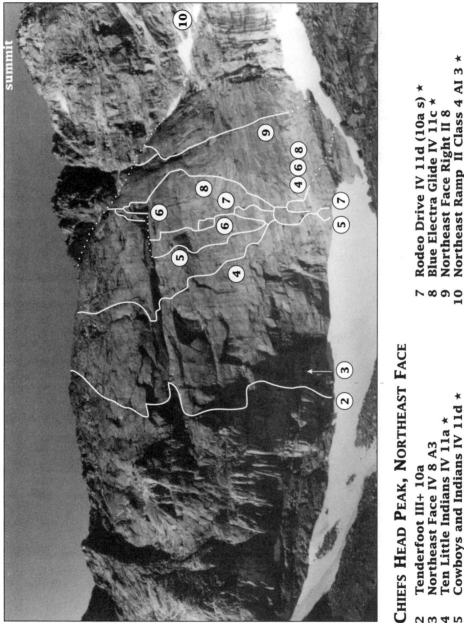

CHIEFS HEAD PEAK, NORTHEAST FACE

2 Tenderfoot III+ 10a
3 Northeast Face IV 8 A3
4 Ten Little Indians IV 11a ★
5 Cowboys and Indians IV 11d ★
6 Risky Business IV 11d vs ★

7 Rodeo Drive IV 11d (10a s) ★
8 Blue Electra Glide IV 11c ★
9 Northeast Face Right II 8
10 Northeast Ramp II Class 4 AI 3 ★

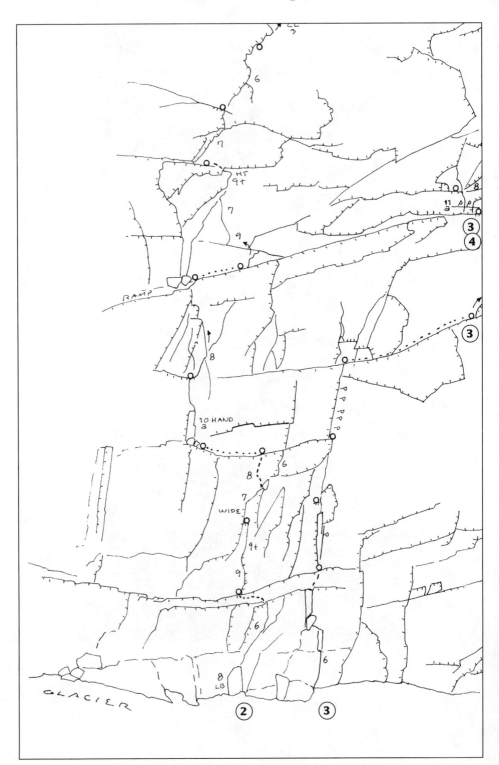

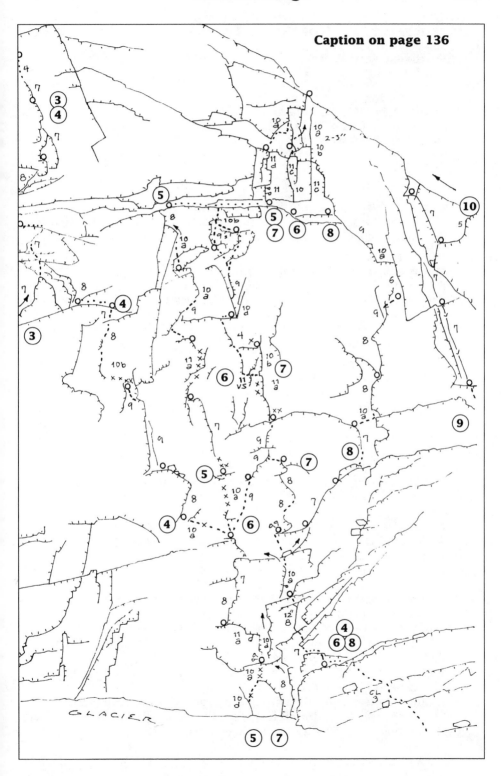

Caption on page 136

CHIEFS HEAD PEAK, NORTHEAST FACE, LEFT AND RIGHT SIDES

2 **Tenderfoot III+ 10a**
3 **Northeast Face IV 8 A3**
4 **Ten Little Indians IV 11a ★**
5 **Cowboys and Indians IV 11d ★**
6 **Risky Business IV 11d vs ★**
7 **Rodeo Drive IV 11d (10a s) ★**
8 **Blue Electra Glide IV 11c ★**
9 **Northeast Face Right II 8**
10 **Northeast Ramp II Class 4 AI3 ★**

1 **East Couloir   II Class 2 AI2 or snow ★**
Climb the obvious snow couloir that leads to the col between Pagoda
Mountain and Chiefs Head, then hike west to the summit.

2 **Tenderfoot   III+ 10a**
FA: Greg Davis and Erik Winkelman, 1993.
This route climbs a series of dihedrals and flakes a short way left of the
Northeast Face. It can be identified by a precarious leaning block above
a right-facing dihedral, about 400 feet.
Begin at a crack about 150 feet left of the *Northeast Face*, and proceed
and shown in the topo. Nine pitches.

3 **Northeast Face   IV 8 A3**
FA: Layton Kor and Bob Bradley, 1963.
Also known as *Center Route* or the *Kor Route*, this was the first line
completed on the wall. Begin near the center of the face, several hundred feet below a huge roof that angles down to the right (down and
left from the cave).
1. Ascend thin cracks and easier broken rock to the base of a vertical
black wall (6, 140 feet).
2. Nail overhangs, then climb to a good stance (8 A3, 140 feet).
3. Climb free for 40 feet, then nail 15 feet to a large ledge (5 A2, 70
feet).
4. Nail 100 feet up the big right-facing dihedral, turn the overhang on
the left and climb free to a large terrace (8 A3, 145 feet).
5. Traverse unroped to the right for 200 feet to clear the overhang
above. Climb free up a chimney/ramp for 30 feet, then up a steep crack
for 20 feet to belay in a corner (7, 50 feet).
6. Climb a flake and cracks 45 feet to a steep slab and ascend it to the
base of the second great roof (8, 140 feet).
7. Nail the left end of the roof, then climb free up and right on qustion-
able flakes to belay behind a large flake (5 A3, 80 feet). This pitch is
shared with *Ten Little Indians* (11a).
8. Climb diagonally to the right around an overhang, then straight up to
a good belay (6, 145 feet).
9. Climb 20 feet right, then straight up for 90 feet (4, 130 feet).
10. Climb straight up for 60 feet, then diagonal up and left for 50 feet
(7, 150 feet). Scramble up to the ridge crest.

The initial pitches to the following five routes are shown as they were established; however, all lead to a long ledge some 300 feet up, and one can mix and match pitches as desired. A #4 Friend is needed for the start to *Cowboys and Indians.*

4 Ten Little Indians   IV 11a ★
FA: Greg Davis and Eric Winkelman, 1991. SR to a #4 Friend.
This high-quality, 12-pitch route takes a steep diagonal line across the center of the wall and joins the *Northeast Face* just below the cave. Scramble in from the right or choose a direct start as shown in the topo.

5 Cowboys and Indians   IV 11d ★
FA: Eric Winkelman and Greg Davis, 1993.
This route takes a direct line up the face to the left of *Risky Business* and is probably the best route on the wall.

6 Risky Business   IV 11d vs ★
FA: Mark Wilford and Jeff Lowe, 1984. SR to a #3.5 Friend.
This was the first free climb and second route completed on the face, 21 years after Kor and Bradley nailed up the original *Northeast Face* route. It takes a direct and audatious line up the right side of the face. Sections of the route have been eclipsed by *Ten Little Indians* and *Rodeo Drive.* I have marked the original line on the topo, and except for a bolt belay and two bolts on the fifth pitch, the route is unchanged and as hairy as ever. The origin of the two-bolt belay is unknown.

7 Rodeo Drive   IV 11d (10a s) ★
FA of original pitches: Greg Davis and Eric Winkelman, 1993. Rack: 2 x RPs, 2 x stoppers, Friends to #3.5.
This excellent route takes a direct line up the right side of the wall. At least four of its pitches overlap *Risky Business*, though this was not known at the time of the first ascent.

8 Blue Electra Glide   IV 11c ★
FA: Greg Davis and Kevin Cooney, 1989. SR plus a selection of pins.
This route was established under the impression that it was the second ascent of *Risky Business,* but only the first pitch and a half turned out to be the same. It thereafter follows a series of left-facing flakes and dihedrals along the right margin of the main face and is a good route.

9 Northeast Face Right   II 8
Begin at the far right side of the face beneath a prominent chimney/dihedral in the upper wall. Scramble up a low-angle section and set the first belay at a continous crack system where a ramp angles up to the right.
1. Climb a nice pitch to a big grassy ledge (6, 150 feet).
2. Continue up the crack past two big ledges and belay in a grassy area (4, 150 feet).
Scramble up to the big crack and chimney system on the upper wall.
3. Climb a long groove and chimney, or a right-facing dihedral just to the left, and belay on a ledge (7, 150 feet).
4. Climb a chimney and belay on a ledge at right (6, 130 feet).

5. Climb a long right-facing dihedral to a ledge at its top (8), or climb a steep ramp/dihedral off the right end of the ledge (6). In either case, join the *Northeast Ramp*, whence one may continue to the summit or descend.

10   Northeast Ramp   II Class 4 AI3 ★

This is a good mountaineering route that ascends the long ramp at the right side of the Northeast Face. The easiest (and longest) approach is to hike around to the southwest side of Spearhead (past Frozen Lake) and scramble up to the col at the base of the Central Rib of Chiefs Head. Drop over on the east side and start up the ramp. After about 100 yards, progress is interrupted by a broad couloir where the ramp seems to have fallen away. Cross this on broken ledges (cl4) and continue up the steepening ramp to the ridge crest. Through midsummer, this is an excellent snow climb that reaches a steepness of 45 degrees in the upper part of the ramp. The ramp can be reached more directly by scrambling up a class 4 couloir from Green Lake on the southeast side of Spearhead.

11   Central Rib   II 7

This route ascends the prominent rib that divides the north side of Chiefs Head into its two great faces. The rib drops north from the summit to a col at 12300 feet, then rises up again to culminate in the Spearhead. Hike around to the southwest side of Spearhead and scramble up to the col. Work around to the right to get up on the ridge crest and follow it for about 1300 feet to the summit. The upper half of the rib is steep and presents a series of short cliffs that can be bypassed on the right.

NORTHWEST FACE

The Northwest Face of Chiefs Head is one of the finest alpine walls in the contiguous United States. The immense and unusually smooth oval face rises a thousand feet above a dormant glacier, and is home to some very aesthetic and very hairy routes. The face is nearly vertical at the bottom but bends back as it rises. The rock is solid and clean with a smattering of ledges, but is lacking in crack systems. Most routes follow shallow discontinuous dihedrals that tend to be wet and mossy with cracks sometimes best suited to pitons. All of the routes but *Birds of Fire* have long runouts and no fixed anchors, with *Seven Arrows* and *Screaming Eagle* the most serious. In the event of storm or other adversity, it is very difficult to escape from these routes. The best climbing conditions exist from late June to late August.

Approach. From the pond below the northeast face of Spearhead, hike over the shoulder just north of the peak to an area of grassy benches above Frozen Lake. Make an ascending traverse beneath the west face of Spearhead and gain a rocky shelf above a small waterfall, then scramble up talus to the base of the wall (about 7 miles from the Glacier Gorge Trailhead). Be prepared to kick steps in snow for the last 200 feet or so (depending on month). All of the routes can be done car-to-car in a long day, but it is wise to bring a headlamp for the walk out. Some parties will want to bivouac.

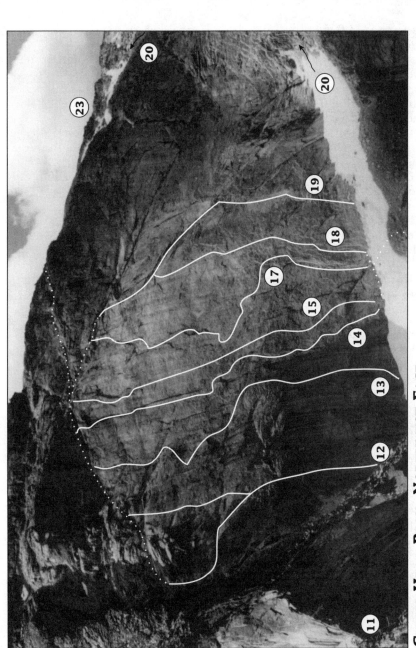

CHIEFS HEAD PEAK, NORTHWEST FACE

11 Central Rib II 7
12 Papoose II 9 s
13 Kachina Winds IV 10a (9 vs)
14 Seven Arrows IV 10b (9 vs) ★

15 Birds of Fire IV 11a (9+ s) ★
17 Center Route IV 10a (9+ s/vs) ★
18 As You Like It IV 10 s
19 Much Ado About Nothing III 8

20 West Ramp I Class 3 ★
23 Northwest Ridge I Class 2 ★

Descent. Make seven long rapppels from the top of *Birds of Fire*. The highest bolt anchor is on a shattered ledge that may be reached from the top of any of the routes. Do not even consider the descent without two 50-meter (165-foot) ropes. CAUTION: The last rappel takes the entire rope and ends precariously on the hand traverse at the start to *Seven Arrows*. It also is possible, though decidedly more trouble, to downclimb the *West Ramp* (below).

12   Papoose   II 9 s
FA: John Harlin and Kent Wheeler, 1980.
This route takes a line on the shaded left side of the wall about 50 feet left of a large right-facing dihedral and about 400 feet left of *Seven Arrows*.
Begin down and left of a 20-foot slanting corner near the center of the smooth, grey face.
1. Climb up through the corner to a ledge, walk right, and belay (8). This ledge is a short way up and left from a light-colored spot in the rock.
2. Climb a long pitch straight up the face to a small ledge (8, 160 feet).
3. Follow a right-facing dihedral to a big ledge halfway up the face (7, 100 feet).
4. Climb straight up the slab for a long pitch to a ledge (9 s).
5. Continue straight up the wall (9 s) or follow a ramp that climbs left to the edge of the face (7).
It is possible to avoid the last two pitches by following ramps up and left from the big ledge at the beginning of the fourth pitch. From the upper left edge of the face, scramble up and right along grassy ledges and rappel *Birds of Fire*.

13   Kachina Winds   IV 10a (9 vs)
FA: Bob Horan and John Baldwin, 1992.
This improvisational route ascends the steep face left of *Seven Arrows* for four pitches, then veers up and left along ramps and dihedrals to the rim of the face.
Begin about 200 feet left from the L-shaped flake at the start to *Birds of Fire*.
1. Climb up onto a ledge/ramp, work up and right and belay on a pinnacle (8).
2. Climb a left-facing flake and belay on a sloping stance (9).
3. Climb a long pitch straight up the face, work through some roofs, and belay (9).
4. Work up and left along a ramp and belay at the end of the rope (6).
5. Climb up and left across a smooth slab (crux), pass some flakes, and belay on a stance beneath a long roof (10a).
6. Work up and right beneath the roof, climb past its right side, and belay on a big ledge (8).
7. Work up and left, then climb straight up the wall to the big broken ledge at the top of the wall (5). Scramble up and right to reach the rappel route on *Birds of Fire*.

14 Seven Arrows   IV 10b (9 vs) ★

FA: Charlie Fowler and John Harlin, 1980. SR to a #2 Friend with a few KBs and LAs.

This coveted route takes a left-leaning line on the lower face, then follows a black water streak straight to the top. Retreat is difficult. At one or two points along the lower half of the route it may be possible to reach belay anchors on *Birds of Fire*; otherwise, there are no anchors. Begin about 100 feet left of *Center Route* at a 25-foot flake that is shaped like a fat L or the state of Louisiana. This flake is reached most easily by traversing ledges left from the start to *Center Route*. It is partially burried by snow in early summer.

1a. From the L-shaped flake, climb up and left along the right edge of another flake, then continue up past a tiny ledge (fixed pin) and along a shallow left-facing corner to a stance on the right where one can place a sling over a horn (10b, 140 feet).

1b. Do a short initial pitch and belay atop the flake, then stretch the next lead to the second belay on *Birds of Fire* (165 feet).

2. In either case, continue in the left-facing flake system to a semi-sling belay (9, about 90 feet from the belay on *Birds*).

3. Continue up the corner, then go up and right to a grassy ledge (10a, 150 feet).

4. Move up and left over easy ground to a big ledge; belay to the left of the long water streak (7, 140 feet).

5. Climb flakes straight up the face to the left of the water streak. At 120 feet it is possible to belay, but a better belay is reached after 180 feet (9 vs).

6. Begin up a right-facing corner, then go right under a flake and up its right edge to the next ledge (9 s, 90 feet).

7. Climb a right-facing dihedral that fades into the face near the left edge of a roof. Turn the roof, move up and left, then straight up to the large, shattered ledge at the top of the face (10b, 120).

15 Birds of Fire   IV 11a (9+ s) ★

FA: Richard Rossiter, Joyce Rossiter, and Rob Woolf, 1988. Light SR to a #3 Friend with 6 QD.

This route ascends the center of the face to its zenith. The climbing is characterized by sustained face and friction work on superb rock. The hardest moves are protected by bolts, but runouts will be encountered on easier ground. From Frozen Lake, a long white streak is vaguely discernable on the upper half of the wall, to the right of the black streak on *Seven Arrows*. This is a curiously unlichened stretch of granite that yields 300 feet of peerless face climbing on the fifth and sixth pitches. Begin from the L-shaped flake as for *Seven Arrows*.

1. Move up and right past two bolts and belay from cams under a roof (10a, 90 feet).

2. Turn the roof and work straight up to a stance with a bolt (optional first belay). Continue up to a narrow ledge and traverse left until it is appropriate to work up and left again to a good ledge with a two-bolt anchor (10b, 150feet).

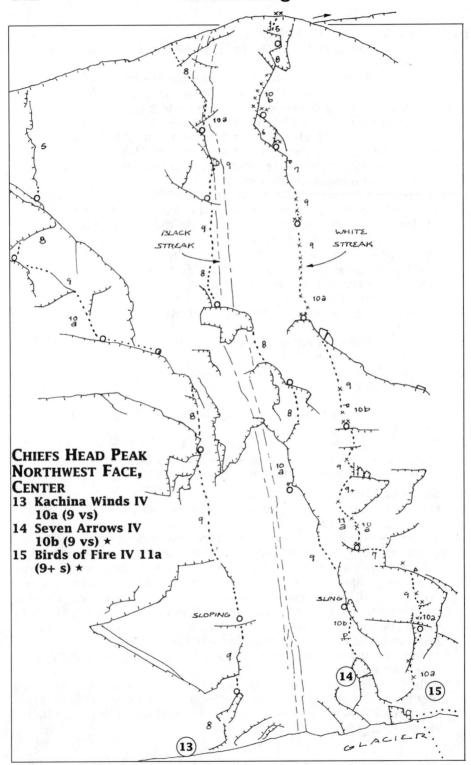

BLACK STREAK

WHITE STREAK

CHIEFS HEAD PEAK
NORTHWEST FACE,
CENTER
13 Kachina Winds IV
   10a (9 vs)
14 Seven Arrows IV
   10b (9 vs) ★
15 Birds of Fire IV 11a
   (9+ s) ★

SLOPING

SLING

GLACIER

13

14

15

3. Step right and climb straight up to a tiny roof, move left and up past a bolt (crux), then go more or less straight up over thin ground to the higher of two good ledges (11a, 140 feet).

4. Look for a bolt followed by a fixed pin. Climb up and eventually a bit left over steep rock to the long, curving ledge that runs across the middle of the face, then scramble up and left to its high point (10b, 150 feet).

5. Work straight up the White Streak past several bolts to a small stance with a bolt anchor (10a, 150 feet).

6. Continue straight up past 2 bolts and eventually a fixed pin, then move up and left to a bolt anchor (9, 150 feet).

7. Angle up and left along flakes to the bottom of a large, right-facing dihedral (7, 70 feet).

8. Move left out of the dihedral and climb the smooth face past five bolts (sustained lieback off the arête). Work up and right, turn a small roof (8), and belay at the top of a wide crack or on a ledge 15 feet higher (10b, 140 feet).

9. Climb straight up to the bolt anchor at the top of the wall (6, 50 feet).

16   Screaming Eagle   IV 10d vs
FA: Charlie Fowler and Dan McGee, 1987. SR plus extra small nuts, a selection of thin pitons, and a keyhole hanger.

This difficult and poorly protected route trends up and right from the center of the face. Dan McGee comments on the first ascent: "The climbing was excellent, but there was no pro. I'd get to a belay ledge and just be glad I was still alive." Charlie Fowler: "Anyone who goes up to do this route should bring a bolt kit!" Begin with a left-angling ramp at the bottom of *Center Route* and proceed as shown in the topo.

17   Center Route   IV 10a (9+ s/vs) ★
FA: Layton Kor and Bob Culp (IV 5.9 A2), 1961. FFA: Billy Westbay and Dan McClure, 1975. SR to a #3 Friend. Bring a #4 Friend to go straight up the dihedral on the second pitch.

Also known as *Path of the Elders,* this is the standard free version of the original *Northwest Face* route. The line is disjunct and most of the pitches are runout, but the aura and beauty of the face will override any whining and leave a lasting sense of satisfaction.

Begin at a conspicuous, left-facing dihedral system about 100 feet right from the L-shaped flake at the start to *Birds of Fire*. Note also a ramp that rises to the left from the bottom of the dihedral: this is an alternate start to *Birds of Fire* (7).

1. Climb the dihedral and belay at a stance (5, 160 feet).

2. Continue up the corner through an overhanging section with a wide crack (10a, usually wet) or exit the dihedral below the wide section and climb the face on the right to belay beside a huge, rectangular flake (9 s, 155 feet).

3. Make a long, leftward traverse across a flake/ledge system that transects the wall and belay at some blocks (8, 160 feet).

4. Continue left across the ledge and belay beneath some small, right-facing dihedrals up on the wall (cl3, 90 feet).

5. Run the pitch from the ledge or bring two short Lost Arrows for a small ledge higher up (which is recommended since it's the last pro for a long way — consider leaving the pins for a permanent anchor). From the small ledge, traverse right about 50 feet, then up to gain a shallow corner. Climb the corner about 30 feet, traverse right across a slab, and belay in another right-facing dihedral (9 s, 165+ feet from the main ledge).

6. Climb the dihedral past an old, ringed angle piton and belay about 50 feet short of a roof (8, 100 feet).

7. Climb almost straight right for 70 feet (9+, no pro), gain a thin crack with some fixed pins in a right-facing dihedral and belay in a niche (9+ s/vs, 120 feet). One also may traverse right beneath the roof at the top of the dihedral but it is just as stimulating.

8. Follow the dihedral system to the top of the wall (7, 150 feet).

17a Northwest Face   9 A2

This is thought to be the original line of the route. From the bottom of the initial dihedral, climb straight up the slab past "decaying fixed pro" for two harrowing pitches to the ledge at mid-face. Begin the traverse left as for the standard free version but after a few moves, climb a difficult and poorly protected right-facing dihedral (10a s) to a good ledge and share a belay with *Screaming Eagle*. Follow the ledge up and left to gain the free line at the fifth pitch.

17b Super Indirect   9 s

Begin as for *Screaming Eagle* with the ramp that rises to the left, but from the top of the flake system, work up and right to a poor belay stance. Climb up and left to belay at a flake below a blank wall (maybe the second belay on *Screaming Eagle*). Make a long traverse right to a bolt and join the original line of the *Northwest Face*.

18   As You Like It   IV 10 s

FA: Eric Doub and G. Russel, 1980.

This line begins right of *Center Route*, and then goes right of *Screaming Eagle* on the upper half of the face. This description may have a missing pitch. Begin in an area of left-facing flake/dihedrals about 50 feet right of *Center Route*.

1. Climb a crack for 60 feet, then move right to another crack and follow it to a ledge.

2. Follow another crack system, then angle up and right to belay at a left-angling crack.

3. Climb the crack (9) followed by some nebulous terrain and belay after 160 feet (this is probably along the flake/ledge system that runs across the middle of the face).

4. Work up and right along the ledge system, then climb a blank slab (10 s) and continue to a small ledge.

5. A less difficult pitch intersects *Much Ado About Nothing* and leads to a ledge that is followed to the right edge of the face. Scramble up and left along a ledge system to the rappel route.

CHIEFS HEAD PEAK, NORTH-
WEST FACE, RIGHT SIDE
16 Screaming Eagle IV 10d vs

17 Center Route IV 10a (9+ s/vs) ★
18 As You Like It IV 10 s
19 Much Ado About Nothing III

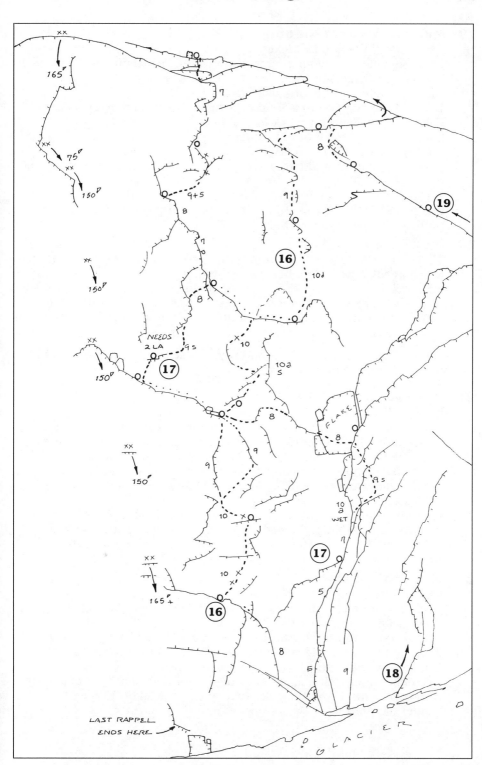

19　Much Ado About Nothing　　III 8
FA: Dan McClure and M. Kleker.
This route climbs the long ramp system along the right side of the wall.
Begin in a left-facing corner directly below a large white spot that is
shaped like the profile of a head facing left.
1. Climb the dihedral to a V, take its right branch, and belay on a
flake/ledge in the white rock of the "neck." (6, 150 feet).
2. Follow a left-facing flake through the "head" and continue up to a
series of ledges (7, 150 feet).
3. and 4. Climb up and left along a ramp and belay near its end (5, 300
feet).
5. Climb up along a left-facing flake, then up and right to a grassy ledge
that leads off the face (8, 100 feet). Scramble up and left to the rappel
route at the high point of the face.

20　West Ramp　　I Class 3
This is the best downclimb from routes on the Northwest Face, but it is
also a good shortcut for the *Northwest Ridge*. From the bottom of the
main Northwest Face, hike up and right along a big ramp for about 1000
feet. At a cairn, and when it looks easy, scramble up and left to the
crest of the northwest ridge and follow it to the summit. By mid-August,
this route is usually passable without snow travel.

The following two routes lie about midway between the main Northwest Face
of Chiefs Head and Stoneman Pass.

21　April Fools　　II M6 ★
FA: Eric Winkelman and Michael Bearzi, 1994.
This route climbs a conspicuous left-facing dihedral, remeniscent of
Athlete's Feat in Boulder Canyon, just left of a smooth wall with a long
roof. There is some hazard of avalanche from a shelf above the route.
1. Climb a stepped left-facing dihedral with a mossy crack and belay on
a traingular snow patch (M6, 75 feet). In late spring, much of this pitch
will be burried.
2. Climb steep snow to a roof. Climb out right under the roof and hook
a thin runnel on the right wall, then climb a shallow, one-foot-wide
groove for about 100 feet and belay on the right (M6, 150 feet).
Rappel the route.

22　May Day　　II M5
FA: Bill Myers and Eric Winkelman, 1994.
This route ascends a prominent gully/chimney about 50 feet right of a
smooth wall with a long roof.
1. Traverse left into the gully along a sloping ledge (M3, 40 feet).
2. Climb up the left side of the gully passing an overhang near the top,
and belay at right on a long ledge (M5, 130 feet).
3. Climb a right-facing dihedral to the left of the chimney for about 60
feet, then continue up the gully to a large ledge (M4+, 150 feet).
Rappel the route.

23 Northwest Ridge   I Class 2 ★

This is the long ridge that runs southeast from Stone Man Pass to the summit. Follow the approach for the Northwest Face routes (see above). From the talus field south of Frozen Lake, make an ascending traverse to Stone Man Pass, the col between Chiefs Head Peak and McHenrys Peak. Just south of the col is a curious spire called the Stone Man. Stay on the right side of the crest to avoid cliffs and pinnacles until the ridge broadens, then hike easily to the summit. This ridge also may be reached from from the Lion Lake Trail in Wild Basin.

SPEARHEAD

Spearhead (12575) is the striking island spire in the center of the cirque above Black Lake. It is quite steep on three sides and has a dramatic, pointed summit. The north ridge and sheer northeast face are visible during most of the approach and lend inspiration on the 6-mile march up Glacier Gorge. The serrated south ridge is continuous with the north rib of Chiefs Head Peak, reaching a nadir at 12300 feet. The 800-foot northeast face has a bevy of fine routes, and the *North Ridge* is one of the best moderate climbs in Rocky Mountain National Park. The junction between the southeast and northeast faces forms a rounded prow or nose that also features excellent climbing. A long horizontal bench called Middle Earth Ledge runs across most of the northeast face about 160 feet above the talus. Approach via the Glacier Gorge Trail.

Descent A. Gain the ledge that runs across the top of the northeast face and follow it south (toward the Northeast Face of Chiefs Head) until it is possible to descend northeast along a steep ramp (Class 4, see *Southeast Ramp*). This descent is not recommended in wet or icy conditions. An alternative is to continue south until it is possible to descend a talus slope toward Green Lake.

Descent B. All routes arrive at a long ledge system that traverses the top of the northeast face about a hundred feet below the summit. This ledge extends southward to a cliffy talus slope above Green Lake. The easiest return to the bottom of the peak is to follow the ledge out onto the north ridge and descend the talus field on the west side to the grassy benches above Frozen Lake (cl2). This option is especially useful if gear is left at the bottom of the North Ridge.

SOUTHEAST FACE

The following routes are located on the southeast face of Spearhead.

1 Southeast Ramp   I Class 4

This route provides an interesting scramble to the summit as well as a means of descent. Hike around to the left side of the smooth southeast face and to the top of a talus fan. Scramble 800 feet up and left along a steep ramp to an area of broken ledges and talus. Be careful of loose rock. Work up and right to a broad ledge system and follow it north across the top of the northeast face to the north ridge. Cross to the west side of the crest and scramble southward up to the summit.

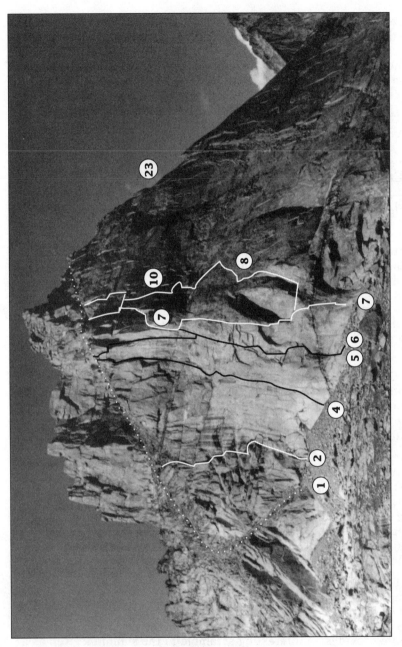

Spearhead, Southeast Face

1 Southeast Ramp I Class 4
2 Border Patrol II 8
4 Direct Southeast Face II 10d ★
5 Awesome III 9 ★
6 Fast Prow 9 ★

7 Age Axe III 10b/c ★
8 Scimitar III 10c ★
10 Stone Monkey III 12a ★
23 North Ridge III 6 ★

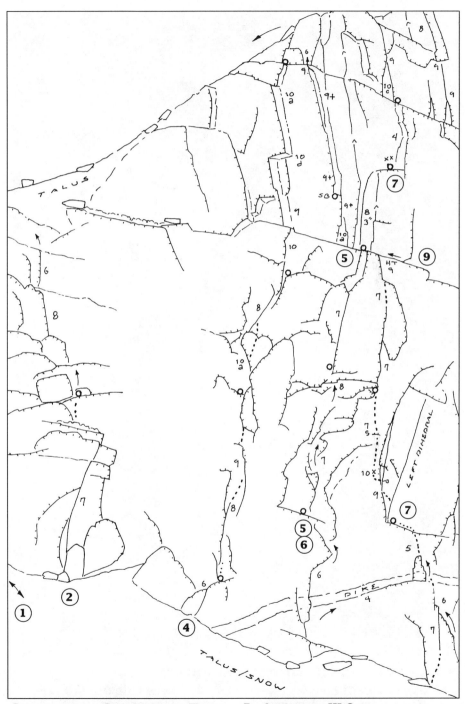

SPEARHEAD, SOUTHEAST FACE

1 Southeast Ranp I Class 4
2 Border Patrol II 8
4 Direct Southeast Face II 10d ★

5 Awesome III 9 ★
6 East Prow 9 ★
7 Age Axe III 10b/c ★
9 Unbelievers III 10c

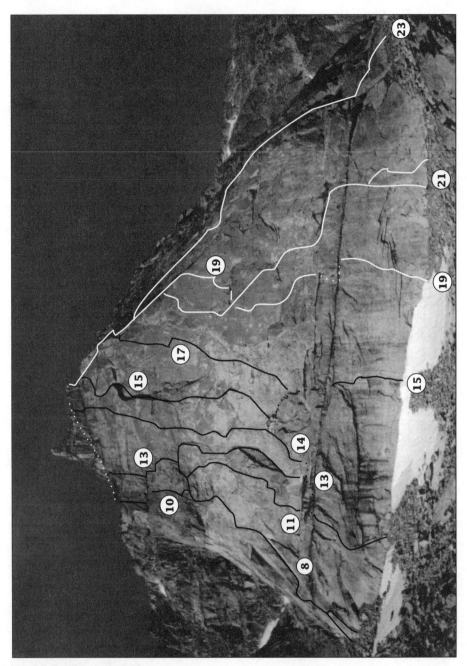

Spearhead, Northeast Face, Overview

  8   Scimitar III 10c ★
10   Stone Monkey III 12a ★
11. Three Stoners III 11b ★
13   Obviously Four Believers
      III 11a ★
14   Spear Me the Details IV 11d ★

15   Sykes Sickle III 9 (7 s) ★
17   Stratospear III 11 ★
19   Burning Spear III 10s
21   The Barb III 10b ★
23   North Ridge III 6 ★

2 Border Patrol II 8
FA: Dan Hare and Jeff Bevan, 1974.
This route climbs up short dihedrals and grassy ledges at the left margin of the southeast face. Begin to the right of a large right-facing dihedral.
1. Climb cracks up a slab to a big, grassy ledge.
2. Climb a right-facing dihedral to the reach the walk-off ledge.

3 Tom Thomas Memorial II 11
FA: Tom Thomas and Thom Byrne, 1988.
This route apparently ascends the southeast face, but its line is not known.

4 Direct Southeast Face II 10d ★
FA: Michael Colacino and Ron Kirk, 1988.
This five-pitch route ascends the right side of the southeast face about 100 feet left of the East Prow. Begin with a thin crack that angles up to the right, then climb more or less straight up the slabby face, and finish with a right-facing dihedral at the top of the wall.

EAST PROW
The following three routes ascend the prow formed by the junction of the southeast and northeast faces.

5 Awesome III 9 ★
FA: Eric Bader and Paul Hauser, 1980. SR plus a selection of pitons.
This route approximately follows the *East Prow* for three pitches, then takes the left side of a long right-facing dihedral to the top of the wall.
4. Follow a difficult, thin crack up and left, and belay in slings on the arête (10a s, 60 feet).
5. Start up the arête, then follow a crack about 3 feet right of the arête to a large roof (9+). Traverse 10 feet around to the left side of the arête, turn the roof (9), and follow a right-facing corner to the walk-off ledge (165 feet).

6 East Prow 9 ★
FA: Dan Hare and Jeff Bevan, c. 1975.
The junction between the southeast and northeast faces forms a beautiful rounded prow. This route begins to the left of the prow in a right-facing dihedral system.
1. Climb the dihedral, then exit left to a grassy ledge (8, 120 feet).
2. Climb straight up along right-facing flakes, work up and left through a roof, and belay on a stance at the bottom of a left-facing dihedral (8, 150 feet).
3. Follow the dihedral to the highest ledge below a long, horizontal fault line where the rock changes color (7, 75 feet).
4 - 6. Continue as for *Age Axe.*

TWIN DIHEDRALS
The following four routes are associated with two, large right-facing dihedrals near the left side of the northeast face, just beyond and above the left end of Middle Earth Ledge. There are three ways to reach a sloping ledge that runs across the bottom of the dihedrals: **A.** Climb in from the left along a

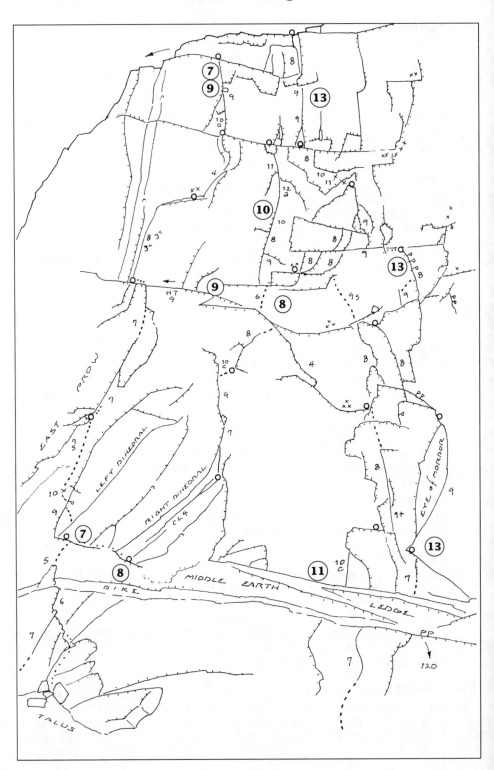

dike (6). **B.** Climb a beautiful finger crack up a slab (7), then work up and left to the left dihedral. **C.** Start up a right-facing dihedral that curves right to form a roof, but exit left along a flake and follow a crack up to the right dihedral (6).

7 Age Axe   III 10b/c ★
FA: Chris Reveley and Ajax Greene, 1975.
This roiute begins in the left of the Twin Dihedrals.
1. Climb an initial pitch to a ledge at the bottom of the left dihedral (6-7, 120 feet).
2. Climb a short way up the dihedral, then move left and climb a crack past a fixed pin (9). Move out left onto the slab and make a difficult move past an old bolt (crux), then climb a moderate slab to a stance on the left (10, 130 feet).
3. Climb up through flakes to where the rock changes color, then move left and belay beneath a three-inch crack in a right-facing dihedral (7, 150 feet).
4. Climb the hand and fist crack to a rubble-strewn ledge with two bolts (8, 100 feet).
5. From the north end of the ledge, climb easy cracks and corners up and right to a long, grassy ledge (4, 90 feet).
6. From the south end of the ledge, climb a steep crack and right-facing corner to a ledge at the top of the wall (10c, 100 feet). Or move the belay 50 feet to the right and do the last pitch of *Obviously Four Believers* (9, 130 feet).

NORTHEAST FACE

The following routes ascend the broad northeast face, which is characterized by the hanging roof/dihedral of *Sykes Sickle*.

8 Scimitar   III 10c ★
FA: Scott Woodruff and Dan Hare, 1975.
This route begins in the right of the Twin Dihedrals.
1. Climb one of the initial pitches (described above) to reach the right dihedral, then scramble up the ramp formed by its right side, and belay at some cracks where the ramp steepens.
2. Climb up and left into a shallow right-facing corner and follow it to a point short of its top (9), then traverse right with marginal pro to a stance beside a left-facing flake (10c, 150 feet).
3. Work up and right over hollow flakes to a grassy ledge, then climb up to a higher ledge on a large rectangular block (8, 130 feet).
Make three long rappels back to the ground or continue with *Stone Monkey* (left) or *Obviously Four Believers* (right).

SPEARHEAD, NORTHEAST FACE, LEFT SIDE
7   **Age Axe III 10b/c ★**
8   **Scimitar III 10c ★**
9   **Unbelievers III 10c**
10 **Stone Monkey III 12a ★**
11 **Three Stoners III 11b ★**
13 **Obviously Four Believers III 11a ★**

9 Unbelievers   III 10c

This route connects *Scimitar* to the upper pitches of *Age Axe*.

3. Follow the third pitch of *Scimitar* to the fist grassy ledge, then work up and left along flakes and ledges to where they end on the right side of the East Prow.

4. Hand traverse left around the nose and belay as for *Age Axe*.

5. Climb a hand and fist crack up a left-facing dihedral and belay on a grassy bench with two bolts (8, 130 feet).

5. Climb easy cracks up and right to a long, grassy ledge (4, 90 feet).

6. Climb the steep crack above the left end of the ledge (10c, 100 feet).

10 Stone Monkey   III 12a ★

FA: Chip Chase and Dan Stone, 1985.

This route presents one of the best single pitches on Spearhead.

3. Climb *Scimitar* to a grassy ledge atop a rectangular block.

4. Undercling up and left into a hand crack (9) that is followed as it tapers to a seam (12a), and continue (11) to a long grassy ledge (140 feet).

5. Move the belay to the left and climb the last pitch of *Age Axe* (10c, 100 feet), or move to the right and climb the last pitch of *Obviously Four Believers* (9, 130 feet).

EYE OF MORDOR

The following three routes are associated with the Eye of Mordor, a large, spindle-shaped, right-facing dihedral above Middle Earth Ledge, about 200 feet right of the Twin Dihedrals. An initial pitch is necessary to reach all three routes: Begin below and left of the Eye of Mordor. Scramble up a short, right-facing dihedral to a ledge with a block and belay. Follow a crack up and left, then back right and continue to Middle Earth Ledge (6, 150 feet).

11 Three Stoners   III 11b ★

FA: Nichols and party, date unknown; alternate start: Charlie Fowler and Kent Lugbill, 1981.

This route follows steep cracks and flakes left of the Eye of Mordor and joins *Scimitar* or *Obviously Four Believers* halfway up the face. Begin on Middle Earth Ledge beneath a vertical finger crack about 70 feet left from the Eye of Mordor.

1a. Climb the crack and a left-facing flake to a ledge (10c, 60 feet).

1b. Climb a crack about 30 feet right of the initial finger crack and reach the same ledge (9).

2. Climb a short, left-facing corner and a crack to a good ledge (9, 140 feet).

Climb up and left to join *Scimitar* or *Stone Monkeys* or climb straight up to join *Obviously Four Believers*.

12 All Two Obvious   IV 12a ★

FA: Greg Davis and Erik Winkelman, 1993; of second pitch: Dan Stone and Jeff Achey, c. 1985. Double set of RPs, double stoppers, TCUs, #0.5 to 3 Friends.

This beautiful route begins just left of *Obviously Four Believers*, then crosses that route at its third pitch and continues up the steep wall to the right. The two upper pitches follow shallow left-facing dihedrals on excellent rock and are primarily protected by bolts. Rappel the route or walk off.

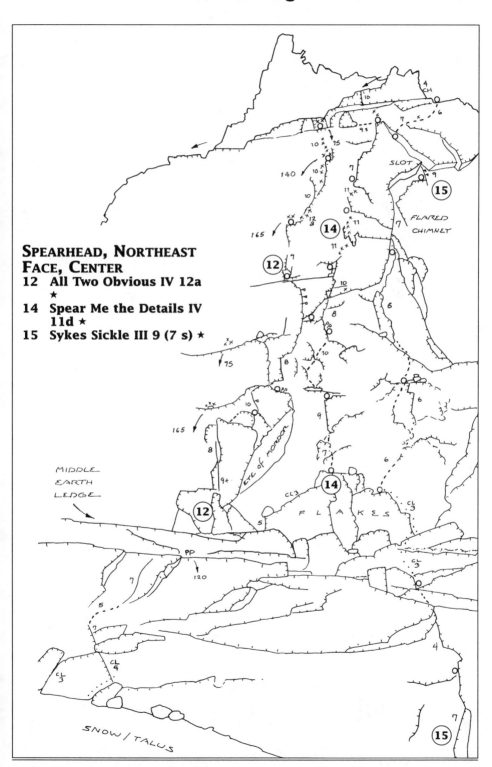

SPEARHEAD, NORTHEAST
FACE, CENTER
12 All Two Obvious IV 12a
    ★
14 Spear Me the Details IV
    11d ★
15 Sykes Sickle III 9 (7 s) ★

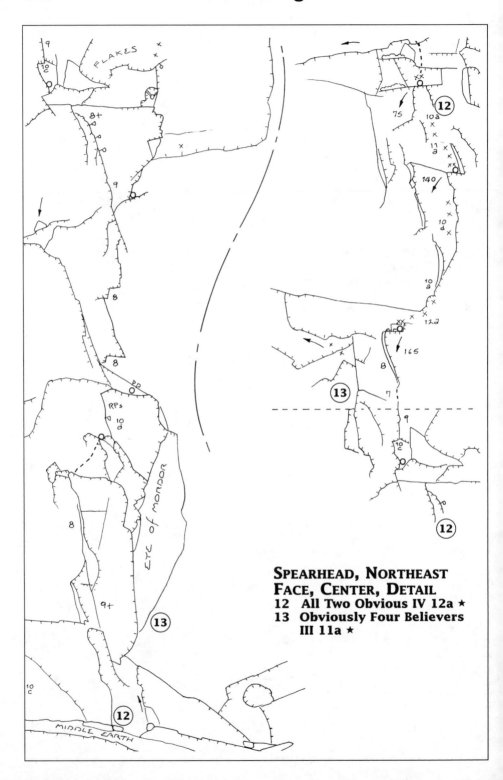

SPEARHEAD, NORTHEAST FACE, CENTER, DETAIL
12   All Two Obvious IV 12a ★
13   Obviously Four Believers III 11a ★

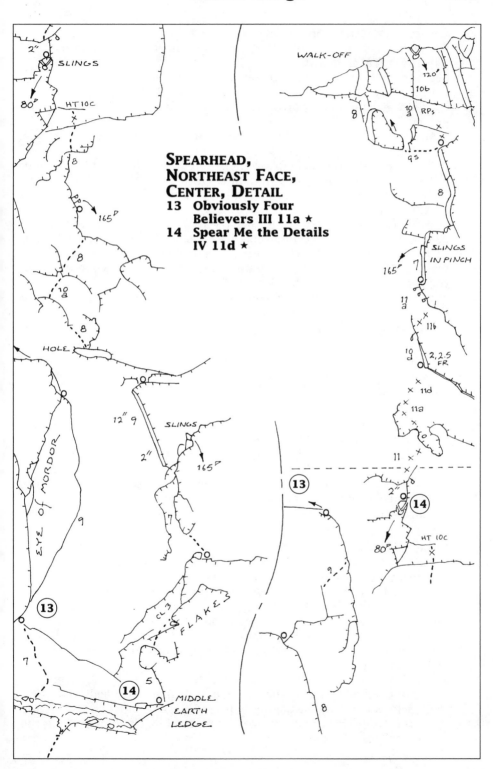

2"
SLINGS
80°
HT 10C
8
165°
8
10
a
8
HOLE
12" 9
SLINGS
2"
165°
EYE OF MORDOR
9
13
7
CL 3
FLAKE
14
5
MIDDLE
EARTH
LEDGE

**SPEARHEAD,
NORTHEAST FACE,
CENTER, DETAIL**
13 Obviously Four
    Believers III 11a ★
14 Spear Me the Details
    IV 11d ★

WALK-OFF
120°
10b
8
10
a RPs
9 s
8
SLINGS
IN PINCH
165° 7
11
a
x 11b
10
d 2,2.5
   FR
x
x 11d
x
x 11a
o
11 x x
2"
14
HT 10C
80° x
13
9
8

13 Obviously Four Believers   III 11a ★

FA: Michael Covington, John Marts, Rick Petrillo, and Jim Stanton (V 5.8 A4), 1967. FFA: unknown.

Begin from Middle Earth Ledge beneath the Eye of Mordor.

1. Climb a crack to the lower corner of the Eye (7, 45 feet).

2. Climb the crack along the right side of the Eye and belay on a ledge up and left (9, 165 feet).

3. Work up and left and follow a right-facing flake to a ledge at its top (8, 120 feet).

4. Work up and right past a short crack into a right-facing dihedral and follow it to a sling belay at a horzontal crack (9, 100 feet).

5. Traverse straight left to a crack, then jam up to belay on a pedestal (9, 130 feet).

6. Work up and left past a bolt, turn a roof (crux), and go up the face past another bolt to a second roof. Traverse left beneath the roof (10a), then climb a short left-facing corner to a long grassy ledge (11a, 100 feet). It also is possible to climb up and right from the second bolt and traverse left to the same belay (11).

7. Climb a slot followed by a hand crack, go left around a roof, and continue to the walk-off ledge (9, 130 feet).

13a Short Crack   12a

FA: Jeff Lowe and George Lowe, 1983.

From the walk-off ledge, climb a 35-foot crack above the finish to *Obviously Four Believers*. The crack ends at a ledge. It was led with some aid, then toproped.

14 Spear Me the Details   IV 11d ★

FA: Greg Davis and Neal Beidleman, 1991. The first four pitches were climbed by Ed Webster and Joe Frank, c. 1986.

This excellent route takes a steep line to the right of *Obviously Four Believers* and finishes along the walk-off ledge about 50 feet left of *Sykes Sickle*. Do the initial pitch (described above) to reach Middle Earth Ledge, then scramble up and right to the bottom of a short, left-facing dihedral about 50 feet right of the Eye of Mordor. Proceed as shown in the topo.

15 Sykes' Sickle   III 9 (7s) ★

FA: Richard Sykes, John Wharton, David Isles, and Dave Rearick, 1958. FFA: Royal Robbins and Steve Komito, 1964.

This area classic ascends the obvious right-facing dihedral and roof in the upper right side of the northeast face. The original line followed left-facing flakes up and right from Middle Earth Ledge, then cut left into the Sickle Dihedral. The Robbins-Komito version is described. Begin with The Door, a curious detached flake directly beneath the Sickle Dihedral.

1. Climb the left side of The Door and belay at a stance (7, 80 feet).

2. Continue in a left-facing flake system to Middle Earth Ledge (4, 90 feet). Scramble up and left along shattered flakes to a ledge at their top (cl 3, 150 feet). This point also may be reached by climbing in from the left as for *Spear Me the Details*.

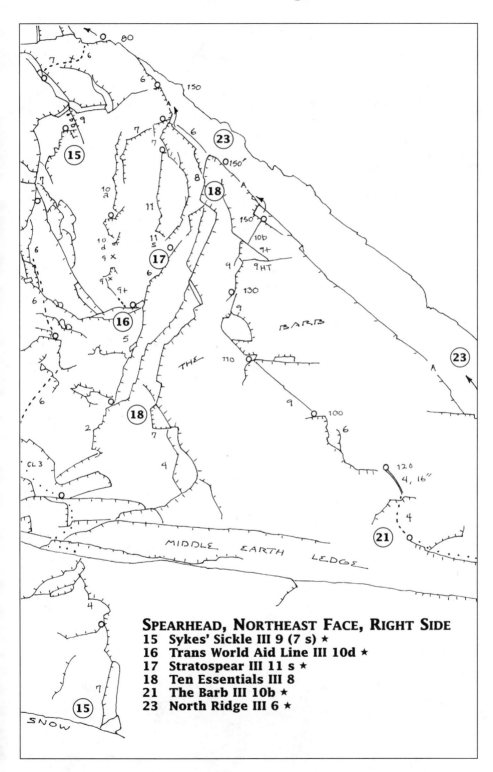

SPEARHEAD, NORTHEAST FACE, RIGHT SIDE
15 Sykes' Sickle III 9 (7 s) ★
16 Trans World Aid Line III 10d ★
17 Stratospear III 11 s ★
18 Ten Essentials III 8
21 The Barb III 10b ★
23 North Ridge III 6 ★

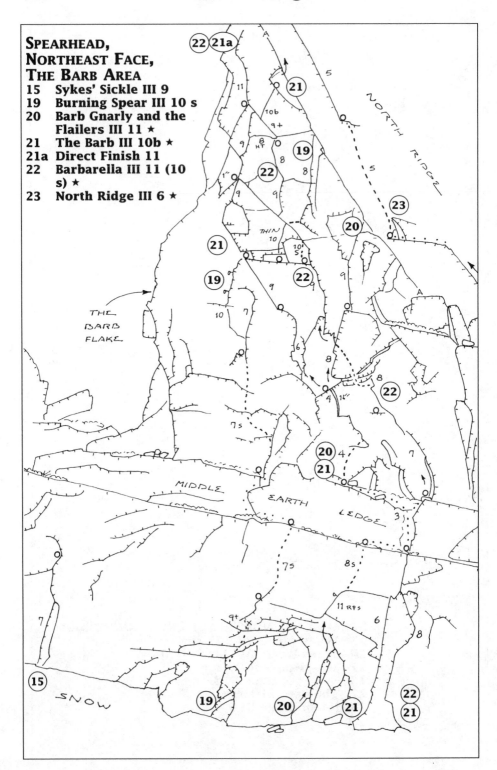

SPEARHEAD,
NORTHEAST FACE,
THE BARB AREA
15   Sykes' Sickle III 9
19   Burning Spear III 10 s
20   Barb Gnarly and the
      Flailers III 11 ★
21   The Barb III 10b ★
21a Direct Finish 11
22   Barbarella III 11 (10
      s) ★
23   North Ridge III 6 ★

3. Climb up and right via thin flakes and friction and belay at the bottom of the Sickle Dihedral (7, 150 feet).
4. Climb the dihedral to a stance at the bottom of a flared chimney (6).
5. Climb the chimney until it is possible to stem right to a series of flakes that lead up and right to a ledge beneath the Sickle Roof (7).
6. Move right into a crack, then climb straight up past fixed pins through a slot in the roof (9) and belay in a crack system after 100 feet.
7. Continue up the crack system a short way, then break right across the slab past a lone bolt (7s) and continue up and right to the walk-off ledge.

16 Trans World Aid Line   III 10d ★
This is the free version of an aid route that lies between *Sykes' Sickle* and *Stratospear.* The route's history is not known. The name is offered as a convenience.
Follow *Sykes' Sickle* to the grassy benches in the middle of the northeast face.
1. Climb a crack up and left, then work straight up the face past some fixed pro and belay on a flake (10d, 100 feet).
2. Follow a left-facing flake/dihedral for about 90 feet, then traverse up and right along flakes and join the *North Ridge* (10a, 150 feet).

17 Stratospear   III 11 s ★
FA: Osborn and Fargo, 1981. FFA: Tim Coats and Bret Ruckman, 1987.
This is a free version of the aid climb *Believe It or Not* (IV 9 A3). Begin with the first three pitches of the *Ten Essentials*, then break left into a clean, left-facing dihedral system high on the wall. This dihedral requires difficult stemming protected by tiny RPs, and leads to the last two pitches of the *North Ridge*.

18 Ten Essentials   III 8
FA: Chris Reveley and Jim Erickson, 1974.
Left of the massive triangular flake called The Barb, a series of left-facing flake/dihedrals runs up the wall. Reach Middle Earth Ledge as for *Sykes' Sickle*, then follow the left of the dihedrals for three pitches.
From here, work up and right and climb a beautiful, curving left-facing dihedral. Merge with the *North Ridge* and continue for two more pitches to the walk-off ledge.

THE BARB FLAKE
The following routes ascend a gigantic flake at the right side of the northeast face. All descriptions begin from the talus below Middle Earth Ledge.

19 Burning Spear   III 10 s
FA: Larry Coats and Steve Grossman, 1987; of fifth pitch variation, Ed Webster and Curt Fry, 1987.
A sporting route requiring bold face climbing, this line starts to the left, then crosses *The Barb* at mid-face and continues up and right to the *North Ridge*.
Begin midway between *Sykes' Sickle* and *The Barb* at a curious flake that may be likened to a left-facing profile of Cleopatra...or not. Climb the flake, proceed through a series of shallow roofs, pass a bolt (9+), and

The author, free solo on *Age Axe*.   Photo: Gail Efron

continue up slabs (7 s) to Middle Earth Ledge. Climb up and left above two short, left-facing corners (7 s), then up to a ledge beneath a long, left-facing dihedral. Climb the dihedral (7), then work up the face and belay as for *The Barb*. A variation to this pitch called *Stormrider* (10) climbs cracks out to the left of the dihedral. Now, work up and right in a difficult crack (10) and gain another left-facing dihedral which is followed to the right edge of The Barb Flake (8).

20   Barb Gnarly and The Flailers   III 11 ★
FA: Larry Coats and Bret Ruckman, 1987.
Begin about 30 feet left of *The Barb* at some left-facing flakes. Climb up through the roof at a right-leaning crack and past a fixed pin to Middle Earth Ledge (11, 160 feet). The route apparently continues with *The Barb* for two pitches, then breaks right and follows a steep left-facing dihedral (9) to join the *North Ridge*.

21   The Barb   III 10b ★
FA: Walter Fricke and Charlie Logan, 1970. FFA: Dan McClure and Robert Gulley, c. 1975. SR to a #3 Friend.
Classic. Begin beneath an odd flake at the right end of some roofs. The flake is straight on the left and curved on the right side of the northeast face.
1. Climb the left (6) or right (8) side of the flake and continue to the lower tier of Middle Earth Ledge (160 feet).
2. Scramble up to the next tier and traverse 50 feet left to belay at a flake (cl 4, 130 feet).
3. Climb up via flakes and a 16-inch slot and belay at its top (4, 120 feet).
4. Move left and climb the left of two right-facing corners (6, 100 feet).
5. Work up and left along a thin crack and belay on a ledge beneath a roof (9, 110 feet).
6. Climb through an A-shaped roof and follow a one-inch crack to a stance in a left-facing corner (9, 130 feet).
7a. Climb the corner to its top, then move down and right to a thin crack that angles up and right. Climb the crack to a ramp and belay (10b, 150 feet).
7b. Start up the dihedral, but before reaching the top, traverse right to a hand crack that angles up and left to the crux crack (9+).
8. Turn a small roof and go up a ramp for 40 feet, step around the edge of The Barb Flake at a tiny horn, and continue up to belay at a flake/ledge.
9 and 10. Climb the last two pitches of the *North Ridge*.

21A Direct Finish   11
FA: Bill Feiges, 1970s.
Climb to the high point on pitch 7a and belay at an awkward stance. Climb a steep left-facing dihedral to the top of The Barb Flake.

22   Barbarella   III 11 (10 s) ★
FA: Tim Coats and Steve Grossman, 1987.
Reach Middle Earth Ledge as for *The Barb*. Climb up into a left-leaning, left-facing dihedral system and continue at a diagonal to a long ledge at

mid-face shared with *The Barb*. From the middle of the ledge, turn a roof (10s) and follow a series of cracks up and left to where they intersect *The Barb* just below its crux. Continue up and left into a large, left-facing dihedral and follow it to the top of The Barb flake.

23   **North Ridge**   **III 6** ★
FA: Chuck Schobinger and Pete Soby, 1958.
This route ascends the long ridge that forms the right margin of the northeast face. The rock on the upper half of this route is excellent and the climbing is exhilarating. The route described above the big ledge at mid-face is the most direct and aesthetic line. Easier varitions exist to the right and merge with the upper half of the seventh pitch.
Begin from high ground at the bottom of the north ridge.
1. Scramble up and left across an easy slab and belay at the bottom of a short steep slot (2). This is the left of two similar slots.
2. Climb the slot and belay at the base of a V-shaped dihedral (4, 120 feet).
3. Climb the V, then continue up an easy, right-facing dihedral and belay (4, 140 feet).
4. Continue up the easy corner to a big ledge and belay at its east (left) end (cl4, 140 feet).
5. Climb a flawless slab to a belay on a small ledge (5, 150 feet).
6. Climb a shallow, right-facing corner and step left to a belay on a square-cut ledge (5, 150 feet).
7. This is a great pitch. From the left side of the ledge, climb an exposed left-facing dihedral (6), then traverse right to a larger left-facing dihedral that is followed to a small stance on the ridge crest (6, 150 feet).
8. Climb an awkward slot to a level section in the ridge (6), then tackle a short crack (4) to reach a belay on a big bench (6, 150 feet).
From here, one may scramble 150 feet up broken terrain to the summit or hike down the talus field on the west side (see Descent B).

23a **Direct Start**   **8** ★
This is the most easthetic and desirable line for the lower half of the route. Climb the crack and corner system on the left side of the arête a short way left of the regular route. After two pitches, climb the arête until it is obvious to exit right to the big ledge at the top of the regular fourth pitch.

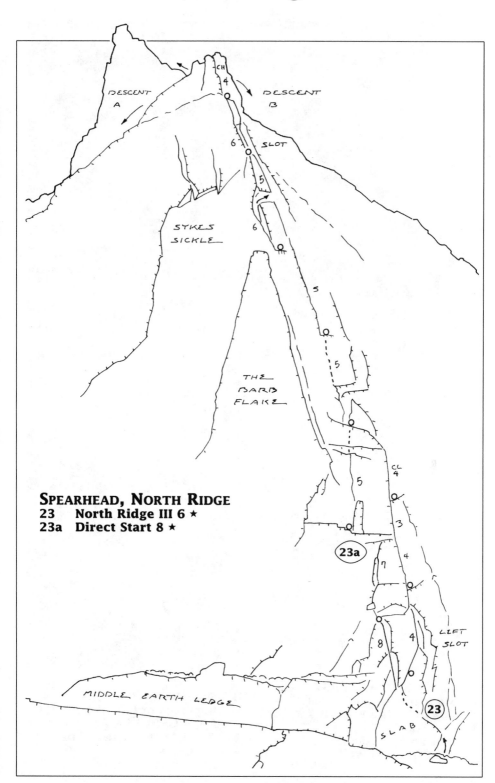

SPEARHEAD, NORTH RIDGE
23   North Ridge III 6 ★
23a   Direct Start 8 ★

McHenrys Peak, East Face

1   Stoneman Ridge II Class 3 ★
2   Constellation Prize II 7
3   Dog Star III 8 ★
Black Lake Ice Climbs
4   West Gully II WI 4 ★

5   Snow Bench II 4 AI2+
6   Big Mac Couloir III 6 A1 AI4
7   Right Gully III 8 A1 AI4
8   Arrowhead Arête II 6 or
     Class 4 ★

MCHENRYS PEAK

McHenrys Peak (13327) towers above Black Lake at the western extreme of the Spearhead Cirque. It is one of the few peaks along the Continental Divide that is steep enough all around to actually look like a mountain from any viewpoint. The easiest route on McHenrys Peak is the *Southeast Ridge*, which is also the easiest descent from the summit. All of the routes on the east side of the peak are approached from the Spearhead Cirque; the north face is approached via the Solitude Lake Trail.

1 Stoneman Ridge   II Class 3 ★

This route ascends the southeast ridge of McHenrys Peak. Approach as for the Northwest Face of Chiefs Head Peak. From the shelf above Frozen Lake, hike up talus or snow to Stoneman Pass (just right of the curious pinnacle on the skyline called The Stoneman). From the pass, head northwest up the ridge to the summit. An ice ax and mountain boots are needed to reach the pass until late summer when enough snow has melted to allow passage up the rocks on the left.

EAST BUTTRESS

The following three routes ascend the large, triangular buttress just right of Stoneman Pass.

2 Constellation Prize   II 7

FA: Richard Page and Taliaferro, 1979.

This route begins at a striped block some 400 feet left from the prow of the buttress. Work up and left for two pitches along a ramp, then climb a dihedral/chimney to a slabby area at mid-face. Follow a mossy groove up the slabs for two pitches to a ledge. Work up and left and follow a series of large, right-leaning ramps to the ridge crest.

3 Dog Star   III 8 ★

FA: Larry Hamilton and Dakers Gowans, 1974.

This route follows a series of dihedrals just left of the prow of the buttress. Begin at the left side of a massive block. Climb a short corner, then traverse up and left along grassy ledges to the bottom of a steep wall. Climb a crack at left followed by a clean, black dihedral which leads to a slabby area one-third of the way up. Work up the slabs and a prominent left-facing dihhedral to gain the left end of a large ramp that angles up to the right. Move right on the ramp until beneath a left-facing dihedral that is capped by a roof. Climb the dihedral and roof, then continue directly up the wall for two pitches to a final steep section. Start up the wall, then angle up and left along a ramp to reach the ridge crest.

4 LV 426   III 11b ★

FA: Jeff Lowe and Teri Ebel, 1994.

This route ascends the prow of the buttress via moderate ramps and corners, but finishes with a fantastic right-facing dihedral on the eighth pitch. Begin from the snow directly below a red left-facing dihedral on the prow. Climb a pitch just right of the prow, then veer right in a large open book dihedral (7). Continue up ramps and corners on the right side of the prow for several pitches and gain a ledge at the base of a steep right-facing dihedral. Climb the dihedral (11b), then exit left near its top

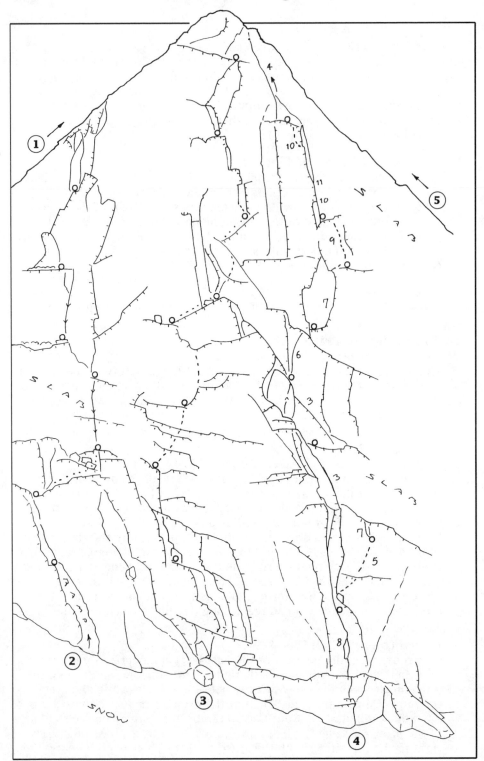

and climb a crack (10) to a bench. A moderate pitch leads to the top of the buttress.

5 Snow Bench II 4 AI2+
FA: Kuncl and Deeming, 1965.
Begin at the bottom of the east face almost directly below the summit. The objective is the long snow gully that angles up and left across the face. Climb a long rock pitch to enter the gully, then follow it southward to a notch on the southeast ridge. Continue up the ridge to the summit.

6 Big Mac Couloir III 6 A1 AI4
FA: Joe Hladick and Scott Kimball, 1979.
This route ascends the steep couloir at the left side of the large buttress in mid face, down and right from the summit. Gain the long, diagonal snow gully as for the preceding route, then turn right up the steep couloir at the left of a prominent gendarme. The couloir will be mixed snow and ice with some rock climbing depending on season. At the top of the couloir, move right to the top of the central buttress, then climb the head wall to the summit.

7 Right Gully III 8 A1 AI4
FA: Kaelin and party.
This route follows the gully along the right side of the central buttress. Begin as for *Snow Bench,* then traverse right to enter the gully. Gain the top of the central buttress and climb the head wall to the summit.

8 Arrowhead Arête II 6 or Class 4 ★
FA: Ritterbush, Ehlert, and Sawyer, 1957.
This route ascends the northeast ridge of McHenrys Peak and has the same approach options as the *Arrowhead Arête* on the Arrowhead (see below). It is in fact the same ridge; the route simply goes the other direction from the low point. From the Spearhead Cirque, two obvious pitches lead up and right to the low point in the ridge (6). From Solitude Lake, hike about 0.5 mile up the valley and scramble to the ridge crest (cl 4). From here, scramble southwest up the narrow crest to the summit. Avoid steeper sections on the right.

8A.Variation 7
Climb a series of chimneys up the right side of the east face to a prominent notch on the ridge (four pitches).

9 Direct North Face III M4 AI4
FA: Bill Feiges and Peter Metcalf, 1979.
Approach via the Solitude Lake Trail and hike to the head of the valley. Climb a rotten chimney that leads to a 45-degree couloir. Climb ice or snow up the couloir and pass a chockstone at its top. There are three distinct snow and icefields with steep rock bands between. Ten pitches.

McHENRYS PEAK, EAST BUTTRESS

1	Stoneman Ridge II Class 3 ★	4	LV 426 III 11b ★
2	Constellation Prize II 7	5	Snow Bench II4 AI2+
3	Dog Star III 8 ★		

Arrowhead Spire

From Black Lake

ARROWHEAD, SOUTH FACE
1 **Arrowhead Arête II 6 or Class 4**
2 **Artemis II 9**
3 **Airhead III 12a**
4 **South Ramp II 4**
5 **South Face II 9**
9 **East Face II 4 ★**

10 McHenrys Notch Couloir   II Class 4 AI3 ★

This alpine route ascends a classic couloir and the northwest ridge of McHenrys Peak. Best conditions are mid to late summer. Approach via the Solitude Lake Trail and hike to the head of the valley. Climb the prominent couloir at the right side of the north face and reach a deep cleft on the ridge crest (McHenrys Notch). Scramble southeast up the ridge to the summit. From the notch, one also may scramble south to Powell Peak and traverse Thatchtop to descend, or continue northwest to the Andrews Glacier.

ARROWHEAD

Arrowhead (12645) is a summit on the northeast ridge of McHenrys Peak in the manner of Spearhead on the north rib of Chiefs Head Peak. Arrowhead seems to have been named for a large pinnacle on its southeast side that is prominent from the Glacier Gorge Trail below Black Lake. Once, pointing out this feature to a friend, she said, "It looks more like something else to me!"

Approach. For routes on the south face, it is possible to hike directly up the steep slope from Black Lake. One also may approach as for Spearhead (see above) and countour around the basin beneath McHenrys Peak. For routes on the east ridge and north face, it is more practical to take the primitve Solitude Lake Trail (see under Glacier Gorge) and proceed from there. The easiest descent from the summit is to scramble down the *Regular Route* (see below).

1 Arrowhead Arête   II 6 or Class 4

This route climbs the long ridge west of the summit and may be approached from the north or south. This is the same ridge as *Arrowhead Arête* on McHenrys Peak, but going the other way from the low point. From Solitude Lake, hike west about 0.5 mile and scramble to the low point in the ridge (cl 4). From the Spearhead Cirque, contour around below McHenrys Peak until beneath the low point in the ridge, whence two pitches lead up and right to the crest (6). From here, hike eastward to the summit.

2 Artemis   II 9

FA: Larry Hamilton and T. Griese, 1975.
Begin on the south side of Arrowhead Arête about 100 feet right from the low point. Two moderate pitches up slabs lead to a large left-facing dihedral. Two pitches up the dihedral lead to the ridge crest.

3 Airhead   III 12a ★

FA: Eric Winkelman and Michael Bearzi, 1994. SR to #4 Friend, mostly small pieces.
This route climbs a hanging left-facing dihedral about 600 feet right of the McHenrys-Arrowhead col.
Scramble about 300 feet up moderate slab to a ledge below a large left-facing dihedral.
1. Bridge up corner with thin crack sometimes climbing on right wall of dihedral to a small stance (11a, 120 feet).
2. Continue up dihedral to a ledge on right (10d, 80 feet).

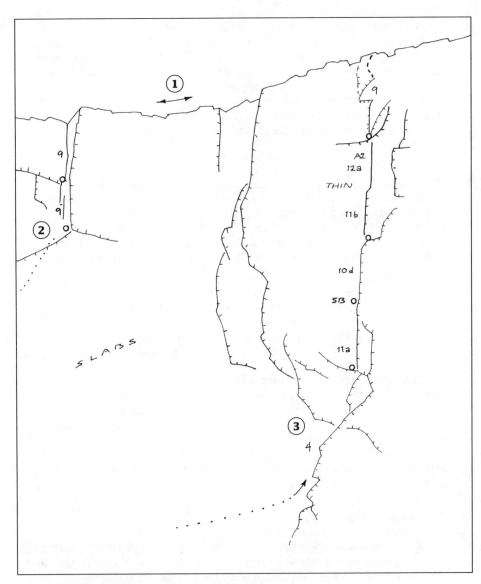

ARROWHEAD, SOUTH FACE, LEFT SIDE
1 **Arrowhead Arête II 6 or Class 4**
2 **Artemis II 9**
3 **Airhead III 12a** ★

3. Climb a shallow left-facing dihedral, turn a small roof, and up a very thin crack in face to a big ledge (12a, 120 feet). This is a very sustained pitch.

4. Traverse 20 feet left, then climb a right-arching, right-facing dihedral to a roof. Turn the roof and continue past several more roofs to crest of ridge (9 loose, 70 feet).

4 South Ramp II 4

Begin well to the right of the preceding route, beneath the main south face. Scramble up a long ramp that angles up to the right until below the summit tower. Follow the ramp around to the north side and climb to the top.

5 South Face II 9

This route climbs the left side of the south face below the ramp. Near the left side of the face is a deep chimney; about 200 feet right of this is a curving dihedral. Begin about 10 feet right of the dihedral. Climb two shallow, left-facing corners, then a larger dihedral that slants up to the left. Turn an overhang on the left and climb easily up to the *South Ramp*.

6 South Face Right II 9

Begin in the next left-facing dihedral system to the right of the preceding line. Climb the dihedral past the left side of a roof. Where the corner angles left, move up and right to reach another dihedral that leads to the *South Ramp*.

7 Warhead III 9

FA: Hamilton, Griese, and Byrd, 1975.

This route climbs the right side of the south face begining from its low point. This is still to the left of the pillar for which the peak is named. Begin beside a large flake at the bottom of a slab. Climb a pitch up the slab to a grassy ledge. Follow shallow grooves up slabs, then climb a flake on the right to the base of a dihedral formed by an arch. Climb the dihedral up and left to a ledge (9). Climb through the arch at a black flake, then go up and left across a slab to a ledge beneath a second arch. Continue up and left across a slab to a rotten section that is climbed at left to a ledge. Start up a dihedral, then climb the face on the right to a ledge that is level with pinnacles to the left. Climb a shallow corner past a roof and follow a steep wall to the top.

8 Manic Laughter III 9

FA: Brink and Warren, 1980.

This route climbs the east side of the large buttress to the right of the Arrowhead Tower. It is most easily reached by "hiking" directly up through the trees and scrub vegetation from Black Lake, but this is not as fun one might think. Climb a low-angle slab, then follow a right-facing dihedral system up to a big ledge beneath a large overhang in a huge dihedral (three pitches). Climb a chimney behind a flake at right and gain a higher ledge, then jam a wide crack past the end of the roof and belay at a good stance. Continue up the dihedral system to a large, grassy ledge. Go 40 feet right on the ledge, then climb another dihedral to a chimney that leads to easy ground.

9   East Face   II 4 ★
This route climbs the narrow face just left (south) of the northeast ridge.
Approach directly from Black Lake or take the Solitude Lake Trail and
traverse south to begin. Climb up via slabs and ledges to a broad shelf
beneath a steeper section. Traverse right onto the northeast ridge and
continue to the summit.

10   Hourglass Couloir   II M4 ★
This route ascends the long chimney above the south side of Solitude
Lake. It is best climbed from late winter to late spring. About halfway
up, the couloir branches; the route takes the right branch. About 40 feet
above the branch, climb a vertical 2-foot-wide chimney for 60 feet,
above which the difficulties ease.

11   Sister Sweetly   III 8 W14
FA: Jon Allan and Clay Wadman.
This winter/spring route climbs a couloir several hundred feet right of
the *Hour Glass Couloir.* The first ascent party used a 60-meter rope.
1. (8 W12, 60 meters). 2. (W14, 60 meters). 3. Up gully for 60 meters. 4.
Straight up (8 W13). 5. Up slabs (6). 6. Go up and left to summit (4 W13,
300 meters).

12   Regular Route II Class 3
Hike to Solitude Lake and continue up the valley for about 0.5 mile.
Scramble southeast up a long gully directly to the summit.

Spearhead Cirque Traverse. A dramatic traverse of the peaks surrounding
Spearhead has been made by a number of dauntless individuals. The follow-
ing version was completed by Bill Briggs on 3 September 1984: Glacier Gorge
Trailhead to Longs Peaks via *The Trough*, then a traverse of Pagoda Peak,
Chiefs Head Peak, McHenrys Peak, Taylor Peak, Powell Peak, Flattop Mountain,
and back to the Glacier Gorge Trailhead. One may also begin with the *East
Face* on the Arrowhead and finish with Longs Peak, or the reverse.

Triple Crown. Gerry Roach's Triple Crown is another classic: Chiefs Head,
Alice, and McHenrys in one fell swoop. Can be done from Wild Basin or
Glacier Gorge.

The Great Wheel. This version follows the entire rim of Glacier Gorge. Begin
with the *Regular Route* on Thatchtop Mountain and gain the Continental
Divide. Head southeast over Powell Peak and cross McHenrys Notch, then traverse McHenrys Peak, Chiefs Head Peak, Pagoda Peak, Longs Peak, Storm Peak,
and finish with Half Mountain.

LOCH VALE

Loch Vale climbs westward from the bottom of Glacier Gorge and is among the most beautiful and accessible of the glacier valleys in Rocky Mountain National Park. The Sky Pond Cirque lies at the head of the valley ringed by the precipitous walls of Thatchtop, Powell Peak, Taylor Peak, and the Cathedral Spires. The pristine tarn Sky Pond resides in the center of the cirque and is the highest of three spectacular lakes in the upper end of the valley. Just below Sky Pond at tree line is the Lake of Glass or Glass Lake. The Lowest and largest of the lakes is The Loch. Icy Brook, descends northeast from these lakes to join Glacier Creek. One can expect to find many hikers and climbers in this area. The *South Face* route on the Petit Grepon draws crowds all by itself.

Loch Vale Trail. This trail branches right from a signed junction along the Glacier Gorge Trail (1.9 miles from the trailhead) and leads to The Loch in 2.7 miles (total). The trail continues along the north shore of The Loch, and in another half mile, goes left at a junction with the Andrews Glacier Trail. It then curves southward beneath Cathedral Wall, and climbs along a waterfall to reach Glass Lake at the entrance to the upper valley. A more rugged trail proceeds along the north side of Glass Lake, and at 4.6 miles, reaches Sky Pond in the heart of the cirque.

Andrews Glacier Trail. This trail branches right from a junction 3.4 miles along the Loch Vale Trail, then climbs along Andrews Creek and reaches the Andrews Glacier about 4.5 miles from the Glacier Gorge Trailhead. It is not difficult to kick steps up the Andrews Glacier and reach the Continental Divide, but a slip could have unpleasant consequences. An ice ax is recommended.

The Gash. About 0.7 mile up the Andrews Glacier Trail, a rugged valley called The Gash climbs southward to the East Col, the notch between the Saber and the Sharkstooth. This boulder-strewn valley is the primary approach to routes on the Sharkstooth and provides the the easiest (and longest) return from the Saber and Petit Grepon.

THATCHTOP
Thatchtop (12668) is the large, bulky mountain that separates Glacier Gorge from Loch Vale. Its summit is about a mile northeast from Powell Peak, the latter of which straddles the Continental Divide. Beyond an athletic summit scramble, Thatchtop has not drawn the interest of rock climbers, but it has a fine collection winter ice climbs on its east and north faces.

EAST FACE
The following winter ice climbs are located on the cliffy east face above Mills Lake. Follow the Glacier Gorge Trail to Mills Lake, and plow up the long slope to the beginning of the ice.

1   Overflow   WI3
FA: R. Rossiter, Ralph Baldwin, and Tim Hogan, 1977.
Follow the Glacier Gorge Trail past Jewel Lake and continue until a 75-foot ice flow can be seen through the trees low on the east slope of Thatchtop. Rappel from a tree to get down.

2   All Mixed Up   III WI4 ★
This route is also known as *The White Spider.* From the north end of Mills Lake, wallow up the slope for several hundred feet to the foot of the ice. Climb several easy pitches and arrive at a large bench. Escape to the left (south) or continue with the steep upper section which is the crux of the route. Descend the shoulder to the south of the face.

3   Curtains   II 7 WI4+
FA: Milan Proska and John Marrs, 1984.
This is a curtain of ice that forms to the right of *All Mixed Up.*

4   Pipe Organ   II 7 WI4+
FA: Milan Proska and John Marrs, 1984.
This is a 100-foot fang that sometimes forms to the right of *Curtains.*

5   Dazed and Confused   II WI5 M4
FA: Malcom Daly and Larry Day, early 1980s.
This route begins about 100 yards right and a bit down from *All Mixed Up.* Climb two pitches up runnels followed by a 60-foot pillar.

6   Regular Route   Class 2
This is the peak bagger's route to the summit, normally climbed during summer. Hike the Glacier Gorge Trail past its junction with the Loch Vale Trail and cross the bridge over Icy Brook. Turn right and hike west along Icy Brook for about 100 yards, then bushwhack south up the forested hillside. Enter a gully that allows passage through a cliff band, then scramble up the open shoulder of the northeast ridge for about 0.75 mile to the summit. From the summit, one may continue southeast for a mile along the ever narrowing ridge crest (Class 4) and gain the Continental Divide. The summit of Powell Peak lies 200 yards southeast along the divide.

LOCH VALE GORGE
The following climbs are found along the south side of Icy Brook, about 300 yards beyond the Loch Vale Junction with the Glacier Gorge Trail. They are most easily reached by fording the stream about 50 feet before the first switchback in the Loch Vale Trail.

7   Mixed Emotions   WI5 M5 ★
FA: Alex Lowe and Dave Gustafson, 1981.
This formidable route ascends a steep wall to an ice curtain, and may be the same line as the following. Dry tool up the wall, then hook the curtain and go for it.

8   Middle Finger of Dr. Wazz   WI5 M5 ★×
FA: John Marrs and Dan Bankard, 1984.
This is an ice curtain that ends in the air as sharp fangs or fingers. It is just down and left from a large tree and is about 500 feet above the

stream. Climb a rock band with tools and crampons. Reach up and hook the ice, cut feet loose, and pull up until front points can be engaged. Continue up vertical ice that eases back to 80 degrees after 40 feet. Belay from a big tree and rappel 150 feet back to bottom.

9   Great Pillar   WI4+ ★
FA: (?) John Marrs, 1984.
About 200 feet right of *Dr. Wazz,* a series of icicles ornaments a cliff band. The most dramatic of these dangles 90 feet from the lip of a roof and is just 3 or 4 feet in diameter. From its top, continue up an iceflow until it is possible to traverse right and rappel from trees

NORTH FACE
The following routes are located on the 1000-foot north face of Thatchtop above The Loch. The face is divided horizontally by a sloping ledge system about a third of the way up. Near the middle of the wall, a large tower called the Dark Angel rises between two deep gullies. A smaller pinnacle on the northwest shoulder of the tower lends further identification. Approach via The Loch Vale Trail.

10   Deep Freeze   III 9 WI5+ M5 ★
FA: Alex Lowe and Eric Winkelman, 1982.
Deep Freeze ascends the deep gully on the east side of the Dark Angel and is considered to be one of the finest and hardest ice climbs in the park. The first ascent party reached the upper gully by free-soloing the lower cliff about 50 feet left of a deep chimney in the lower cliff band (6 or 7). The chimney, however, leads directly into the upper gully and provides two engaging pitches (M4+). *Deep Freeze* may also be reached by traversing east from the top of *Necrophilia.* The crux pillar has come to be known as The Necromancer, though the origin of the name is not known.
1 and 2. Two moderate pitches lead to an ice ledge in an alcove (WI3, 250 feet).
3. Climb a very steep and narrow ice pillar to a roof, then pull over a bulge where ice runs through the roof, and belay in the trough above (WI5+, 100 feet). The pillar is usually climbed on the left side where one can stem off the rock, but under auspicious conditions may be be climbed directly to the flow at the roof.
To descend, rappel the route, then traverse to the top of Necrophilia and rappel from fixed anchors to the bottom of the face. One may also continue upward to easier terrain and traverse east about 500 feet, where a long gully leads back down to the bottom of the wall.

11   Necrophilia   II WI5+ ★
FA: Eric Aldrich and Dakers Gowens.
Necrophilia is a 300-foot ice runnel down and right of the Dark Angel. The ice tops out on the long ledge system that spans the wall. Climb a long pitch to a shelf with a piton anchor on the left. Rappel or climb an easier pitch to the big ledge system whence one may traverse east to Deep Freeze. Rock gear may be useful depending on conditions.

THATCHTOP MOUNTAIN   Photo: Greg Sievers
10   <$iDeep Freeze III 9 WI5+ M5 ★
11   Necrophilia II WI5+ ★
12   Upper Wall II WI6

12 Upper Wall   II WI6
FA: Duncan Ferguson.
To the right of the gully along the right side of the Dark Angel, is a big
wall. From mid-winter to spring, it is sometimes possible to climb two
or three pitches of very difficult ice above the main ledge some 300
feet right from the top of *Necrophilia.*

13 Northwest Face   II WI3
FA: R. Grange and R. Greenman, 1981.
To the right of the north face, a long gully leads toward the summit.
Most of this route is of moderate difficulty with some steeper terrain
about halfway up.

The Crypt   WI4
This is an ice curtain on a short wall just north of The Loch.

POWELL PEAK
Powell Peak (13208) lies along the Continental Divide between McHenrys
Peak and Taylor Peak and is due south of Sky Pond.The 800-foot east face
above Solitude Lake, has three recorded routes, at least one of which is
worth a visit. The north face has a few good alpine routes including the spectacular winter ice climb *Vanquished* and the much easier *North Face Icefield*
to its right.

Approach. Reach the east face via the Solitude Lake Trail (see Glacier Gorge)
and the north face via the Loch Vale Trail.

Descent. From the summit, scramble down to the north and eventually
curve around eastward into a gully. Downclimb to where a 50-meter rappel
can be made to the bottom of the gully and the bottom of the east face. It
also is possible to scramble southeast to McHenrys Notch and kick steps
down the couloir to the north. Other options are to traverse Thatchtop and
descend the *Regular Route,* or follow the Continental Divide north past
Taylor Peak and descend the Andrews Glacier. For north face routes, it is possible to kick steps down the east margin of the *North Face Icefield* when it is
covered with seasonal snow. Later in the season, one may scramble down
talus.

EAST FACE
The east face lies at the head of Shelf Creek between McHenrys Peak and
Thatchtop.

1 Snark III 6
FA: Dakers Gowans, J. Byrd, and Larry Hamilton, 1974.
This route climbs the left side of the east face. From the top of the
Solitude Lake Trail, hike past Shelf Lake and Solitude Lake and continue
southwest up the valley to a dormant glacier at the bottom of the face.
Scramble up ledges to begin.
1. Climb a crack system that leads up to the right side of a huge, left-
leaning pillar and belay on a good ledge.

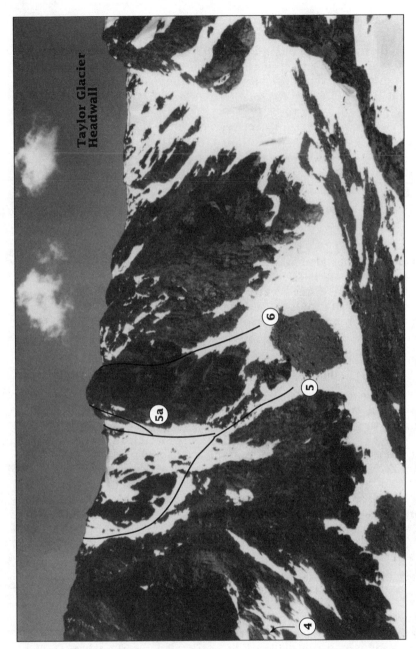

POWELL PEAK, NORTH FACE, RIGHT SIDE

4 Vanquished IV WI5+ M5+ ★
5 North Face Icefield II AI3+ ★
5a Variation
6 North Gully III AI3+ M3+ ★

2. Follow a crack up and right to its end, then go up and left to belay at the bottom of a black gully.

3. Climb the gully, mostly on the left, and belay on a ledge at its top.

4. Climb directly up the wall to a ledge.

5. Walk right on the ledge until it is possible to climb up and left to another ledge.

6. Work right across the steep face, then wander upward to easier terrain. Scramble up to the summit.

2. Early Retirement III 10

FA: Bob Monnet and Terry Murphy, 1996. SR plus several thin and shallow pins.

Begin beneath two parallel vertical cracks, about 300 feet right of the Snark pillar.

1. Climb the left crack, then traverse right along moderate ledges to a belay (10b, 165 feet.)

2. Climb up and slightly right to a long grassy ledge and belay beneath a left facing dihedral (9, 150 feet).

3. Climb up and left to a large detached flake, then traverse right and climb the left-facing dihedral to a belay among blocks (10, 165 feet).

4. Climb up through the blocks, continue straight up moderate terrain, and belay on a big ledge about 35 feet below the summit ridge (8, 165 feet).

5. Angle left to a break in the crest and mantle onto the summit of Powell Peak (5, 80 feet).

3 Corporate Ladder III 11 ★

FA: Bob Monnet and Terry Murphy, 1996. SR with extra small to medium Stoppers, a #3.5 Friend and Camalots to a #3.

Locate a prominent spire that rises above the ridge crest on the right side of the east face cirque, about 0.25 mile right of the previous route. A long left-facing dihedral descends from the spire to the snowfield along the bottom of the face.

Begin up on a grassy ledge to the left of the dihedral and 100 feet right of a precarious flake up on the wall.

1. Climb a seam up a slab and continue up the right of two parallel cracks. Work up left through a loose section followed by a difficult crack, then belay in an alcove (10c, 165 feet).

2. Climb a sustained finger crack in a left-facing corner to a good hold, then continue more easily to a ledge (11, 150 feet).

3. Work up and left over broken terrain and finish with a deep slot. Belay on the narrow ridge crest with a view of the Sky Pond Cirque (8, 160 feet).

To descend, traverse northeast along the ridge to a notch, then follow a gully down to the bottom of the wall.

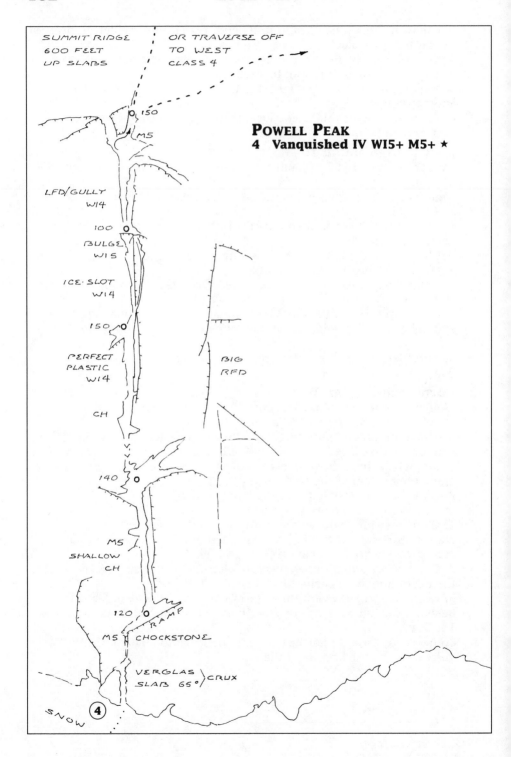

SUMMIT RIDGE
600 FEET
UP SLABS

OR TRAVERSE OFF
TO WEST
CLASS 4

150

M5

POWELL PEAK
4 Vanquished IV WI5+ M5+ ★

LFD/GULLY
WI4

100

BULGE
WI5

ICE·SLOT
WI4

150

PERFECT
PLASTIC
WI4

BIG
RED

CH

140

M5
SHALLOW
CH

120

RAMP

M5   CHOCKSTONE

VERGLAS   CRUX
SLAB 65°

SNOW   (4)

NORTH FACE

The north face of Powell Peak lies south of Sky Pond and is continuous with the west face of Thatchtop.

4   Vanquished   IV WI5+ M5+ ★

FA: Michael Bearzi and Bill Myers, 1991.

This brilliant mixed route ascends the broad slabby buttress due south of Sky Pond and left of the North Face Icefield. It is best climbed in late spring, but autumn may also yield excellent and challenging conditions. Hike straight up to the bottom of the wall from Sky Pond and begin about 75 feet up and left from the low-point. The route follows an ice-packed chimney and corner system 60 feet left a large right-facing dihedral in the middle of the wall. From the top of the fifth pitch, traverse off to the right (cl4, one rappel) or continue straight up to the ridge crest and gain the Continental Divide.

5   North Face Icefield   II AI3+ ★

This elegant snow and ice route ascends the north face of Powell Peak and tops out on the Continental Divide about 200 yards northwest of the summit. It is best climbed in late summer when the seasonal snow has melted or slid and the permanent ice is exposed, but it may be climbed earlier if one is willing to risk the possibility of avalanche. It is reached by hiking south from Sky Pond. The gully on the right affords the steepest line (up to 70 degrees) but may have a cornice at its top. The narrow gully on the left does not usually have a cornice and reaches the divide at about 13000 feet.

5A   Variation

After the first several hundred feet, climb a steep gully in the buttress that forms the right margin of the icefield.

6   North Gully   III AI3+ M3+ ★

FA: Dakers Gowens, 1975.

Just west of the *North Face Icefield* is a long rock rib. This route ascends the gully on the right side of the rib and tops out on the Continental Divide. Climb moderate snow to an overhanging section that is passed via the right wall of the gully (crux). Go back left and continue to the top. In a dry autumn the gully may yield a superb ice climb more than 1500 feet high.

TAYLOR PEAK

Taylor Peak (13153) lies west-southwest of Sky Pond and is the highest peak of the cirque. Its massive 1000-foot east face rises above a hanging snowfield that is accessed by a break in its lower cliffs beneath the Sharkstooth. The prominent cliff band below the snowfield has a single known route at time of writing. Most of the routes are on the main wall or upper east face and are of an alpine nature, characterized by poor rock and mixed climbing. Approach all routes but the *North Ridge* from Sky Pond. To descend from the summit, hike down the *North Ridge* and glissade the Andrews Glacier, or drop down the gully along the north side of the east face and return to Sky Pond.

1 Taylor Glacier Headwall   II AI3 or snow ★
The Taylor Glacier lies to the south of the east face and offers an enjoyable snow climb to the Continental Divide. There are several possible lines of ascent including the gullies on the left and right or weaving about the rock outcrops in the middle. Beware of a cornice at the top of the face. This is an alpine ice climb by late August.

2 Taylor Glacier Buttress   II M2
FA: Michael Covington and B. Hostetler.
This route ascends a left-angling snow ramp in the big buttress at the right side of the Taylor Glacier. It is sometimes possible to make the entire ascent on snow, but some rock climbing may be required about halfway up. The ramp tops out on the Continental Divide.

3 New Sensations   III M5 ★
FA: Michael Bearzi and Bill Myers, 1991.
This route ascends an 800-foot chimney system on the south side of Taylor Peak. From the Taylor Glacier hike northwest into a couloir that separates the Taylor Glacier Buttress from Taylor Peak, and continue for about 300 feet to the bottom of a prominent chimney on the main peak. The primary difficulties are in passing chockstones — up to 10d, but well protected. The route is best climbed in late autumn or late spring.

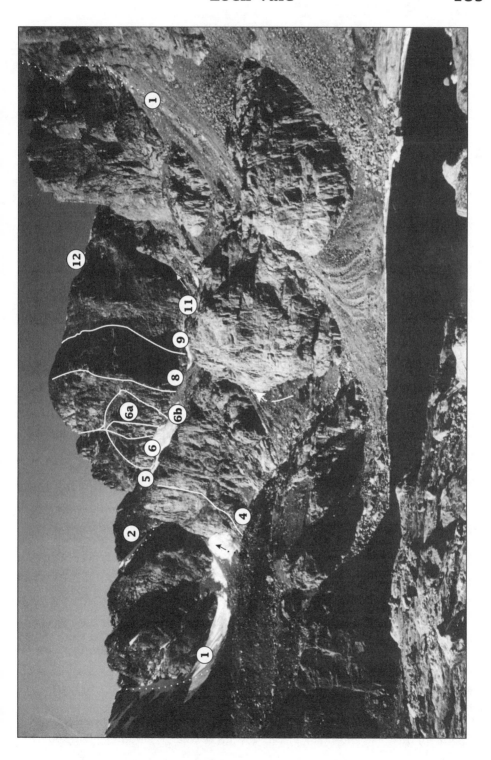

The following route is located on the southeast-facing cliff below the hanging snowfield.

4 South Face   III 10 WI5
FA: Charlie Fowler et al.
Locate an ice-filled chimney near the middle of the wall. Climb steep rock to access the chimney, then continue on ice to the top. Rappel the route or continue to the hanging snowfield.

UPPER EAST FACE
The following routes begin from a big snow bench that angles up and left beneath the main east face.

5 East Face Left   II 4 AI2 M2
FA: Paul Mayrose, 1970.
From Sky Pond, hike up toward the bottom of the Sharkstooth, pass through a gap in the cliffband and gain a hanging snowfield beneath the east face of Taylor Peak. Head southwest up the snowfield to its upper end. Climb steep broken rock up and right and gain a broad gully that leads to a notch on the ridge crest. Scramble to the summit.

6 Quicksilver   III M3
FA: Harry Kent, Michael Covington, Casey Swanson, 1974.
Kick steps up the hanging snowfield as for *East Face Left*, but do not go all the way to its south end. Once below the notch on the south ridge, climb up to a ramp that is followed up and left to the base of a chimney/gully system. Climb the gully to the benches at mid-face and continue more easily to the notch on the south ridge.

6a Quicksilver Variation   9 M5 ★
FA: Rick Strong and John Marrs, winter 1987.
Begin from the snowfield a bit to the right of the regular line. Climb a steep trough up and right about 200 feet and belay at an alcove near the headwall. Go right on a vertical wall with a roof (9), then straight up mixed ice and rock to belay at huge boulder in a snowfield. Angle up and left to join the regular line in the bench area at mid-face.

6b Yet Another Variation
An easier and longer alternative is to climb a broken gully left of the central buttress, then traverse up and left to join the regular line below the notch.

7 Central Buttress Left   III 8 M3 ★
FA: Greg Sievers and Rob Cassidy, 1994.
This route ascends the prominent buttress up the middle of the east face to the summit. Approach as for the original *Central Buttress* route but begin about 200 feet left of a large detached column.
1. Climb any of several light-grey dihedrals for a pitch (8).
2. Continue up small, low-angled dihedrals (7).
3. and 4. Scramble up over ledges along the dished east face just left of the buttress, and work around the left side of a large outcrop on the main buttress and belay at the bottom of a large chimney (cl4, 300 feet).

5. Climb the chimney, turn a roof on the right, then pass a ledge and a 20-foot block (7).

6. and 7. Scramble over blocks and ledges for another 300 feet (cl4).

8. Face climb over horizontal strata and arrive directly at the summit (6, may be done as two short pitches).

8   Central Buttress   III 8 M3 ★

FA: Fonda party, 1950s.

The massive east face is divided into two planes by a long rib that climbs from the hanging snowfield to a point just north of the summit. Begin from the snowfield about 200 feet right of the prow. Climb a chimney and a right-leaning ramp to reach moderate terrain whence one could escape left to join the preceding two routes. Follow the rib for several easy pitches to where the angle steepens. Climb straight up (8 A1) or find an easier line to the side. If climbed during summer, the only snow travel is up the hanging snowfield to reach the bottom of the rib.

9   East Face Right   IV A1 M4

FA: Harry Kent and Joe Hladick, 1970s.

This route ascends the broad gully or bowl between the central buttress and the next prominent rib to the right. Gain the hanging snowfield as for the preceding routes and kick steps to the upper left corner of the snow tongue that reaches up into the bowl. Angle up and right on rock for several pitches toward the rib on the right, then proceed up the middle of the gully until high on the face. Follow the line of least resistance up and left, and pass the final head wall with some aid. Eleven pitches.

10   Far Right Gully   III 8 M3

FA: Kent and Hladick, 1970s.

Gain the hanging snowfield below the east face and begin up the easy gully at the right side of the face. Locate a large chimney on the left side of the gully and climb this for several pitches (8). Easier terrain leads to the ridge crest.

11   North Gully   Class 3

This is the long gully that angles up to the northwest along the right side of the east face. It may be used to descend from the summit or to reach the Continental Divide from Sky Pond.

12   North Ridge   Class 2 ★

The north ridge of Taylor Peak runs along the Continental Divide and offers a spectacular summit hike. It may be approached via the *North Gully* or more easily by hiking south from the top of the Andrews Glacier (1 mile) or from the summit of Flattop Mountain (3 miles). No matter the approach, this is an excellent hike to a commanding summit affording unique views into North Inlet on the west and the Sky Pond cirque on the east.

CATHEDRAL SPIRES

In the high peaks, where most routes ascend massive features such as The Diamond or the northeast face of Spearhead, reaching the summit is not usually an objective. In the precipitous and narrow-topped Cathedral Spires, the summit is the last belay of the climb.

The Cathedral Spires cast a jagged skyline to the north of Sky Pond, and lie along a complex ridge that runs northeast from Taylor Peak and form a divide between the drainages of Andrews Creek and Icy Brook (Loch Vale). The ridge terminates above the confluence of the two valleys in a broad, towering buttress called Cathedral Wall. Any of the routes in the spires may be climbed car-to-car in a day. Note that these routes are numbered consecutively along the ridge except for Cathedral Wall.

1　S-Couloir　II AI2+ or snow
> To the left of the Stilleto, an elegant snow couloir climbs to the ridge crest. From here, it is not difficult to reach the Continental Divide.

STILLETO

From Sky Pond, the Stilleto appears as the next spire west from the Sharkstooth. It is, however, not really a free-standing tower but a narrow buttress that projects southward from the main ridge. A single route ascends the narrow south rib. Approach from Sky Pond. To descend from the summit, it is possible to scramble north and downclimb to the col on the west side of the Sharkstooth where one may continue down The Gash or down the scree gully along the southwest side of the Sharkstooth. It also is possible to hike up to the Continental Divide and descend the Andrews Glacier.

2　Left Gully　II M2+
> Climb the steep chimney and gully system at the immediate left of the Stilleto. A rock step must be passed about halfway up. This route is best climbed late winter through spring.

3　South Rib　II 9
> FA: Page and Kimball.
> Begin with a scramble up the scree gully on the west side of the rib as for the preceding route. Pass a large chockstone and traverse out right to the bottom of a prominent right-facing dihedral. Climb the dihedral to its top and finish via a steep crack in the head wall. Four pitches.

SHARKSTOOTH

The Sharkstooth (12630) is the highest and farthest west of the free-standing towers in the Cathedral Spires and has the most elevation above any col. The narrow buttress to the west is the Stilleto. The Sharkstooth is easily recognized from Sky Pond as the left tower in the impressive triumvirate that includes the Petit Grepon (center) and The Saber (right). Viewed from the Andrews Glacier Trail the Sharkstooth sits directly at the head of The Gash. The pyramidal formation at its left (east) is the Saber. The Petit Grepon is not visible but lies directly behind the East Col (the notch between the

Sharkstooth and The Saber). Routes are described counterclockwise beginning from the East Col.

Approach. Use the Loch Vale-Sky Pond Trail or the Andrews Glacier Trail depending on which route is to be climbed.

Descent. Rappel down the east side from fixed anchors (pitons with slings) and hike out via The Gash. Find the first anchor in an alcove about 75 feet southeast of the summit. Rappel 150 feet to a grassy ledge, then walk north along the ledge about 100 feet to another anchor. Rappel 150 feet to grassy ledges where an easy scramble (class 3) leads down to the East Col. When the snow is gone, a vague path leads down the west side of the gully from the top of The Gash; otherwise, kick steps down the moderately steep snow. If a return to Sky Pond is necessary, see Descent B under the Petit Grepon (below).

East and North Sides. Approach the following routes from The Gash.

4 East Gully I 4 ★

This route ascends a gully in the left side of the east face. From the East Col, scramble up a short ridge and traverse left into the gully.
1. Climb up the gully for 150 feet and belay on a ledge at right (cl4).
2. Climb through a head wall, then continue up easier terrain and belay at a large flake at the next short cliff (4, 130 feet).
3. Climb a short pitch to a grassy area, then scramble 200 feet to the top of the meadow.
4. Move left toward the ridge crest and climb straight up to the first rappel anchor just below the summit ridge (4).
A short scramble leads to the summit.

5 Bivouac Buttress II 7

FA: Magnuson and Schneider, 1982.
This direct route follows a slight rib on the upper east face about 150 feet left of the *Northeast Ridge*, and goes straight up the head wall to the summit. Begin about 200 feet down from the East Col.
1. Climb 150 feet up easy rock to a ledge.
2. Go up and left and climb a steep crack (7).
3. Stay right of a gully, and scramble up grassy ledges to the base of the buttress.
4. Climb about 20 feet to an overhang and pass it on the left, then continue up the rib to the final head wall (7).
5. Wander up the head wall and top out just below the summit cairn.

6 East Face II 4

This is the same route described as *Right Rib* in Walter Fricke's guide (1971). Begin at the bottom of the east face some 300 feet below the East Col. Climb a rope length up easy rock to a grassy ledge, then wander up and slightly right through short cliffs and grassy ledges for a couple of pitches and gain a shelf high on the *Northeast Ridge*. Climb along the left side of the ridge and scramble to the summit (4).

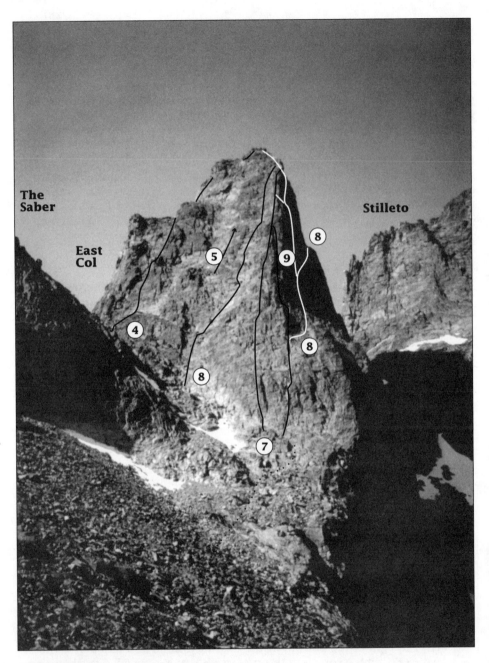

SHARKSTOOTH, FROM THE NORTHEAST
4 East Gully I 4 ★
5 Bivouac Buttress II 7
7 Northeast Ridge II 6 ★
8 North Face III 8 ★
9 Direct North Face III 8 or 9 ★

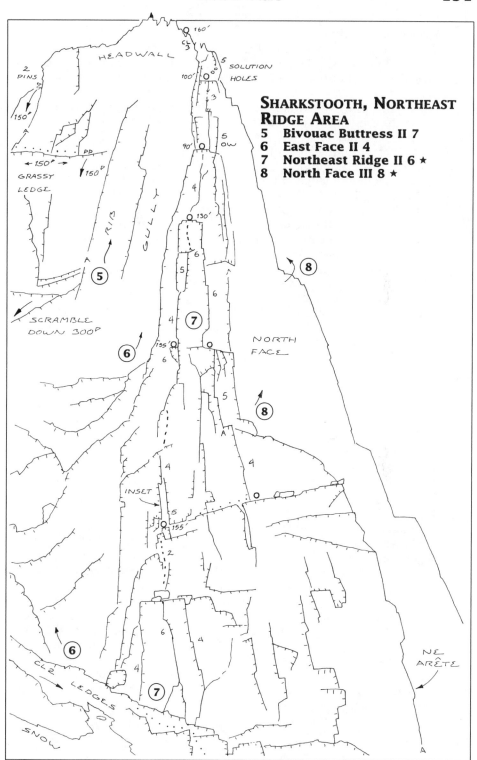

160'
CL
3

2
PINS

HEADWALL

5   SOLUTION
     HOLES

100'

150'

3

5
OW

PP

90'

← 150' →

150°

GRASSY
LEDGE

RIB

GULLY

4

**SHARKSTOOTH, NORTHEAST
RIDGE AREA**
5   Bivouac Buttress II 7
6   East Face II 4
7   Northeast Ridge II 6 ★
8   North Face III 8 ★

130'

6

5

5

6

6

A

⑤

⑧

SCRAMBLE
DOWN 300°

4   ⑦

⑥

155'

6

5

NORTH
FACE

4

4

⑧

A

INSET

4

5

6

155'

2

NE
ARÊTE

⑥

CL 2

LEDGES

4   6   4

4

⑦

SNOW

A

7 Northeast Ridge   II 6 ★

This is the best route on the Sharkstooth and has become an area classic. The line follows the narrow buttress at the right edge of the east face. Of several options for beginning the route, the line described below is the most direct. Some parties start farther right and follow a long, right-facing dihedral system to join the line described at the top of the third pitch, which is also the start to the *North Face.*
Begin from sandy ledges about 300 feet below the East Col and about 75 feet left from the edge of the north face.
1. Climb the left, middle, or right side of an initial buttress, then go up easier terrain to a ledge at the bottom of an inset (4-6, 155 feet).
2. Climb the inset (5), then work up easier ground until a short lieback (6) leads to a belay in a left-facing dihedral (155 feet).
3. Climb the dihedral a short way, then move right and ascend a steep, shallow left-facing corner. Turn the roof at its top and belay on a ledge after about 30 feet (6, 130 feet).
4. Climb an easy pitch up to a big step in the ridge (4, 80 feet).
5. Climb the obvious wide crack and easier rock above to a second step in the ridge (5, 100 feet).
6. Climb the right side of a smooth white face past two solution holes and continue up a right-facing flake to easier ground. Run the rope out and belay on the airy ridge (5, 160 feet).
Scramble the last 80 feet to the summit.

8 North Face   III 8 ★

FA: Tom Hornbein and Cary Houston, 1960s.
Climb the first pitch of the *Northeast Ridge,* then traverse right to the higher of two large grassy ledges; or begin down to the right and climb directly up to the higher ledge in two pitches (5 or 6). Work up and right onto the north face following the easiest line. Continue in a spiral around onto the west face until it is reasonable to climb directly up to the summit. Beware of climbing too high on the north face before rounding the northwest arête; follow the line of least resistance.

9 Direct North Face   III 8 or 9 ★

FA: Richard DuMais and D. Johnston, 1980.
Begin with the first two pitches of the original *North Face.* From the higher of the two grassy ledges, climb up and slightly right onto the north face for three more leads to a ledge high on the face (6). From here, one may traverse left to join the *Northeast Ridge,* however, the line continues upward. From the middle of the ledge, climb a trough/crack for 50 feet, turn a small roof (7 s), and belay on a stance beneath a section of crumbly, white rock. Traverse right around the corner to a small ledge (8) and belay. Climb straight up in a chimney/corner (6) past the right edge of some roofs and belay on a big ledge. Again one can walk left to join the *Northeast Ridge* or continue straight up from the ledge via a steep crack (9). Two more easy pitches lead to the summit.

10 West Fin III 7 A3
FA: Layton Kor and Larry Dalke, 1967.
This route begins from the col on the west side of the Sharkstooth
which is reached by climbing a snow couloir from The Gash.
1. Climb shattered, red rock and a thin crack to a ledge (6, 50 feet).
2. Go left 10 feet, climb up and left across a slab, and go around a corner to a semi-sling belay (6, 45 feet).
3. Traverse 12 feet left and nail a horizontal crack to a small ledge.
Climb past flakes and blocks and nail the overhanging wall for about 50
feet, then traverse 10 feet left to a large ledge (Fin Ledge) on the arête
(A3, 100 feet).
4. Traverse left around the corner to a trough which is followed up and
right to a good ledge (6).
5. and 6. Work up and slightly right to the summit (6).

SOUTH SIDE

Viewed from Sky Pond, the south side of the Sharkstooth is quite impressive.
Unfortunately, the routes that ascend it are somewhat vague lines on some-
what poor rock and are seldom climbed. But with the swelling crowds on the
Petit Grepon and Hallett Peak, these routes look better every season.
Approach from Sky Pond.

11 South Face III 9
FA: Layton Kor and Charlie Roskosz, 1962.
From Sky Pond, scramble up a gully on the left side of a small buttress
to the left of the Petit Grepon. Begin at the southwest corner of the
Sharkstooth.
1. Work slightly left up a steep ramp for 40 feet, then up and right for
60 feet to a grassy terrace. Move the belay to the right.
2. Climb steep cracks to a belay behind a pillar on another grassy ledge.
3. Work up cracks and flakes, make a slight descent, then go up and left
to belay.
4. Go left over a difficult roof and continue to a very exposed belay.
5. Climb straight up shattered rock, jam a vertical white crack, and
belay on the summit ridge.
6. A short easy pitch leads to the summit.

11a South Prow 7 ★✕
Begin a short way up and left from the regular *South Face* route.
1. Climb a steep pitch up the west face to a ledge just left of the ridge
crest (crux).
2. Angle up and right as for the *South Face* and gain a ledge that
extends around to the east side of the buttress.
3 Et cetera. Climb cracks and corners just right of the crest to a ledge in
white rock that runs out across the upper east face. The *South Face*
route goes up the steep, rotten crest on the left. Instead, traverse right
and join the last two pitches of the *East Gully*.

12 Valhalla III 7
FA: L. Smith, B. Cottle, and S. Schneider.

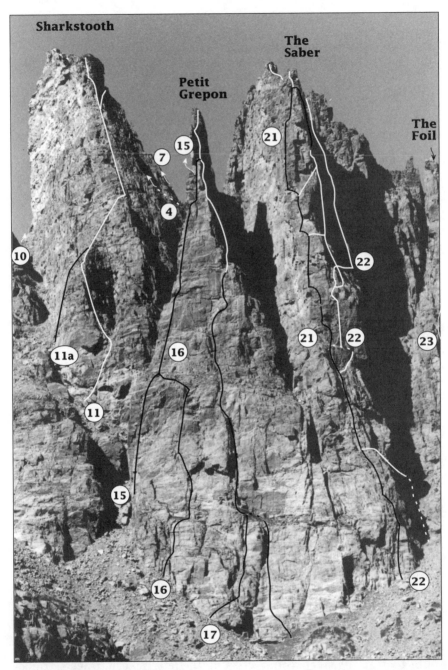

CENTRAL CATHEDRAL SPIRES, FROM THE SOUTH

7	Northeast Ridge II 6 ★	16	Southwest Corner
10	West Fin III 7 A3		III 9 (8 s) ★
11	South Face III 9	17	South Face III 8 ★
11a	South Prow 7 ★	22	Kor Route III 8 ★
15	Davis-Fowler III 10c (8 s) ★	23	South Face III 9 s ★

This route works up the wall between the *South Face* and the *Southeast Ridge*. Scramble up the scree gully past several chockstones as for the *Southeast Ridge*. Climb a short chimney and the face at its right to some ledges. Climb a dihedral or the face at its left and pass a large roof. Make an exposed traverse right and continue up to a big ledge. Gain the southeast ridge and climb it for a pitch and a half. Climb a difficult step (7) or pass it on the left. An easy pitch past some ledges leads to a blocky section with dihedrals on the right side of the ridge (7). A short dihedral (7) leads to an overhang that is passed on the left to reach a ledge. Follow a crack system past several ledges and belay on a big ledge. Work up and right to join the *East Gully*.

13 Southeast Ridge   II 4
FA: Kimball and party, 1979.
This line ascends the east side of the south ridge and joins the *East Gully* about one pitch below the summit ridge. No concise description of this route has been published, and its exact relationship to the previous route is unknown. Begin by scrambling up the scree gully between the Sharkstooth and the Petit Grepon choosing the gully on the left side of a small buttress. Work up the face via cracks and grassy ledges to where the terrain steepens and becomes much more difficult, then work right to join the *East Gully*.

THE PETIT GREPON
The Petit Grepon is named for the Grepon, a famous spire in the French Alps above Chamonix, though it looks more like the Eiffel Tower in Paris. It is easily identified from Sky Pond by its narrow blade-like summit and its central position between the Sharkstooth and The Saber. With a little help from Roper and Steck's *Fifty Classic Climbs of North America*, the excellent *South Face* route has become one of the most popular climbs in the park. The chances of finding yourself and your partner alone on this route during the summer are nil.

Approach. Start out on the Glacier Gorge Trail. After 1.9 miles, change to the Loch Vale Trail and hike to Sky Pond (4.6 miles from the trailhead). The tower rises unmistakably to the northwest of Sky Pond.

Descent A. Make a 50-meter rappel off the north side of the summit into the gully between the Grepon and The Saber. This can be done as well in two half-rope rappels. The easiest way to do the long rappel is to swing right to a ledge after about 140 feet. Walk north along the ledge to the bottom of a deep chimney and climb to its top (5). Unrope and scramble north to the East Col. Kick steps in snow or downclimb rock into The Gash, then continue north down snow or talus and pick up the Andrews Glacier Trail.

Descent B. To reach Sky Pond from the East Col, descend north to the highest talus fields of The Gash, then traverse east beneath the backside of The Saber and some smaller towers to a distinct col (the easterly and larger of two). Scramble south down a loose talus gully, make a short rappel from a dubious bolt, and continue down to Sky Pond. It also is reasonable to descend the narrow gully that passes beneath the east side of The Foil,

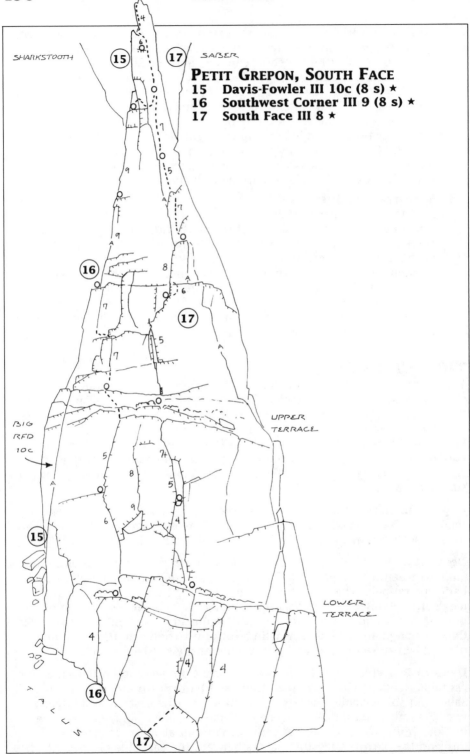

PETIT GREPON, SOUTH FACE
15   Davis-Fowler III 10c (8 s) ★
16   Southwest Corner III 9 (8 s) ★
17   South Face III 8 ★

which requires two short rappels over chockstones. The gullies at the east or west sides of the Petit Grepon are not recommended for descent.

14 West Face   III 10

A route has allegedly been done on the west face but no information is available.

15 Davis-Fowler   III 10c (8 s) ★

FA: (of the first two pitches and probably the FFA of the last pitch) Greg Davis and Charlie Fowler, c. 1978.

This route was previously called the *West-Southwest Face* but, since no such face exists on the spire, it is perhaps less misleading to name it for its originators. Most of this line follows the *Southwest Corner*. Begin in the gully at the west side of the crag beneath a large, right-facing dihedral. Angle in along a crack and climb the dihedral for two pitches (10c), then join the *Southwest Corner* route and follow it to the last belay on the south face. Climb up toward the overhanging prow but work left onto the west face and belay on a good ledge. One more very steep pitch leads up the west face to the summit.

16 Southwest Corner   III 9 (8 s) ★

FA: Bob Culp and Bob Beal (IV 5.8 A3), 1970.

This route is of the same high quality as the *South Face*, but perhaps for its higher rating, has not become so popular. The route goes up the left side of the south face for four pitches, then up and left to the southwest arête. Two long pitches up the arête bring one to a point where it is possible to traverse right and join the *South Face*, two pitches from the top. But it is better to continue up the narrow face for one more pitch before joining the *South Face*. The original line went left beneath the final overhang and finished on the west side with difficult aid climbing.

17 South Face   III 8 ★

FA: William Buckingham and Art Davidson, 1961

Queue up for this classic. The route ascends chimneys and cracks up the center of the south face for four pitches, then veers right to the arête (crux). The final three pitches go up the steep southeast corner of the summit tower and are thoroughly spectacular. There are often three or more parties on this route on any given day from mid-June to mid-September.

Begin at the bottom of the south face a bit right of center.

1. Climb either of two corner/chimney systems to reach the first of two, broad grassy ledges, the First Terrace (4). One also may climb the smooth slab on the right: excellent rock with scanty pro (7s).

2. Move the belay to the base of a large chimney that is ascended to a belay on a chockstone (5).

3. Climb out the left side of the chimney and tackle a difficult crack that leads to the Second Terrace (7). The tone is now set for the rest of the climb.

4. Stem up a smaller chimney, then work up and right to belay on a ramp with a fixed pin (5, poor anchor).

5. Climb straight up a difficult, shallow corner to the right end of a roof (9+) or climb unprotected rock on the right (6) and step back left to the same fate. Work straight up a steep crack (8) to a V-slot that is climbed (8+) to a big ledge on the southeast corner of the spire. Belay from a big block.

6. Climb straight up from the block through a series of left-facing corners until it is possible to traverse left to a belay stance on the very arête (7).

7. Climb a steep crack to a ledge on the east face (7), then go more or less straight up over steep and not-so-well-protected rock to a good ledge just shy of the ridge crest.

8. Climb either of two corners up to the crest, then, staying on the right, proceed easily to the summit (6). One also may climb the arête from the south end of the ledge (6).

18 First Route   II 6
FA: Glendenning party, date unknown.
This was the first route to the summit of the Petit Grepon. From the East Col, scramble east to the large ledge between The Saber and Petit Grepon. Downclimb (4) or rappel the west chimney of two chimneys to a ledge system on the east side of the Grepon. Walk south along the ledge to a right-facing dihedral and set a belay.

1. Climb the dihedral past an overhang/chimney and belay in the notch between the main summit and a pinnacle to the north (5, 75 feet).

2. Go south to the base of the summit tower, work up onto the east face, and follow a crack to the top (6, 75 feet).

19 Pen Knife   I 6
This short route ascends the north side of the northern summit of the Petit Grepon.

THE SABER

Viewed from Sky Pond, The Saber is the long narrow buttress to the right of the Petit Grepon. Viewed from The Gash, its pyramidal summit is seen to the east of the East Col. The south buttress of The Saber is one of the major climbing objectives in Rocky Mountain National Park and features two excellent routes and several variations. The Saber takes its name from the first route on the tower, *The Saber* (now known as the *Kor Route*), established by Layton Kor and Dean Moore in 1962.

Approach. Hike the Loch Vale Trail to Sky Pond, then hike up talus to the bottom of the tower.

Descent. From the summit, downclimb west, then north into The Gash (cl4). Once at the level of the talus field, traverse east just beneath the backside of the Cathedral Spires to a col and descend a scree gully south to Sky Pond (see Descent B under Petit Grepon). One may also hike out via The Gash.

Rappel Route: From the northeast corner of the initial pinnacle of the south buttress, make six 150-foot rappels down the east side and return to Sky Pond. Current condition of the anchors is not known.

Beginning the rappel from the summit of the Petit Grepon.

Initial Pitches. The following routes begin with a 400-foot section of moderate climbing that leads to a big ledge about a third of the way up the buttress. Start at the southeast corner with a "thumb-shaped" formation or higher up in the gully on the right in a grassy meadow. From the grassy meadow:

1. Work up and left along a ramp, then climb straight up to belay on a grassy ledge (4).

2. Climb a large dihedral on the right or (better) step left and climb straight up to a ledge with some large blocks (5).

3. Traverse out left along a crack and climb up to the big ledge (6) or move up to the right and climb a short wall to the right end of the big ledge (6).

Final Pitches. All known routes end on the summit ridge well south of the summit. If the east side rappel route is not taken, one must continue to the summit before beginning descent: From the top of the south buttress, rappel or downclimb into a notch on the north, then climb back up to a level section on the other side (6). Pass a step in the ridge on the right, then climb back up to belay on the crest (5). Pass a small gendarme on the left (west), traverse about 50 feet north along the crest, and climb directly up the crest to the summit (4).

20 Kor-Jennings III 10
FA: Layton Kor and Cliff Jennings, 1966.
Begin this challenging route up in the gully between the Petit Grepon and The Saber above a big chockstone. Traverse right along a ledge, climb a difficult squeeze chimney, and belay on a large flake. Move left and follow steep dihedrals up and slightly right for two pitches. Belay on the arête and finish with *Southwest Corner.*

21 Southwest Corner III 10a (8 s) ★
FA: Chris Reveley and Bob Wade, 1974.
This spectacular route ascends the arête formed by the junction of the west and south faces.
Climb the Initial Pitches and belay in the middle of the big ledge.
1. Climb a small left-facing corner just right of a shallow cave, then veer left into a left-facing dihedral. Climb the corner for about 50 feet (crux), then work up and left to a ledge at the left edge of the face (10a, 150 feet).
2. Climb a stepped left-facing dihedral system with a blocky roof, and continue to a ledge atop a large pillar (8, 150 feet).
3. Traverse straight left to reach cracks that are followed up and right to the left end of a roof (9). Climb a hanging, left-facing dihedral and belay at its top (9, 150 feet).

THE SABER, SOUTH FACE, FROM THE SOUTHEAST

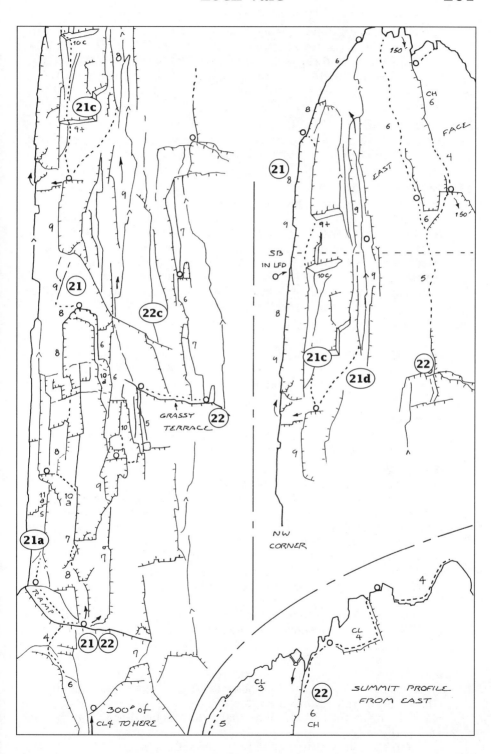

10c

21c

9+

21

8

22c

8

6

10 d 6

9

GRASSY
TERRACE

22

9

5

10

10
a

11
a
s

21a

7

7

8

RAMP

4

21 22

7

6

300° of
CL4 TO HERE

5

6

8

8

9

7

6

21

8

9+

SB
IN LFD

8

4

10c

9

21c

21d

9

NW
CORNER

6

150

8

6

CH
6

FACE

4

EAST

6

150

5

22

4

CL
4

CL
3

22

6
CH

SUMMIT PROFILE
FROM EAST

4. Step down and follow a ledge to the left edge of the face (8). Climb straight up the exposed southwest corner to another ledge (9, 160 feet).
5. Follow cracks and corners to the top of the buttress (7, 100 feet).
6. Scramble up the ridge crest to a high point above a notch (4, 165 feet). Rappel the east face or continue up the ridge to the summit (see Descent).

21a Left Dihedral   11a s

Scramble up a steep ramp from the left end of the big ledge and climb a very difficult left-facing dihedral to the ledge at the top of the second pitch.

21b Snively-Harlin   10 ⋆

FA: Doug Snively and John Harlin, 1980.
This variation is described in other guide books as taking a more difficult line up the lower section, to the left of the easy Initial Pitches. The fourth pitch above the big ledge takes the dihedral to the left of the arête. All other pitches appear to be the same as those climbed by Reveley and Wade in 1974. The line of the route shown in John Harlin's book *The Climber's Guide to North America,* however, shows the entire line in the same position as the *Northwest Corner.*

21c Mother Mica   10c s ⋆

FA: Richard "Skip" Getz and John Marrs, 1988.
Follow the Southwest Corner to the ledge at the top of fourth pitch.
5. Instead of traversing left to the arête, climb straight up through two large roofs (9+ s and 10c s) and rejoin the *Southwest Corner* at its next belay (about 40 feet above the second roof).

21d Stepped Roofs   9 ⋆

From the top of the third pitch, angle up and right and join the steep dihedrals of the *Southeast Corner* variation to the *Kor Route.*

22 Kor Route   III 8 ⋆

FA: Layton Kor and Dean Moore, 1962.
This route, originally called *The Saber,* has gained popularity not only because it is the easiest line on the south buttress, but because it is long, steep, and totally spectacular. The climbing is somewhat difficult for its grade and 11 full pitches are required to reach the summit from the bottom of the buttress. Get an early start.
Climb the Initial Pitches and gain the big ledge 400 feet above the talus. Set the belay beneath a distinct left-facing dihedral near the middle of the ledge.
1. Climb the dihedral to where it fades and continue up to a small roof. Pull left and follow a shorter left-facing dihedral (crux) to a good ledge (8 or 9, 155 feet).
2a. Climb straight up from the belay past a short right-facing dihedral and follow a crack to a long, grassy ledge (10a, 90 feet).
2b. Traverse straight right to a pedestal at the edge of the face, then climb an easy dihedral to the same fate (6).
Move the belay to the bottom of a large left-facing dihedral at the east end of the ledge.
3. Climb the dihedral to a good belay behind a pinnacle (7, 150 feet).

4. Climb a left-facing dihedral and continue up to the higher of two grassy ledges (6, 150 feet).

5. Work up and somewhat right over steep and nebulous terrain and belay on a ledge with some rappel slings (6, 140 feet).

6. Work straight up through a bulge and a V-slot to a sharp notch on the ridge crest. Climb the left (south) side of the notch to do the east face rappels or the right side of the notch to continue to the summit (6, 150 feet). See Final Pitches.

22a South Face   10d ★

1. Climb the first pitch or the Kor Route (8, 155 feet).

2. Climb a dihedral at left (10d) and gain the ledge at the top of the second pitch of the *Southwest Corner*.

3. Climb the *Southwest Corner* to the next ledge (9).

4. Work up and right beneath stepped roofs to the steep dihedrals of the *Southeast Corner* variation, and belay in a corner beneath a large block (9).

5. Climb around the left side of the block, change to the corner on the right, and continue to a ledge at the top of the south face (9). Scramble to the top of the buttress.

22b.Combo   10a ★

From the top of the first pitch, take the 10a variation and follow cracks up and left to the top of a large pillar (6). Join the *Southwest Corner*.

22c Southeast Corner   9 ★

From the grassy bench above the second pitch, climb the vertical southeast corner via steep cracks and dihedrals to the top of the buttress. Four long pitches.

THE FOIL

The Foil is the narrow spire to the east of The Saber. It has a single known route up its south face. Approach directly form Sky Pond. Scramble up the gully on the right side of the buttress to the bottom of a large right-facing dihedral. To descend from the summit, rappel 60 feet off the north side to a notch, then do an easy pitch up to the notch on the ridge crest. Traverse east around the north side of a large pinnacle to a scree gully at its east side, then head down the gully to the south. Initially, make two short rappels to clear chockstones and continue to Sky Pond. One also may descend the next gully to the east with one rappel.

23   South Face   III 9 s ★

FA: Duncan Ferguson and Mark Hesse, 1973.

Begin at the bottom of a large right-facing dihedral at the lower right aspect of the tower.

1. Work up the dihedral and belay at a flake (7).

2. Continue up the corner past some large blocks and a short chimney and belay on a ledge with three fixed pins (7).

3. Move out right, climb straight up the face, then traverse back left and belay in a left-facing dihedral (7).

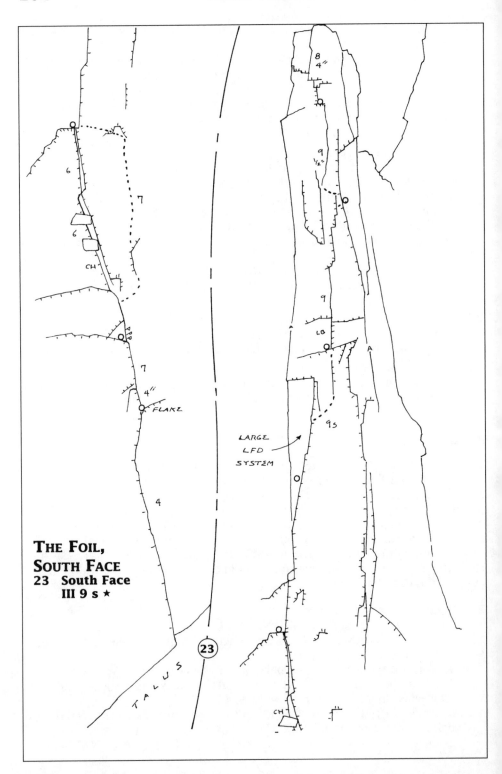

THE FOIL,
SOUTH FACE
23 South Face
III 9 s ★

4. Climb the dihedral to where it fades, then work up and right over unprotected rock and belay on a ledge (9 s).
5. Climb a short corner and a flake/crack, then traverse right and belay in a large dihedral at the right edge of the face (9).
6. Move back left and follow discontinuous cracks to a ledge (9).
7. Work up and left along a corner and climb a 4-inch crack to the top (8).

THE MOON

The Moon is a large, flat-faced pinnacle toward the right end of the Cathedral Spires. It is characterized by a prominent crack that splits the south face. Approach via the gully at its left. To descend from the summit, downclimb to the northwest, then descend the gully that runs past its base.

24 South Face   II 9

FA: Molly Higgins, L. Manson, and Stephanie Atwood, 1975.
Begin at the left of a buttress low on the south side of the pinnacle.
1. Climb a pitch up the buttress (8).
2. Work up and right and belay on grassy ledges beneath dihedrals in the center of the wall.
3. Climb the corners to a ledge beneath a roof (8).
4. Work around the right side of the roof and belay on a ledge a short way up.
5. Climb a wide crack to a ledge, then continue past a false summit and follow a 2-inch crack to the top.

THE JACKNIFE

This is the farthest east of the significant spires on the ridge. It is characterized by a squared off summit and has a vague owl-like shape. Descend via a short rappel on the north side.

25 South Face   II 9

FA: Kimball and Wildberger.
Scramble up gully to the west of the buttress until it is blocked by a chockstone, then cut up and right to some grooves in the middle of the face. Climb a crack on the left and turn a roof near the top of the pitch. Work right and climb another steep crack with a roof.

CATHEDRAL WALL

From the north shoulder of Taylor Peak, the Cathedral Spires ridge runs northeast for nearly a mile and terminates in a massive buttress called Cathedral Wall. The 900-foot northeast face towers above the trail to Sky Pond and is easily seen from The Loch. The south end of the buttress forms two massive ribs separated by a deep cleft. To the left of these is still another rib upon which two routes have been established. The rock on the main wall is very steep and often hard to protect.

Approach. Hike the Lochvale Trail and continue past the cutoff to the Andrews Glacier. Shortly beyond this point, the trail passes near the bottom of the wall.

Descent A. Scramble northwest past the end of the buttress, then descend talus slopes into the Andrews Creek drainage.

Descent B. From the top of the wall, scramble southwest up the Cathedral Spires ridge until it is possible to descend a talus slope and gully to Lake of Glass and the Sky Pond Trail.

FIRST BUTTRESS

This is the smaller buttress left of the two massive ribs at the south end of the main wall. To descend from the top, follow ledges up and left (south), then hike down a broad talus field to Lake of Glass.

1   Blackstar   II 9
FA: Dan Bradford and Angelo de La Cruz, 1985.
Begin below and left of a black water-stained roof.
1. Climb up and right and belay beneath the black roof (4, 150 feet).
2. Cross the black area to a ledge with a tree (2, 40 feet).
3. Follow cracks up and left and belay on a long, narrow ledge (6, 60 feet). It also is possible to move around the corner to the right and climb up to the ledge (5 s).
4. Climb a chimney to a small ledge (7, 40 feet).
5. Climb any of several cracks, pass a small ledge, and belay on a large ledge (8, 120 feet).
6. Work up a chimney and jam an offwidth crack past a chockstone (9, 40 feet).

2   First Buttress   II 6
Begin near the lower right corner of the buttress and climb four pitches up the broken face.

3   Womb with a View   III WI5 M6- ★
FA: Michael Bearzi and Bill Myers, 1991.
This mixed route ascends the deep chimney between the First and Second Buttresses, not to be confused with the similar chimney between the Second and Third Buttresses. It was first climbed in late spring. Begin just left of the initial gully and a cave 100 feet up.

CATHEDRAL WALL, VIEW FROM THE EAST ACROSS THE LOCH
 3   Womb With a View III WI5 M6- ★
 5   Tourist Tragedy III 9 ★
 7   Dalke Route III 9 s ★
 9   Flying Nun III 10b (9 s) ★
10   Kor Route III 9 ★
11   The Pew III 9 s ★
12   Garden Wall III 10

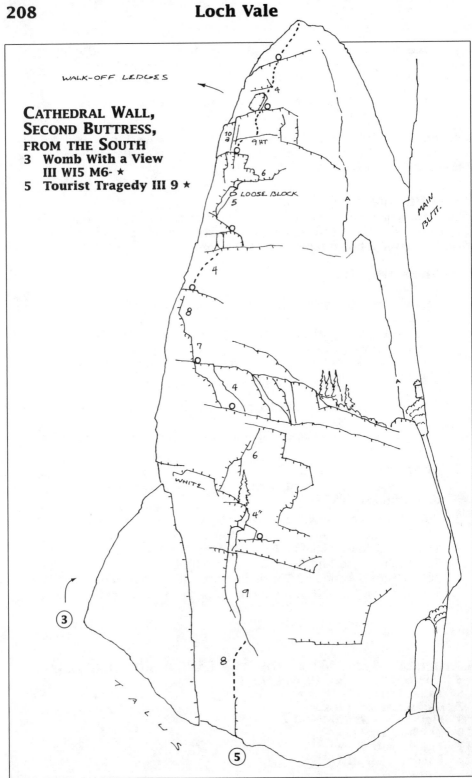

WALK-OFF LEDGES

**Cathedral Wall,
Second Buttress,
from the South**
3 **Womb With a View
    III WI5 M6- ★**
5 **Tourist Tragedy III 9 ★**

4

10 a

9 HT

6

LOOSE BLOCK

5

A

MAIN BUTT.

4

8

7

4

A

6

WHITE

4"

9

3

8

5

Scramble 300 feet up easy rock on the left and belay deep in the main chimney.

1. Climb an ice pillar in a corner.
2. Climb over an ice mushroom.
3. Continue into a huge cave.
4. Climb 30 feet up rock on the right side of the cave, then snag a 15-foot icicle and belay on a small ledge behind it. On the first ascent, Myers cut a hole through the icicle and squeezed through it to reach the ledge. Bearzi was reminded of watching a birth from the inside out, which inspired the route's provocative and punny name.
5. More ice chimneys, chockstones, and corners lead to the top.

SECOND BUTTRESS

The following routes ascend the left of the two massive ribs at the south end of the main wall.

4 Second Buttress   II 7

The exact line of this route is not known. Begin around to the left from a large right-facing dihedral at the bottom of the buttress. Work up and right for two pitches, then head more or less straight up via short cliffs and ledges.

5 Tourist Tragedy   III 9 ★

FA: Richard and Joyce Rossiter, 1984.
This route follows the left side of the Second Buttress to its top.
Begin just right of a large right-facing dihedral midway along the base of the buttress.
1. Work up and right to gain a crack and follow it to a roof, then angle up and right to a ledge (9, 160 feet).
2. Climb up past a tree and follow a right-facing corner up to a ledge (8, 150 feet).
3. Follow a ramp up and left and belay at the bottom of a right- facing dihedral (4, 75 feet).
4. Climb the corner and a short steep crack to a ledge (8, 100 feet).
5. Climb the next step in the ridge via a chimney and belay on a grassy ledge (4, 90 feet).
6. Climb a right-facing dihedral, turn the roof at its top, and continue to a ledge beneath a steep wall (8, 100 feet).
7a. Start up a crack, but traverse out right until it is possible climb straight up to a big ledge (8, 80 feet).
7b. Climb straight up the crack (10a).
8. Climb the right side of a leaning pillar, turn a small roof, and run the rope out to scrambling terrain (6, 160 feet).

THIRD BUTTRESS AND MAIN WALL

The following routes ascend the right of the two big ribs and the broad east-facing wall that continues to the right.

6 Winchester   III 10 s ★

FA: K. Wheeler and John Harlin, 1980.

This route ascends the far left (west) side of the Third Buttress. Begin at the bottom of the deep cleft between the Second and Third Buttresses.
1. Climb a left-facing corner/chimney to a big ledge (7).
2. Climb an open book dihedral that curves left to form a roof, turn the roof on the left, and belay on a ledge that is even with a grassy platform in the big chimney (8).
3. Climb a corner up and right and follow a thin crack to belay under a roof (9).
4. Turn the roof, then climb up and left across a steep face with poor pro and belay at a stance at the bottom of a corner (10 s).
5. Climb a long left-facing dihedral and belay at its top (9).
6. Climb straight up near the left edge of the wall and belay at the bottom of a large recess (8).
7. Climb up through the recess to easy terrain (6).

7   Dalke Route   III 9 s ★
FA: Larry and Roger Dalke, 1966.
This route originally was named *Pillar East* (III 5.8 A3) and involved some aid on the last pitch. It begins at the far left side of the Third Buttress as for the preceding route but thereafter stays to the right. All pitches are 50 meters long.
1. Climb a right-leaning corner/chimney to a big ledge (7). Move the belay right to the near side of a large block.
2. Climb more or less straight up the wall past a ledge with a bush and belay on a higher ledge beneath an area of light-colored rock (9 s).
3a. The original line apparently continued straight up through the roofs above and traversed right to gain a crack and groove system along the right side of a huge pillar (8).
3b. Traverse right from the belay to gain the same system, then runout the rope and belay on a small, grassy ledge (8).
4. Continue up the groove/dihedral and belay on ledges at the upper right corner of the pillar (8).
5. Traverse right and slightly down to reach a pedestal with a "coffin sized block." Climb straight up a steep crack to a point below some loose blocks then traverse up and right to the prow (9 s). Runout the rope and belay on a ledge.
6. Climb a chimney or the face on the right to reach scrambling terrain (7).

7a Variation
Start the route by climbing past the left edge of the big roof (6).

7b Variation
Climb straight up the wall from the top of the fourth pitch (9 s).

7c Variation
From the top of the fourth pitch, work up and left to join *Winchester* (8) or escape into the big chimney (7).

8   Alter Boy   III 9 s ★
FA: Billy Westbay and Doug Snively, 1981.
This route begins at the left side of the east face beneath a large overhang.

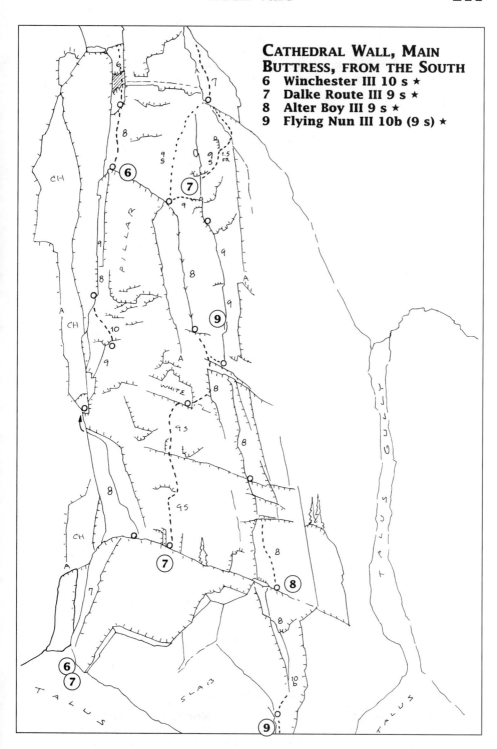

CATHEDRAL WALL, MAIN
BUTTRESS, FROM THE SOUTH
6 Winchester III 10 s ★
7 Dalke Route III 9 s ★
8 Alter Boy III 9 s ★
9 Flying Nun III 10b (9 s) ★

1. Climb a slab up to the roof, hand traverse left at a break and belay on a ledge (8).
2 and 3. Climb a right-facing dihedral system for two pitches and belay at an area of grassy ledges halfway up the face (8).
4. Climb straight up from the left end of the ledges and belay at the top of a massive pillar on the south buttress (8). This is the fourth pitch of the *Dalke Route.*
5. Climb up and right across the blank wall, pass a flake, and exit right onto the upper east face (9 s).
6. A long moderate pitch leads to the top (7).

9 Flying Nun   III 10b (9 s) ★
FA: Greg Davis and Charlie Fowler, 1986.
This variation straightens out the line of *Alter Boy* and comprises one of the best routes on Cathedral Wall. Begin beneath the big roof at the southeast corner of the buttress. Scramble up a ramp along the right side of a slab and belay.
1. Step right and climb a thin crack (crux), then continue up the right side of the arête and belay on a ledge (10b).
2.and 3. Climb the corners above as for *Alter Boy,* but belay at right beneath a massive left-facing open-book dihedral (8).
4. Climb up into the corner and follow a hand crack to a stance (9, 150 feet).
5. Continue up the dihedral past a difficult thin section and exit right as for the *Dalke Route* (9 or harder).
6. A long moderate pitch leads to the top (7).

10 Kor Route   III 9 ★
FA: Layton Kor and a friend from Wyoming, 1963.
This route, originally named *Cathedral Wall,* was the first on the buttress. Begin about 100 feet up and right from the big overhang at the southeast corner, beneath a massive left-facing dihedral with trees at its top.
1. Follow a crack up and left into a right-leaning roof/corner system and belay (7).
2. Follow the corner up and right and belay at the bottom of the big dihedral (9).
3. Climb a steep crack in the left wall of the dihedral, move right, and belay on a ledge with a tree (9).
4. Climb the right-leaning arch behind the tree, then work up and left to a right-facing dihedral that is followed to a grassy ledge (7).
5. Climb an indistinct corner past two pins, then swing out left on jugs (8 s) and traverse to a stance beneath a black roof.

CATHEDRAL WALL, MAIN BUTTRESS, FROM THE EAST

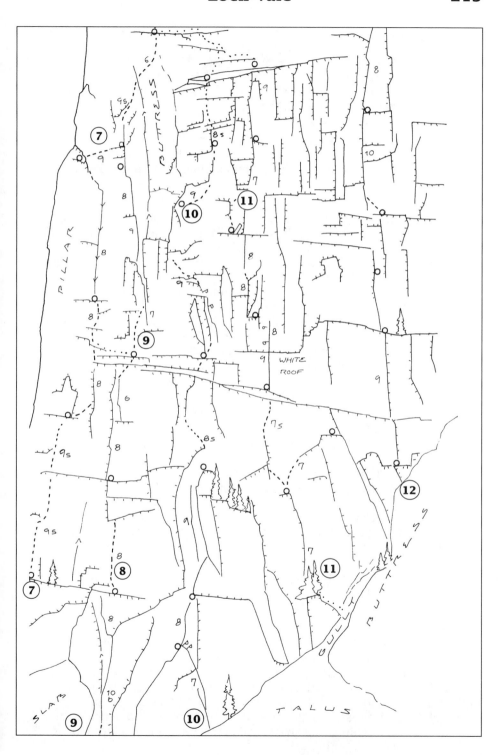

6. Climb a right-facing corner up to the roof, turn it on the right, and work up to a semi-sling belay at a small stance (9; wires and a #2.5 Friend).

7. Start up a right-facing dihedral toward another roof but exit left, then work up the face to a left-facing dihedral that is followed to a ledge (8 s). Scramble right and up to the top.

10a Black Roofs   11c s

FA: John Marrs and Cris Ann Crysdale, 1987.

From the grassy ledge at the top of the fourth pitch, work up and left (about 30 feet left of the regular line) and climb through the black roofs. Two pitches.

11   The Pew   III 9 s ★

FA: Tim and Larry Coats, 1988. SR with lots of small wires.

Begin at a recess in the wall about 200 feet up and right from the *Kor Route* between two large dihedrals that face each other.

1. Climb a crack to a ledge with a dead tree, then work up and right to a ledge in a large left-facing dihedral (7).

2. Move up and right out of the dihedral, then work up and left to a long grassy ledge (7 s).

3. Climb a crack straight up through a long flat roof, continue up past two pins, and up left to belay on a ledge in a left-facing corner (9).

4. Move left into another left-facing dihedral. Climb the corner, then work up and slightly left to a ledge with a large detached flake (8).

5. Follow a short crack up and left, then work up right and climb a stepped right-facing dihedral, stem up to a roof that is turned on the right, and belay on a ledge (9). Scramble to the top of the buttress.

12   Garden Wall   III 10

FA: Joe Hladick and Scott Kimball, 1979.

This route is characterized by a long, left-facing dihedral, low on the wall. Begin in the gully that angles up along the right side of the face.

1. An easy pitch leads up to the bottom of the dihedral.

2. Climb the long dihedral and belay on a ledge at its top (9).

3. Climb cracks at left and belay beneath an overhang.

4. Climb past the roof and continue for a long pitch to belay beneath another roof (9).

5. Work up to the roof, pass it on the left, and belay on a ledge (10).

6. Climb a slab between two corners (8) and continue up easier terrain to a big ledge.

OTIS PEAK

Otis Peak (12486) sits along the Continental Divide with its long east ridge separating the Andrews Creek drainage from Chaos Canyon. The summit is an easy scramble from the west and can be reached via the Andrews Glacier or the Flattop Mountain Trail. It also is reasonable to scramble up the east ridge from the vicinity of Lake Haiyaya. The south face of Otis presents a series of steep buttresses, some of which have eroded into detached spires and offer good climbing. The striking pinnacle on the north face (above

Chaos Canyon) is called the Turkey Monster. It was climbed with some aid by Charlie Logan and Larry Van Slyke, c. 1975.

ZOWIE

Zowie is the left of two prominent towers along the south face of Otis, which viewed from the south bears a striking resemblance to the Petit Grepon. Approach via the Loch Vale Trail and go right on the Andrews Creek Trail. Hike about 0.6 mile past the junction to where the narrow summit is seen against the sky, and scramble up to the bottom of the south face. To descend from the summit, reverse the *Standard Route*: Make a 150-foot rappel north to a notch, then scramble down a steep gully to the west. One or two short rappels are required to clear chockstones in the gully.

1   Standard Route   II 8+

FA: (?) Glendenning and Fonda, early 1950s.

This is the original route on the tower. Scramble up the gully along the left side of the tower to the notch at its top. Climb a broken chimney to reach a ledge at the base of the summit tower, then traverse around the east side and belay beneath a steep crack on the south face. Climb the wide crack past two small roofs (crux).

2   South Face   II 8+ ★

FA: Brian Poling and Barry Harper, 1968. SR to a #4 Friend.

This route is fun and has become vaguely popular.

1 and 2. Climb a chimney system up the left side of the south face (4). Move the belay east to the bottom of a crack near the right side of the south face.

3. Climb the crack for a long pitch and belay on a higher ledge (6).

4. Continue up the right side of the south face to a ledge at the base of the summit tower (5).

5. Traverse around onto the east face and climb cracks to a ledge beneath the final wide crack of the *Standard Route* (6).

6. Climb the crack past two small roofs to reach the summit (8+).

2a   Variation

From the long ledge atop the second pitch, climb a crack on the left, then go up and left to a ledge beneath a right(?)-facing dihedral. Climb the dihedral and cracks above to reach the ledge at the bottom of the last pitch. On the last pitch it is possible to leave the crack about halfway up and climb the face out to the right (9).

2b   Variation

The final wide crack may be avoided by jamming a steep crack around on the south side of the summit tower (8+).

2c   Direct   8 s ★

FA: Dougald McDonald and Kate Bartlett, 1996.

Climb the "flatiron" at the lower right side of the south face and join the *South Face* route at the east end of the long horizontal ledge. 2-3 pitches.

ZOWIE AND WHAM, FROM THE SOUTHWEST
1   Standard Route II 8+
2   South Face II 8+ ★
2a   Variation
2c   Direct 8 s ★
3   South Face II 7

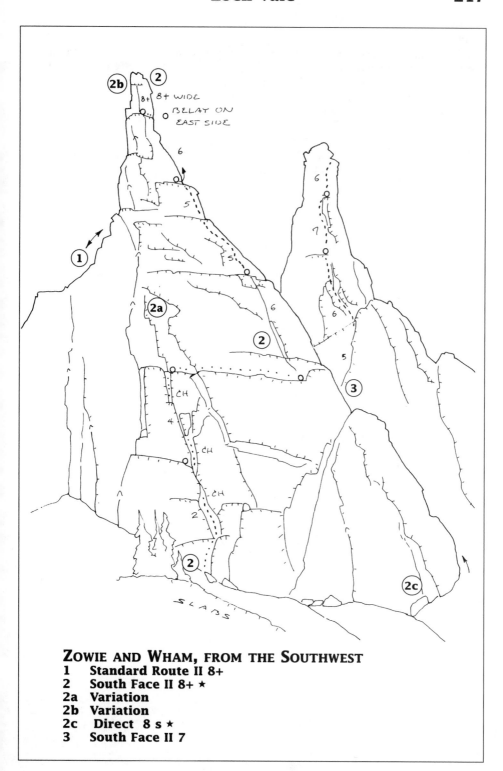

ZOWIE AND WHAM, FROM THE SOUTHWEST
1   Standard Route II 8+
2   South Face II 8+ ★
2a   Variation
2b   Variation
2c   Direct 8 s ★
3   South Face II 7

WHAM

Wham is the long, narrow tower immediately northeast of Zowie. It has a single known route up its southwest face. Approach via the gully between the two towers. To descend from the summit, make several long rappels west into the gully.

3   South Face   II 7

FA: Bob Culp and Ken Parker, c. 1961.

Climb several indistinct pitches up to the summit overhangs and veer right through these to reach the top.

The author on the *Kor Route*, The Saber.   Photo: Bonnie Von Grebe.

Gail Effron on the *Love Route*, Hallet Peak.

TYNDALL GORGE

Bear Lake (9450), at the mouth of Tyndall Gorge, is a very busy tourist area as well as the point of departure for climbers and hikers en route to Hallett Peak, Flattop Mountain, Notchtop Mountain, Emerald Lake, Odessa Lake, the Continental Divide, and many other destinations. It is also an alternate trail-head for Glacier Gorge and Loch Vale. To reach the Bear Lake area from Estes Park, drive west on Highway 36 to the Beaver Meadows Entrance Station. Continue for another 0.2 mile, then turn south (left) on Bear Lake Road and drive 9.4 miles to a large parking lot at its end. The following trails begin from a paved walkway at the west end of the lot.

Glacier Gorge Link-Up. This trail begins from the first junction on the left and goes left again where the Dream Lake Trail goes right. It reaches the regular Glacier Gorge Trailhead in 0.4 mile.

Dream Lake Trail. This trail begins as for the preceding, but goes right at the second junction. It passes Nymph Lake in 0.5 mile and reaches Dream Lake in 1.1 miles. The trail continues past the north shore of Dream Lake and reaches its end at Emerald Lake 1.8 miles from Bear Lake. This trail is used to reach the north face of Hallett Peak, the south face of Flattop Mountain, and Tyndall Glacier.

Lake Haiyaha Trail. The north end of this trail begins from the Dream Lake Trail, just east of Dream Lake. It curves around the east ridge of Hallett Peak, passes a junction, and reaches Lake Haiyaha and Chaos Canyon in 1.1 miles. From the junction, the trail continues southeast for another mile and joins the Glacier Gorge Trail near its junction with the Loch Vale Trail. This trail may be used to reach the south side of Hallett Peak.

Flattop Mountain Trail. This trail begins from the northeast side of a paved walkway that circumnavigates Bear Lake. It reaches a junction with the Bierstadt Lake Trail in 0.3 mile and a junction with the Fern Lake Trail in 0.8 mile. It reaches the summit of Flattop Mountain in 4.4 miles. The Bierstadt Lake Trail does not lead to any climbing objectives. The Fern Lake Trail is listed under Odessa Gorge.

HALLETT PEAK

The sharp northern profile of Hallett Peak (12713) is a hallmark of Rocky Mountain National Park and is no doubt among the most photographed features in Colorado. The domed summit sits on the Continental Divide between Chaos Canyon (on the south) and Tyndall Gorge (on the north), and may be reached by an easy hike from the summit of Flattop Mountain. The 1000-foot-high north face towers above Emerald Lake and presents several of the most popular climbs in the park.

Deep clefts divide the north face into three distinct facets or "buttresses" which are numbered from east to west. The First Buttress is less steep and continuous than the others and its routes are less often climbed. The promi-

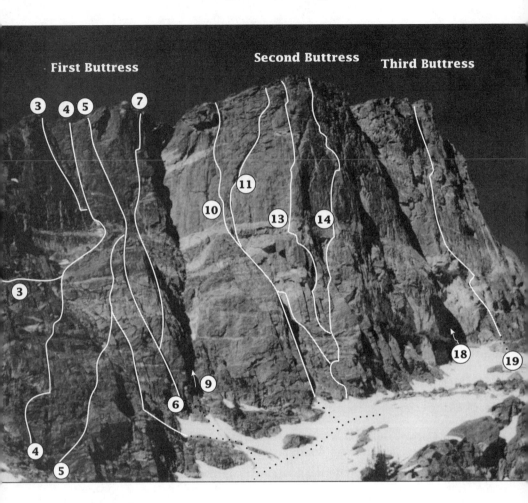

HALLETT PEAK, NORTH FACE, VIEWED FROM EMERALD LAKE
 3 Standard Route II 5
 4 Finch Route II 8
 5 Center Route II 6 ★
 6 Great Dihedral II 7 ★
 7 Magistrate II 7
 9 Hallett Chimney II 6 M4
10 Love Route III 9 ★
11 Englishman's Route III 8 ★
13 Culp-Bossier III 8 ★
14 Jackson-Johnson III 9 ★
18 The Slit III 8
19 Northcutt-Carter III 7 ★

nent Second Buttress features the cleanest, sheerest rock and is easily identified by a long, blunt prow at the junction of its northeast and north planes. The all-time classic *Culp-Bossier* route ascends this exposed prow. The massive Third Buttress has fewer routes but is home to *Northcutt-Carter,* the most popular route on Hallett Peak.

Approach. Follow the Dream Lake Trail to Emeral Lake, then scramble south over giant boulders and gain a moraine bench. Veer west and hike up talus or snow to the foot of the north face — about a 90-minute walk from Bear Lake.

Descent A. For routes on the First Buttress, it is probably more expedient to downclimb the *East Ridge* (cl4). This may require one short rappel to reach a col in the ridge, whence a steep gully leads back to the bottom of the north face. If the gully is full of snow it is possible to scramble down rocks on its west side.

Descent B. For routes on the Second and Third Buttresses, the *West Gully* (cl3) provides the fastest descent and least arduous return to the bottom of the face where extra gear and clothing are typically stashed. To reach the top of the West Gully, hike west along the rim of the north face to a small saddle just west of the Third Buttress. From here, descend a deep scree gully that drops down to the north. After several hundred feet, the gully veers right — do not go this way. Scramble up to a notch on the left (west) and continue down another gully to the talus slope along the bottom of the north face.

If a return to the bottom of the face is not required, one also may hike up over the summit and north along the Continental Divide to the Flattop Trail which goes back to Bear Lake. This is a long, beautiful walk (about 7 miles) and affords excellent views of the north face of Hallett Peak and the route just climbed.

SOUTH BUTTRESS

The south side of Hallett Peak presents a prominent buttress that rises above Chaos Canyon and Lake Haiyaha. Only one route is known on this feature. Follow the Dream Lake Trail and the Lake Haiyaha Trail to Lake Haiyaha in Choas Canyon, then clamber west over giant boulders and up talus to the bottom of the buttress. To descend from the top of the buttress, downclimb the East Ridge route to a col, then drop down a gully to the south (Chaos Canyon) or the north (Tyndall Gorge) as desired.

1   South Buttress   II 8
FA: Duncan Ferguson.
Follow a system of cracks and corners a short way left from the prow of the buttress. Protection is not so hot. Seven pitches.

FIRST BUTTRESS

The First Buttress is the farthest east of the three major facets of the north face, and is defined by a long couloir and col on the east and the Hallett Chimney on the west. The routes on this feature are less severe and continuous as those on the other two buttresses.

2   East Ridge   I Class 4

This enjoyable mountaineer's route may be approached from Lake Haiyaha on the south or Emerald Lake on the north, the latter of which is shorter and easier. From Emerald lake, hike up talus or snow to the south and kick steps up the couloir just east of the First Buttress. From the col atop the couloir, climb the east ridge to the broad, sloping shoulder above the north buttresses and continue westward to the domed summit. Descend by reversing the route or scramble down the steep gully just west of the Third Buttress. See *West Gully.*

INITIAL PITCHES

The following three routes are described with various traditional beginnings on the broken buttress down and left from the upper head wall. However, the best start to all of them, including Magistrate, is the Great Dihedral.

3   Standard Route   II 5

Also known as the *First Buttress Route.* Begin about 300 feet up and left from the low point of the buttress. Climb to the top of a small buttress, then angle up and right over ledges and short steps for several hunderd feet into a bowl in the middle of the wall. Scramble up and right the right to the highest of the white bands that span the wall, then go up and left to a large grassy ledge at the lower right side of a prominent tower. Climb the left of two right-facing dihedrals/chimneys to the top of the face.

4   Finch Route   II 8

This route climgs a prominent dihedral/chimney in the head wall, 50 feet right of the preceding route. Begin at a right-facing dihedral, about 200 feet up and left from the low point of the buttress. Climb the dihedral, then scramble up and right to the big white band that spans the face, and gain a broken ledge at the bottom of the dihedral/chimney system.
1. Climb a right-facing dihedral and belay on a good ledge (6, 75 feet).
2. Climb the difficult corner above to another ledge (8, 150 feet).
3. Climb the gully above to the right and continue up a right-facing dihedral (7, 150 feet). One may also climb the face to the right (7 s).
4. A short easy pitch leads to the top.

5   Center Route   II 6 ★

Begin at a slab just down and right from the preceding route. Climb the slab, then work up and right over broken terrain and cross a broad gully system in the middle of the face. Climb cracks and shallow corners up a large rounded buttress on the right side of the gully, then scramble to the highest ledges above the white band, about 100 feet left of Hallett Chimney. A clean right-facing dihedral, 50 or 60 feet left of the *Great Dihedral,* leads directly into the line on the rounded buttress and provides a superior start (7). Climb an easy pitch up and right toward a ramp, then up and left in a right-facing corner and belay beside some blocks (4). Climb a right-facing chimney/dihedral and belay above a little pillar (5). Climb a shallow right-facing dihedral and crack system to the top of the wall (6).

6 Great Dihedral II 7 ★
This is a good route and can be combined with any of the crack systems on the upper head wall. Hike up to the bottom of Hallett Chimney, then scramble up and left into the bottom of a prominent right-facing dihedral in the lower buttress. Climb two or three pitches up the dihedral, then scramble up broken slabs to the grassy ledges above the big white band. Choose a line on the head wall.

7 Magistrate II 7
FA: Jeff Bevan and party, 1972.
Begin with the *Great Dihedral*, but after the first pitch in the main dihedral, break right at a faint ramp and follow shallow corners on the right side of the crest to a low-angled area about halfway up. Note: It may be possible to enter this corner system from its bottom by starting about 100 feet up the *Hallett Chimney*. Work up and right over slabs to the highest white band, above which a ramp angles up to the right. Start up the ramp, then follow a curving crack through a prominent roof, and belay above on a ledge. Follow the crack system to a ledge at the bottom of a big right-facing dihedral. A long lead up the dihedral brings one to the top of the wall.

8 Dunrite Flake II 7
FA: Ken Duncan and B. Ebrite, 1975.
Climb the *Hallett Chimney* to the highest of the white bands, then break left and gain a large flake on the First Buttress. Climb two pitches along the flake and belay at its top by a large block. Follow cracks up and left througha big roof and finish as for *Magistrate*. It is not known how this route differs from a variation to the *Hallett Chimney* completed c. 1957 by Herbie Keishold, Erwin Hegewald, and Ernie Kuncl that is described in Walter Fricke's guide book (1971).

9 Hallett Chimney II 6 M4
FA: Glendenning party 1951.
This route ascends the deep chimney between the First and Second Buttresses of Hallet Peak. It is best approached as a winter climb and, despite its rating, has gained a reputaion for difficult mixed climbing and grisly epics. The initial chimney is relatively easy, but it becomes more difficult higher up (above the big white band). Some large chockstones provide the main challenges.

SECOND BUTTRESS

The massive middle buttress is characerized by its prominent northeast prow and a large horizontal band of white rock that spans the buttress at mid-height. A rappel route exists in the big dihedral that forms the first half of the Love Route. This allows an escape from any route that reaches the grassy terrace above the long white band. Look for clusters of slings every 150 feet or so along the dihedral.

10 Love Route III 9 ★
FA: Carl Love, Bill Hurlihee, Dean Eggett, 1957.
The lower left side of the Second Buttress forms a smaller triangular buttress that ends at the white band. The first half of the *Love Route*

ascends the huge loose dihedral formed by the right side of the buttress. This description begins with the first 200 feet of the *Hesse-Ferguson* and avoids the lower corner. The entire corner can be avoided by climbing the *Hesse-Ferguson* or *Culp-Bossier* to the terrace below the white band.

1. Climb the pink wall about 20 feet right of the smaller dihedrals (80 feet right of the big dihedral) and follow a grassy right-facing dihedral for 130 feet. Step left and climb 30 feet to a good stance (6, 160 feet).

2. and 3. Work up and left and follow the big dihedral to a belay alcove at its top (cl4, 300 feet).

4. Traverse right and climb a steep wall out of the alcove (6) or traverse left onto the prow of the triangular buttress and climb straight up to the same fate. Continue up steepening rock to a belay ledge above the white band (6, 160 feet).

5. Climb up and slightly right for 90 feet, then work up and left and belay at the edge of a ramp that angles up to the right (7, 160 feet).

6. Climb up the ramp, then follow a slight rib to a good ledge with a fixed pin (4, 50 feet).

7. Climb directly up to a black dihedral at the right side of a large overhang. Climb the vertical corner past several fixed pins and gain the slabs above the roof (crux). Climb through another roof (6) or go around it on the right and continue easily to the top of the wall (9, 150 feet).

11 Englishman's Route   III 8 ★

FA: John Wharton and David Isles, c. 1958.

This route begins as for the *Love Route,* then climbs along the huge, arching dihedral that splits the upper northeast face.

1-3. Follow the *Love Route* to the terrace below the white band (6).

4. Climb the big right-arching dihedral/chimney and belay on a small ledge (7).

5. Continue up the dihedral/chimney and belay at some blocks (6).

6. Climb straight up a crack to a roof, then traverse left to a crack that leads to the top of the wall (8).

11a Variation

On pitch six, climb straight up to the roof, then angle up and right and climb a right-facing corner to the top of the wall (9).

11b Variation

On pitch six, traverse right to the *Hesse-Ferguson,* climb a shallow left-facing dihedral to the upper roofs, then traverse left and finish with the preceding variation.

HALLETT PEAK, NORTH FACE

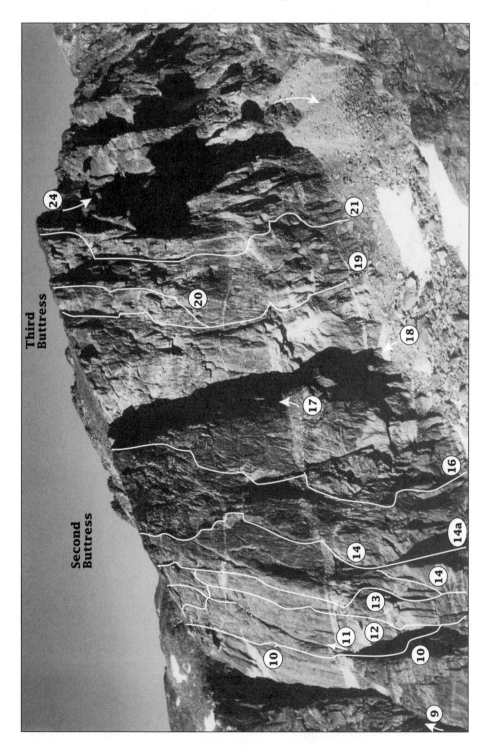

HALLETT PEAK, NORTH FACE, SECOND BUTTRESS, LEFT SIDE

9   Hallett Chimney II 6 M4
10   Love Route III 9 ★
11   Englishman's Route III 8 ★
12   Hesse-Ferguson III 9 ★
13   Culp-Bossier III 8 ★
13c Dark Side 9 ★
14   Jackson-Johnson III 9 ★

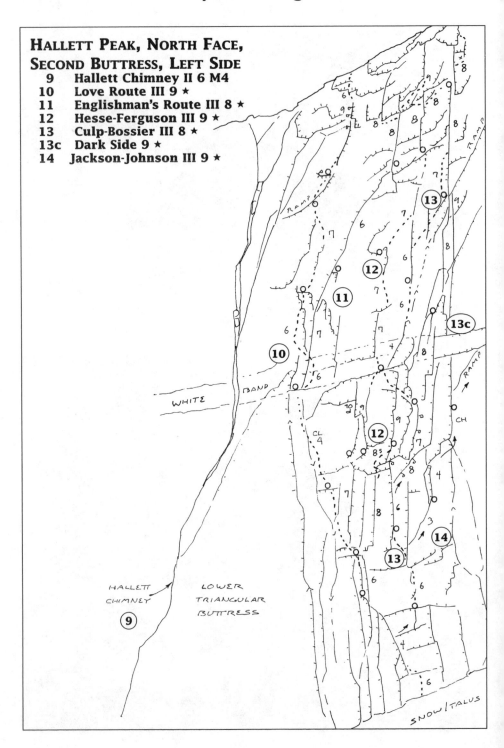

11c Variation: Turner Cut-Off 8

FA: Jack Turner and Bob Boucher, 1962.
6. Traverse right along a white band all the way to *Culp-Bossier* and finish with its last two pitches.

12 Hesse-Ferguson III 9 ★

FA: Mark Hesse and Duncan Ferguson, 1974.
This steep route ascends the second buttress half a rope left of the *Culp-Bossier* all the way to its last pitch where it either goes right to join *Culp-Bossier* or left to join the *Englishman's Route*. Begin at the pink band as for *Culp-Bossier.*
1. Climb through the pink band, then follow a grassy right-facing dihedral for 130 feet. Step left and climb 30 feet to a stance (6, 160 feet).
2. Climb the left of two small dihedrals and continue up easy ground to a grassy ledge. From the left side of the ledge, climb a left-facing dihedral and pass a white roof on the left, then go up and right to stance in the right of two left-facing dihedrals (7, 165 feet).
3. Climb the dihedral and turn a large, square roof, then follow a crack to the terrace at mid-face (9, 80 feet).
4. Climb a shallow right-facing dihedral to a roof that is passed on the right, then continue up the face to belay at a flake (7 s, 150 feet).
5. Climb the face up and slightly right and belay at a white band (8, 150 feet).
6a. Climb a shallow left-facing dihedral to a diagonal roof, then traverse up and right beneath the roof to join *Culp-Bossier* (8, 100 feet).
6b. From the top of the dihedral, traverse left and follow a shallow right-facing dihedral to the top of the wall (9).
7 (from 6a). Climb the last pitch of *Culp-Bossier* (8, 100 feet).

12a. Left Roof 10d

FA: Roger Briggs, c. 1979.
2. Climb through the white roof on the second pitch, then belay on a narrow grassy ledge.
3. Climb the left of two left-facing dihedrals and turn the large white roof at its top (10d).

12b Barnyard Traverse 8 s

Once above the white roof on the second pitch, traverse 50 feet up and right across a hanging slab and join Right Dihedral.

12c Right Dihedral 9 ★

From the grassy ledge on the second pitch, step right and climb a right-facing dihedral to a roof (8). Turn the roof, then go up and right across a slab (8 s) and belay in another right-facing dihedral. Climb the dihedral (9) and go left to the grassy terrace at mid-face.

13 Culp-Bossier III 8 ★

FA: Bob Culp and Tex Bossier, 1961.
Classic. This great route ascends a series of steep dihedrals to reach the big white band, then ascends the left side of the nose to the top of the Second Buttress. Begin at a pink band about 20 feet right of some small dihedrals (about 90 feet right of the big dihedral of the *Love Route*).

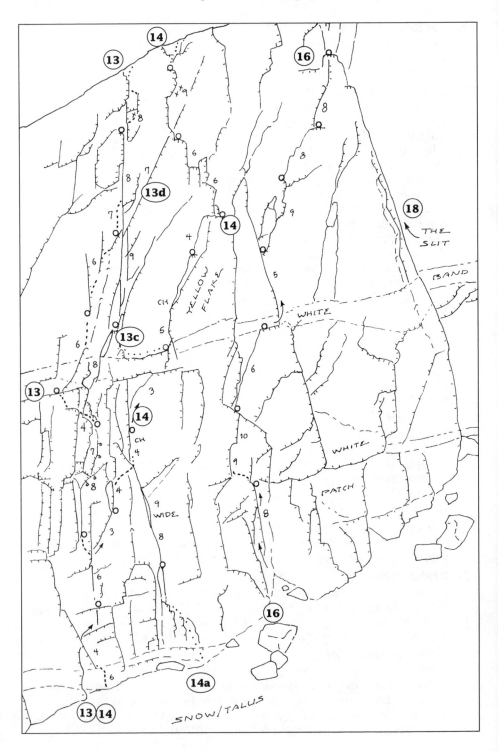

1. Climb through the pink band, then follow a right-facing dihedral for about 40 feet. Traverse right along a narrow grassy ledge to a crack, then climb to a higher ledge and belay (6, 140 feet).
2. Continue straight up into a right-facing dihedral, then work up and left into another right-facing dihedral and belay at a stance (5, 100 feet).
3. Climb the dihedral to where it branches, then work up and right past some fixed pins, turn a roof (8), and climb another dihedral to a stance (8, 150 feet).
4. Climb up and left through short corners and belay just left of the nose on a big terrace below the band of white rock (4, 75 feet).
5. Climb a small left-facing corner and the face above to belay at the bottom of a shallow dihedral (6, 140 feet).
6. Climb the shallow corner, then work up and right to belay in a niche (6 s, 120 feet).
7. Climb the face just left of a right-facing dihedral to a roof (7 s), step right, and follow a steep crack to a stance (8, 150 feet).
8. Work out right to a bolt, go up past a roof (8), then back left to the crack and belay on a good ledge at left (8, 90 feet). Scramble to the summit plateau.

13a Variation
Climb straight up though the white roof on the third pitch (11a), and follow a steep right-facing dihedral (9) to the terrace at mid-face.

13b Variation
On the fifth and sixth pitches, climb straight up the rounded prow for 300 feet and rejoin the regular line (8 s).

13c Dark Side   9 ★
FA: Tink Wilson and Dan Davis, c. 1960.
This variation may be reached from *Culp-Bossier* or *Jackson-Johnson*.
4. From the top of the regular fourth pitch, follow a crack up and right to a stance in a huge right-facing dihedral just right of the prow (7). From the top of the fourth pitch of *Jackson-Johnson*, traverse left along a ledge, then climb up to the same belay.
6. Climb a steep crack through an overhang and gain the ramp that connects *Culp-Bossier* with *Jackson-Johnson* (9). Finish with either route.

13d Ramp   7
From the top of the sixth pitch, follow a long ramp up and right to join *Jackson-Johnson* at the beginning of the crux pitch.

HALLETT PEAK, SECOND BUTTRESS, RIGHT SIDE
13	Culp-Bossier III 8 ★	
13c	Dark Side 9 ★	
13d	Ramp 7	
14	Jackson-Johnson III 9 ★	
14a	Direct Start 9	
16	Direct Second Buttress III 10a ★	
18	The Slit III 8	

14 Jackson-Johnson   III 9 ★

FA: Dallas Jackson and Dale Johnson, 1957.

This famous route begins as for *Culp-Bossier* but branches right on the second pitch. The last long pitch is the crux. The route is characterized by a 200-foot-high yellowish flake above the white band.

1. Climb through the pink band, then follow a right-facing dihedral for about 40 feet. Traverse right along a narrow grassy ledge to a crack, then climb to a higher ledge and belay (6, 140 feet).
2. Continue straight up into a right-racing dihedral, then branch right into a right-facing flake/dihedral, and belay at a block (5, 150 feet).
3. Go right around the arête and belay up in a chimney (4, 140 feet).
4. Continue up the chimney, then go up and right along a slab and belay at the bottom of a higher chimney that runs along the left side of the big yellow flake. This belay is just above the white band (4, 150 feet).
5. Climb the chimney/dihedral along the edge of the flake to a stance (5, 145 feet).
6. Continue up the chimney to a big ledge atop the flake (4, 50 feet).
7. Follow a stepped, left-facing dihedral system up and left to a ledge (6, 150 feet).
8. Climb a right-facing dihedral for about 50 feet, then work up and right past two bolts (crux) where the corner leans right. Continue as the corner again goes straight up and belay at left (9, 120 feet).
9. A short, easy pitch leads to the summit plateau (3, 40 feet).

14a Direct Start   9

Begin about 100 feet right of the regular start and climb a large right-facing dihedral for two or three pitches and merge with the regular fourth pitch.

14b Headwall   8

6-8. From the ledge atop the big flake, wander up the head wall to the right of the regular line.

14c Upper Ramp   7

The diagonal fault that creates the *Ramp* variation to *Culp-Bossier,* continues up and right from the beginning of the crux pitch of *Jackson-Johnson.* This may be followed to the top of the wall.

15 Bliss-Carlson   III 7

FA: R. Bliss and D. Carlson, 1972.

This route is seldom climbed, and its exact line is not known.

Begin from a grassy ledge, 75 above the talus, at the bottom of next dihedral right from the direct start to *Jackson-Johnson.* (It is about 320 feet from the first belay to a grassy ledge at the lower left corner of the big yellow flake. The fourth pitch of *Jackson-Johnson* passes the left end of this ledge).

1. Climb the dihedral past a small roof, continue up a crack, and belay on a ledge (6, 120 feet).
2. A long moderate pitch goes up the face and some small dihedrals to merge with *Jackson-Johnson* .
3. Climb a dihedral and belay beneath a steep wall.
4. Climb around the right side of the wall (7) and continue to a belay on the big terrace just left of the prow of the buttress.

5-7. Climb the face just left of the prow to a ledge beneath the summit overhang.

8. An easy groove leads to the top of the wall.

16 Direct Second Buttress III 10a ★

FA: Layton Kor and Tex Bossier, 1963.

This is a steep and excellent route up the middle of the Second Buttress. The route described was climbed by Jeff Lowe and Terry Ebel during the summer of 1994. Its exact relationship to the original line is not known. Kor made more than one attempt on this part of the wall and developed at least two independent starts. One of these has three bolts (possibly without hangers) used to aid through the initial roofs; the other was rated 5.8.

Begin at the third dihedral right of the direct start to *Jackson-Johnson* and below the left side of a large white spot 150 feet up on the wall.

1. Start up the corner, then veer right in a smaller dihedral to the next corner system and continue to a belay stance (8, 150 feet).

2. Start up the corner, then traverse left and climb an arching, right-facing corner with a fixed pin, exit left and follow a shollow dihedral to the top of a large ramp (10a, 120 feet).

3. Start up a dihedral, but veer right and follow a crack to stance (6, 120 feet).

4. Traverse right, then climb a right-facing dihedral (5, 140 feet).

5. Follow a crack system up and right past a roof, then climb another corner past a small roof to a stance (9, 130 feet).

6. Follow a crack up and right to a ledge (8, 90 feet).

7. Continue up and right along the crack system, then follow a left-facing dihedral to a ledge (8, 100 feet).

8. Climb up and slightly left along cracks to a notch at the top of the face (6, 100 feet).

17 Kor-Benneson III 9 s

Climb the first pitch of the *Direct Second Buttress*, then work up and right to a grassy ledge in a cleft about 20 feet above the white spot (which may be the line of the original *Direct*). Angle up and right to low-angled rock along the big white band and traverse to the right edge of the face. Climb straight up for about five pitches.

18 The Slit III 8

This route ascends the chimney/dihedral between the Second and Third Buttresses. It is characterized by steep, wet rock with poor protection and is not recommended. The chimney splits at the top and the route takes the left branch.

THIRD BUTTRESS

This is the right of the three north buttresses, famous for route-finding difficulties and, of course, the *Northcutt-Carter* route.

19 Northcutt-Carter III 7 ★

FA: Ray Northcutt and Harvey Carter, 1956.

Classic. This was the first major route completed on the wall (other than *Hallett Chimney*,) and perhaps for that reason as much as its position and length, has always drawn a lot of traffic. It is a bit easier than the other lines but is famous for route-finding debacles. The line takes the left side of the Third Buttress. It has good sunlight in the morning through most of the summer but, like The Diamond, goes into shadow by about 11 A.M. In early June, the exit chimney at the top of the wall will likely contain snow and ice.

Scramble up snow or scree ledges to the bottom of a broken dihedral about 25 feet right of a break in a prominent white band that runs across the bottom of the wall. This is about 300 feet right of *The Slit.*

1. Climb the corner for about 80 feet, then move to the left side of a vague prow and continue to a slab with slings around a horn (4, 120 feet).

2. Start up the steep corner above the belay, but after about 10 feet, traverse straight left and climb a white open book to a crack/flake that angles right, then hand-traverse up and right to a good ledge (4, 150 feet). Caution: A common error is to continue up the steep corner above the belay (see *Faux Pas*).

3. Traverse left above an overhang for 40 feet to a small right-facing dihedral. Climb the dihedral for 80 feet, then step left into another small dihedral that forms the right side of a pillar and belay near its top (6, 150 feet).

4. Climb straight up from the top of the pillar along a shallow right-facing dihedral, into a left-facing dihedral, and belay in an alcove beneath a roof (5, 140 feet).

5. Turn the roof on the right and follow steep cracks for 100 feet to a grassy ledge (optional belay), then go up and right to a larger grassy ledge (7, 160 feet).

6. Climb straight up a small dihedral with a fixed angle piton (6), pass a bulge, and climb through an area of red rock (best along the right side of a detached pillar). Continue past a fixed pin into a steep chimney and belay on a small platform 10 feet beneath a roof (6, 160 feet).

7. Climb through the left side of the roof and follow the broken chimney to the top of the face (5, 150 feet).

19a.Faux Pax   9+

On the second pitch, climb straight up into a steep left-facing dihedral with a roof and good crack (fixed pin). Turn the roof (8) and climb a steep slab to a two-pin anchor with slings (apparently set for retreat). Continue up and right through an overhang (9+), then go up and left to the belay at the top of the regular second pitch.

19b Dihedral   7

This is the line of the original route.

3. Continue left past the pillar into a large right-facing dihedral system (6, 130 feet).

4. Climb the diheral and on a ramp beneath a huge double overhang (7, 160 feet).

5. From the far right end of the ramp, traverse up and right and join the regular fifth pitch at the lower of two grassy ledges, then continue to the upper ledge and belay (7, 140 feet).

19c Chouinard-Weeks   8 s

FA: Yvon Chouinard and Ken Weeks, 1959.

3. Traverse up and left to a short right-facing dihedral that continues as a long crack. Follow this crack straight up the wall and belay at a stance (7, 120 feet).

4. Stay with the crack and belay at the bottom of a right-facing dihedral (7, 150 feet).

5. Step left out of the dihedral and follow cracks up the steep face to the top of the regular fifth pitch (8, 150 feet).

20   Orange Beyond   III 9 ★

FA: Malcom Daly and Michael Finsterwald, 1976.

This steep variation branches right from the last pitch of the *Chouinard-Weeks* and continues as an independent line on the big yellow (orange) buttress above. The following description begins from the pillar at the top of the third pitch of *Northcutt-Carter*, but the *Chouinard Weeks* offers a more direct approach.

4. Climb the crack for about 90 feet, then break right beneath some roofs, and belay near the bottom of a right-facing dihedral on the *Chouinard-Weeks* (7, 150 feet).

5. Work up and right across a ramp, up a short steep section, then up and right again to a belay beneath another right-facing dihedral (6, 160 feet).

6. Climb the dihedral, turn the roof at its top, and continue up the crack system to another, smaller ramp (9, 150 feet).

7. Climb to the upper end of the ramp and follow a vertical crack and chimney to a ledge (9, optional belay). Climb a right-facing dihedral to the summit plateau (9, 160 feet).

21   Kor-Van Tongeren   III 9

FA: Layton Kor and Butch Van Tongeren, 1962.

This route ascends the right side of the Third Buttress and features a large, black chimney easily visible from the ground. Begin about 300 feet right of *Northcutt-Carter* beneath a break in the overhangs.

1. Climb a ramp up and right to a small ledge beneath a vertical black wall. Climb the wall for 40 feet, then work up and left to a marginal stance on a slab.

2. Work up and left to a big grassy terrace, then traverse left 50 feet and belay beneath a long left-facing groove/dihedral in white rock that is about 50 feet left of a prominent left-facing dihedral.

3. Climb the groove/dihedral to a belay on a tiny pillar (6, 100 feet).

4. Continue up the groove, then veer left into a black chimney and belay at a wide spot after about 50 feet (7, 140 feet).

5. Climb the chimney and belay on a chockstone (8, 150 feet).

6. Climb to near the top of the chimney and exit in a flared, overhanging crack on the right (9, 140 feet).

Scramble up and right for about 150 feet to the base of a large, left-facing dihedral/chimney.

7. Climb the dihedral/chimney to the summit plateau (9, 120 feet).

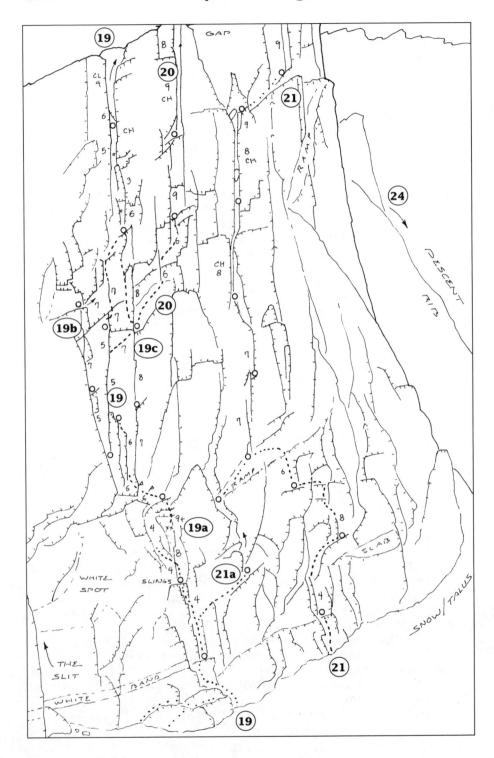

21a Left Start 8

Scramble up and right onto a grassy ledge about 50 feet right of *Northcutt-Carter*.

1. Climb a small right-facing dihedral to a roof, then follow a vague ramp up and right and belay at the base of a conspicuous diagonal slot.
2. Climb up and left and turn a roof in a shallow right-facing corner system, then continue up and left past a smaller roof and follow mossy cracks to a large white ramp that angles up to the right. Move up and right along the ramp and belay as for the regular route.

It may be possible to climb the slot and follow a shallow groove directly up to the same belay.

21b M&M 9+ ★

FA: Steve Morris and John Marrs, 1987.

From the big white ramp, climb the steep wall about 30 feet left of the regular line for two long, excellent pitches (both 9+ and somewhat runout). Veer right and join the main line.

22 Mayrose-Bucknam III 8

FA: Paul Mayrose and Bob Bucknam, c. 1961.

This route is thought to begin with the first two pitches of *Kor-Van Tongeren*. The rock is good except at the bottom. From the big ramp at the top of the second pitch, continue up and right to the spur at the west edge of the face. Climb directly up the spur (7) and pass three or four pinnacles en route. The final obstacle is a smooth, 60-foot, west-facing wall that is passed via a solitary crack (8).

23 North Face Traverse III 9

FA: Larry Bruce and Mark Hesse.

This route traverses all three buttresses at about mid-height. Begin by climbing up to the slabs in the middle of the First Buttress, then traverse west, mostly along the big white band, for about 12 pitches, and finish in the *West Gully*.

24 West Gully Class 3

This is a scrambler's route to the summit of Hallett Peak and is the most common descent from the north face routes. As an ascent, hike scree beneath the north face to a double talus fan just beyond the third buttress. Slog up the right fan and follow the gully for nearly 1000 feet to the summit plateau. Hike west over tundra to reach the summit.

Hallett Peak, Third Buttress

19	Northcutt-Carter III 7 ★	20	Orange Beyond III 9 ★
19a	Faux Pax 9+	21	Kor-Van Tongeren III 9
19b	Dihedral 7	21a	Left Start 8
19c	Chouinard-Weeks 8 s	24	West Gully Class 3

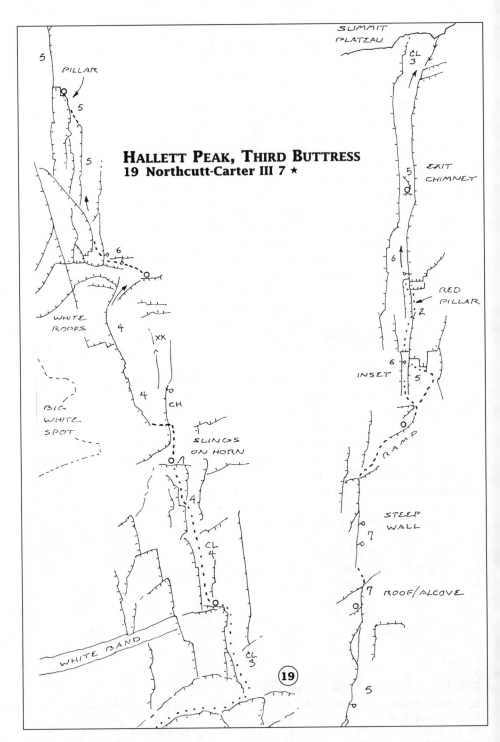

HALLETT PEAK, THIRD BUTTRESS
19 Northcutt-Carter III 7 ★

John Marrs climbing *The Squid.*   Photo: J. Marrs Collection.

FLATTOP MOUNTAIN

Flattop Mountain (12324) is unique in Rocky Mountain National Park in that a major hiking trail leads all the way to its summit, which is so broad and flat that it is difficult to ascertain the actual high point. Because of its relatively easy access, it also has more human visitors than any other summit in the park. From Bear Lake, it is about 4.4 miles and 2867 feet in elevation to the top. From a climber's perspective, the rock climbs on this mountain are nothing to write home about, but the snow and ice climbs are varied and interesting.

Tyndall Glacier   AI2 or snow

The Tyndall Glacier—that is, the tiny remnant of the great Pleistocene glacier that created Tyndall Gorge—resides at the far west end of the chasm between Hallett Peak and Flattop Mountain. Approach as for the north face of Hallett Peak (see above). Once below the north face, continue west over talus or snow and climb the glacier to the Continental Divide. Crampons may be needed in late summer.

DRAGONS TOOTH

Also known as Tyndall Spire, Dragons Tooth is the left of the two most prominent ribs on the south side of Flattop Mountain. Viewed from Emerald Lake, its narrow profile suggests a free-standing tower, but it is actually the southeast end of a long rib. Approach from Emerald Lake by hiking up a talus fan to its base. To descend from the summit, scramble off to the north and gain the Flattop Plateau; continue north to reach the Flattop Trail.

1   **South Ridge   II 7**
    This route supposedly ascends the skyline ridge as seen from Emerald Lake. However, this "ridge" turns out to be a long, grassy ramp that climbs across the south face and leads to the southwest side of the summit.

2   **Southeast Buttress   II 7**
    FA: Richard Rossiter, Linda Willing, and Steve Ross, 1979.
    This route ascends the buttress just left of the gully between the Dragon's Tooth and the Dragon's Tail. The first half of the route is Class 4 but the upper pitches are more interesting. The route finishes on the south side of the summit.

3   **East Face   II 7 A3**
    Climb the gully along the right side of the southeast buttress until directly beneath the summit tower, then head straight up. The last pitch follows a crack up a narrow, slightly overhanging wall.

4   **Dragons Tooth Couloir   II AI2+ or snow**
    Climb the long snow couloir between the Dragons Tooth and the Dragons Tail and top out on the Flattop plateau. This route is best climbed during early summer. Beware of avalanches.

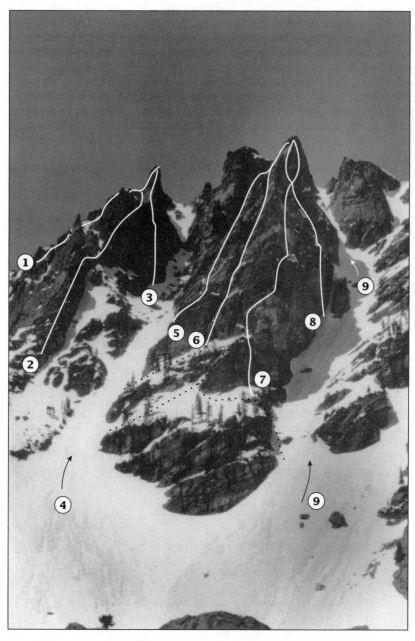

FLATTOP MOUNTAIN, DRAGONS TAIL, FROM THE EAST

1	South Ridge II 7	6	Old Route III 7
2	Southeast Buttress II 7	7	South Ridge III 7
3	East Face II 7 A3	8	Mosquito Wall III 8
4	Dragons Tooth Couloir II AI2+ or snow	9	Dragon Tail Couloir II M2+ AI3 or steep snow ★
5	West Slab III 7		

DRAGONS TAIL

This is the prominent buttress that rises to the northwest of Emerald Lake. It is bound on both sides by steep snow couloirs and is at least 600 feet high. A short hike from the north shore of Emerald Lake leads to the foot of the buttress. To escape from the summit, drop into the notch on the north side and climb back up to the ridge crest, then continue north past several towers and notches to the Flattop Plateau.

5   West Slab   III 7
FA: Molly Higgins and Harry Kent.
Begin a short way up the Dragons Tooth Couloir and traverse out onto the upper of two, large tree-covered ledges. From the east side of the ledge, scramble up and right for several hundred feet until steeper terrain forces the use of a rope. Follow cracks and slabs up the left side of the buttress and gain the notch between the summit and a large tower on the right, then climb up to the summit. Eight pitches.

6   Old Route   III 7
FA: Buckingham and Boucher, 1954.
The exact line of this route is not known; it is presumed to begin at the left side of the buttress, probably on the lower of the two, large tree-covered ledges. Work up and right toward the crest and climb to the top of the initial tower, then proceed to the summit.

7   South Ridge   III 7
FA: Richard DuMais and D. Johnston, 1980.
This route ascends the ridge directly above Emerald Lake. From the lake, hike up talus or snow to the bottom of the Dragons Tail Couloir, then scramble up and left onto a forested ledge and go left to the right of two grooves.
1. Climb the groove to a brushy ledge (5, 150 feet).
2. Climb the right side of a chimney, then go right to a big ramp on the prow of the buttress.
Scramble up and right along the ramp to the southeast edge of the prow.
3. Climb a short wall just right of the edge and continue up to a notch with loose blocks.
Traverse right on a big ledge for about 200 feet.
4. Climb a short wall to gain another ledge (7). Continue right along the ledge until directly beneath the notch on the south ridge high above.
5. Climb an easy lead up and right to a steeper section.
6. Climb corners on the right (6) and continue with steep flakes and dihedrals.
7. Climb a distinct left-facing dihedral (7), then continue more easily to the summit.

8   Mosquito Wall   III 8
FA: Paul Mayrose and Bob Bradley, 1964.
This route ascends the middle of the steep, southeast-facing wall above the Dragon's Tail Couloir. Begin several hundred feet up and below a chimney formed by a rock outcrop in the couloir.

1. Scramble up broken rock to a prominent crack, then climb the face at left and the crack past a bulge with a bolt and continue to a big ledge (8).
2a. The original line procedes from the left end of the ledge. Climb up to a small ledge, then work up and right and gain a large, grassy ledge. Climb around the right side of a roof and gain a big ledge (7).
2b. From the right end of the ledge, climb a dihedral to the same fate (7).
3. Start up left, the walk right on ledges to a short wall that is passed via a crack. Gain another ledge and travere right to the end of the rope.
4. Work up and right and gain a large terrace. This pitch may be longer than 160 feet. Walk up the terrace to a chimney.
5. Climb the chimney to the notch between the first tower on the ridge and the summit (6), then scramble to the top.

9   Dragons Tail Couloir   II M2+ AI3 or steep snow ★
This excellent route ascends the long, curving couloir along the right side of the Dragon's Tail. It is best climbed from early June to July; the gully faces south and does not hold snow through summer. Kick steps up snow and stay left at a bifurcation. The upper section of the couloir is the most difficult with some short rock steps and the possiblity of hard ice instead of snow. The couloir tops out on the Flattop plateau a short way from the trail. Beware of avalanche.

EMERALD LAKE ICE CLIMBS
On the lower south slope of Flattop Mountain, a few hundred feet northeast of Emerald Lake, some transient ice forms on a cliff band. There are three very difficult routes of one and two pitches that form up briefly if at all. Since the routes face south into the sun, an early start on a cold day is recommended. The right-facing dihedral is The Squid.

10   Tentacles   WI5
This rarely formed route ascends ice smears up the cliff about 100 feet left of *The Squid*.

11   The Squid   II WI5 ★
FA: Duncan Ferguson and Doug Snively, 1974.
This is the most well-known of the Emerald Lake ice climbs.
1. Ascend an overhanging, right-facing dihedral that may require some stemming on bare rock with crampons, then move up and right and climb a large, free-hanging icicle.
2. A short, steep flow leads to the top of the face.

12   Calamari   II WI4-5
FA: Alex Lowe, Erik Winkleman, and Sandy Stewart, 1982.
This route is about 150 feet right of *The Squid.* In optimal conditions it is the easier and more extensive of the three routes. When less filled in, some difficult rock climbing may be required to reach the ice (9 s).

John Marrs nearing the top of *Jaws* (page 257). Photo: J. Marrs Collection.

ODESSA GORGE

Odessa Gorge begins from the cirque of the Ptarmigan Glacier and descends north-northeast for about 1.7 miles to a forested bench above Fern Lake. Odessa Lake sits in the floor of the gorge at the confluence with Tourmaline Gorge, the narrow valley between Knobtop Mountain and Gabletop Mountain. The Fern Lake Trail runs along Joe Mills Mountain on the east side of Odessa Gorge with Notchtop, the Little Matterhorn, and The Gable being the significant landmarks on the west side. With the exception of Notchtop Mountain, the rock climbing in this area has not gained popularity. A few winter ice climbs, however, have become well-known; foremost among these is *Grace Falls* below Notchtop and *Jaws* along the Fern Lake Trail.

Fern Lake Trail. This trail is 8.5 miles long and has trailheads at Bear Lake (south end) and Moraine Park (north end). The south end is initially congruent with the Flattop Mountain Trail, then branches right at 0.8 mile. At 2.8 miles, the trail passes over a saddle between Joe Mills Mountain and Notchtop Mountain. It then descends past the Little Matterhorn, Odessa Lake, and reaches Fern Lake at 4.7 miles. It is 3.8 miles from Fern Lake to the Fern Lake Trailhead in Moraine Park.

If one begins from the Moraine Park trailhead, the first significant landmark is Arch Rocks, giant boulders that tower over the trail at about 1.3 miles. There also is a designated campsite just beyond the rocks on the north side of the trail. At about 1.8 miles is The Pool where the Fern Lake Trail crosses the Big Thompson River and begins its climb southwest to Fern Lake.

To reach the Moraine Park trailhead, take Highway 36 into Rocky Mountain National Park and after about 2 miles, turn left on Bear Lake Road. Drive another 2 miles and turn right (west) on the road to Moraine Park Campground. After about a half mile, turn left on another road and follow it to the Fern Lake Trailhead (at the west end of the road). During winter, the last mile of the road is closed to autos. To reach the trailhead at Bear Lake, drive all the way to the end of Bear Lake Road.

Lake Helene Trail. A short way south of the saddle between Joe Mills Mountain and Flattop Mountain, a well-developed but unsigned footpath branches west (left), passes Lake Helene, and continues to a small tarn below the south ridge of Notchtop in 0.7 mile.

PTARMIGAN GLACIER CIRQUE

The Ptarmigan Glacier occupies the beautiful cirque between Flattop Mountain and Notchtop Mountain. The glacier itself is not very steep, but to its south, more on the north face of Flattop, three snow and ice gullies climb from the bottom of the cirque to the Continental Divide. Two of these reach angles of 60 to 75 degrees. During summer, the gullies are fun snow climbs, but by late August most of the seasonal snow is melted off exposing hard, grey alpine ice. Approach as for Notchtop Mountain (see below). Descend via the Ptarmigan Glacier or pick up the Tonahutu Creek Trail from the top and follow it south to the Flattop Mountain Trail, whence one may return to Bear Lake.

1 **East Couloir   II AI3 or snow ★**
This is the farthest left of the three prominent gullies on the north face of Flattop. Climb snow or ice up to 60 degrees and top out on the Continental Divide due north from the summit of Flattop Mountain.

2 **The Hourglass   II AI4 or steep snow ★**
The middle couloir is the longest and best of the three; it gains almost 1000 feet in elevation and approaches an angle of 75 degrees near its top. The climb ends on the Continental Divide a few yards from the Tonahutu Creek Trail.

3 **West Couloir   II AI3 or snow ★**
This is the farthest right (north) of the three couloirs. Its notable feature is a narrow channel (about 3 feet wide by 60 degrees) in the upper half of the route. A variation traverses left above the hiatus, then climbs rock and snow to the divide.

4 **Ptarmigan Glacier   AI2 or snow**
At the farthest west arc of the cirque is the humble remnant of the Pleistocene glacier that carved Odessa Gorge. The south side of the glacier is less steep and affords an easy ascent to the Continental Divide.

NOTCHTOP MOUNTAIN

The massive buttress of Notchtop Mountain (12160+) sits just east of the Continental Divide at the head of Odessa Gorge. The peak is not visible from most areas of the park but can be seen in profile from Deer Ridge Junction or at close range from the high point of the Fern Lake Trail. The sheer south ridge of the buttress terminates in a narrow summit that is separated from the higher, main summit by a sharp notch for which the peak is named. This smaller summit is known as the Notch Spire (12129). The hanging gully below and east of the notch is called the East Meadow. A prominent northeast ridge separates the vertical east face from the broad cirque of the north face.

Approach. From Bear Lake, hike the Fern Lake Trail and then the Lake Helene Trail to the foot of the objective. It is impractical to begin from Moraine Park.

Descent. From the top of the Notch Spire, downclimb 30 feet west (cl3), gain a scree-covered ledge, and follow it north to the notch between the Notch Spire and the main summit. Scramble north up the east side of the crest and gain the true summit of Notchtop Mountain. From the summit, follow a grassy ramp down along the west side of the crest to the top of the *West Gully*, then hike down the gully (cl2) and return to the Fern Lake Trail.

It also is easy to reach the Continental Divide: From the col atop the *West Gully*, scramble up to a narrow ledge and traverse 50 feet left to easier ter-

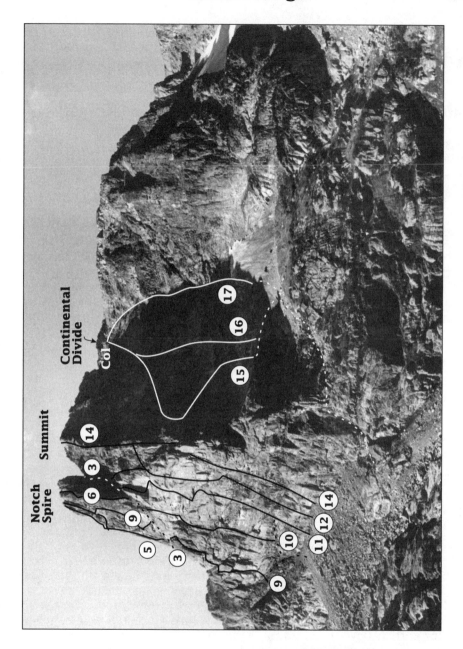

NOTCHTOP MOUNTAIN, FROM THE NORTHEAST

3 Spiral Route II 4 ★
5 Direct South Ridge III 9 ★
6 East Buttress II 9 ★
9 Religion III 8
10 Optimismus III 9 ★
11 White Room III 11 vs

12 Topnotch III 11c ★
14 Northeast Ridge III 8
15 North Face Left III 7 AI4
16 Direct North Face III 8 AI4
17 North Face III 6 WI3 AI4 ★

rain (cl4). Follow the ridge crest westward for several hundred feet, then move left to a break in the cliffband and scramble to the divide plateau. Hike west to pick up the Tonahutu Trail, then follow it south to the Flattop Mountain Trail and descend to Bear Lake.

SOUTH SIDE

The following routes begin from a pristine tarn below the south ridge of Notchtop. From Lake Helene, follow a primitive path 0.4 mile southwest to the tarn.

1   West Gully   Class 3

From the tarn below the south ridge, hike up into the steep grassy gully on the west side of the Notch Spire. After several hundred feet veer left to avoid a steep section, then continue to the col between the Continental Divide and the summit (cl3). From here, follow the narrow ridge crest about 200 feet southeast to the true summit which is about 50 feet higher than the summit of the Notch Spire. The summit (and the Notch Spire) may be reached most easily, however, by following a grassy ramp along the top of the west face that leads directly to the summit (see Descent). To reach the Notch Spire, scramble down to the notch and traverse about 30 feet across a ledge on the west side, then scramble 50 feet to the top (cl3).

2   West Face   III 9

FA: Bob Culp and Larry Dalke, 1960s..

The steep and impressive southwest face is located to the left of the south ridge and directly above the west gully. Only one route is known to have been climbed here. Begin as for the *Spiral Route* (below) and climb the first two moderate pitches to a ledge that is followed around onto the west face. It also is possible to climb straight up to this point. Climb five pitches up steep cracks and shallow dihedrals to the summit of the Notch Spire.

3   Spiral Route   II 4 ★

Never difficult, but developing great exposure, this route almost circumnavigates the Notch Spire before reaching its summit. From the tarn beneath the south ridge, hike up toward the *West Gully*, then cut right to gain a rocky shelf above the initial cliffs of the south ridge. Three moderate pitches lead up and right to grassy ledges beneath the south ridge. From here, follow a long grassy ledge system up and right across the east side of the spire to the East Meadow. Scramble west up the meadow following the easiest line. Avoid any temptation to veer off to the north. Above the meadow, the terrain steepens. Continue up through short cliffs and ledges (cl3 or 4) to the notch, or go up and left along a ramp, then back right to the notch. Look for old fixed pins. From the notch, drop down a short way on the west side, traverse a ledge about 50 feet to the south, then scramble to the summit of the Notch Spire (cl3).

4   South Ridge   III 9 ★

FA: Charles Schobinger and Al Auten, 1958.

Classic. This spectacular route ascends the steep and exposed south arête of the Notch Spire. Similar to the *Flying Buttress* on Mount Meeker, there are enough variations to comprise two or three separate routes; the best line stays just right of the crest and is described below as the *Direct South Ridge*.

Climb the first two pitches of the *Spiral Route* (4), traverse around to the east side of the crest, then scramble up and left to the highest ledge.

1a. Climb up and left toward the arête and belay on a small ledge (6, 80 feet).

1b. Climb up and left into the right-facing dihedral. Halfway up the corner, climb around to the left side of the arête and belay in a crack system (7, 155 feet).

2a. Make airy moves out left to a flake on the west side of the arête, then climb a crack up the steep face and belay on a small ledge just left of the arête (7, 145 feet).

2b. Continue up cracks and shallow dihedrals and belay at the top of the third pitch (7, 150 feet).

3. Climb a shallow dihedral followed by easier, blocky terrain and belay at a platform on the arête (7, 90 feet).

4. Traverse left and climb a chimney/crack that leads to an exposed, incut stance that straddles the arête (6, 100 feet).

5. Follow steep cracks up the wall on the east side to a ledge beneath an open book dihedral (9, 150 feet).

6. Climb the dihedral and follow easier ground to the summit (7, 150 feet).

4a   West Side   9

From the point where the regular line first reaches the west side of the arête, it is possible to follow a continuous crack and corner system straight up for four pitches to the summit. The last long pitch is the hardest: Take the left of two very steep dihedrals and follow it to a bulge, then work up and right to the top of the right dihedral and climb to the summit of the Notch Spire. The right dihedral is easier.

4b.   Original Finish   8

4. From the platform atop the third pitch, traverse out right across a slab and climb a steep crack up to a ledge at the bottom of a large, right-facing dihedral (8, 150 feet).

5. Follow the dihedral to the summit (5, 150 feet).

5   Direct South Ridge   III 9 ★

Begin as for the regular *South Ridge*.

1. Climb up and left toward a right-facing dihedral that is capped by a roof and belay at a stance before reaching it (6, 100 feet).

2. Climb the dihedal and turn the roof(9), then pass a smaller roof on the right and work up and left to belay on a sloping stance 6 feet right of the crest.

3. Climb straight up a prominent crack through a triangular roof and belay on a small ledge (8, 90 feet).

4. Follow a crack up to the crest of the ridge, then traverse around to a ledge on the west side (7).

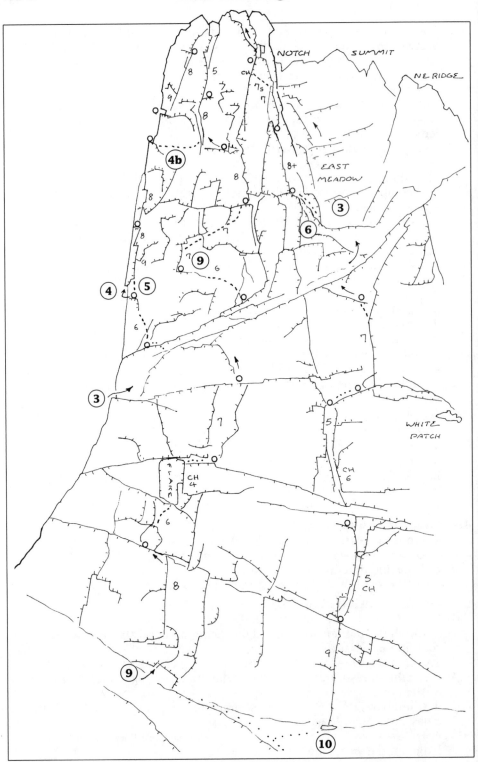

5. Climb a chimney and short right-facing dihedral, then traverse right to an incut stance on the crest from which a ledge continues a short way around on the east side (6, 100 feet).

6. From the ledge, climb up and right on a steep wall and pass a roof on the right. Climb a crack through a right-facing corner and belay at a stance 30 feet above the roof (9).

7. Climb straight up into a dihedral/chimney that leads to the top of the Notch Spire (7, 100 feet).

The following three lines are located on the northeast aspect of the Notch Spire and may be approached from any route that leads to the diagonal ramp of the Spiral Route.

6   East Buttress   II 9 ★
FA: Richard DuMais and Steve Komito, 1987.

This excellent route climbs the steep northeast corner of the Notch Spire. The position of the route in the topo is based on a sketch left at Neptune Mountaineering (labeled *Dyno Honers From Planet X*) and on a "stylized" drawing I received from Richard DuMais. The text also is based on a note that accompanied the drawing.

Gain the bottom of the East Meadow and scramble up to a terrace where a ramp leads up and left to a right-facing dihedral system.

1. Traverse up and left and belay at the base of a distinct right-facing dihedral (5). It also is possible to climb straight up to the belay in a lower dihedral (10).

2. Climb the dihedral and belay behind a flake at its top (8 or 9).

3. Climb to the top of a thin crack, then traverse up and left on knobby rock, step around the corner, and climb a chimney to a notch (7).

4. Climb a short wall (7, no pro), then follow a gully to the summit.

7   Relief Train   II 7
FA: Harrell and Olsen, 1982.

Scramble up along the south side of the East Meadow to the base of a prominent dihedral that is the farthest right of several and has a bulging overhang. Climb the dihedral to the roof (7), then go left and climb the face to a belay on a mossy ledge. Follow a crack and gully system to the top of the Notch Spire (6).

Notchtop Mountain, Notch Spire, East Face
3   Spiral Route II 4 ★
4   South Ridge III 9 ★
4b Original Finish 8
5   Direct South Ridge III 9 ★
6   East Buttress II 9 ★
9   Religion III 8
10 Optimismus III 9 ★

8 Mornin' II 7
FA: Magnuson and Schneider, 1983.
Ascend easy ledges up the East Meadow to the base of steep wall with a right-facing dihedral. Climb the corner to a good ledge and belay. Climb a short gully, then move right and follow broken rock for a long pitch. Move up, then veer left for about 100 feet. A short easy pitch leads to the summit of the Notch Spire.

EAST FACE
The following routes ascend the impressive face between the south ridge and the northeast ridge.

9 Religion III 8
FA: Larry Hamilton and K. Bell, 1973.
This steep and little-known route ascends the entire east face of the Notch Spire. Begin from a ramp at the south side of the east face and beneath the left of three right-facing dihedrals.
1. Climb a crack to reach the dihedral, then continue to a roof at its top. Go left (8) to a small ledge (optional belay), then climb a shallow right-facing dihedral to a big grassy ledge with a huge detached flake (6).
2. Climb an easy chimney and belay at the base of large, right-facing dihedral.
3. Climb the dihedral to a grassy ledge (7), and continue up a short cliff to the grassy ramp of the Spiral Route.
Move up the ramp to a large block that leans against the wall and belay at its top.
4. Angle up and left to a grassy ledge beneath a short dihedral.
5. Climb part way up the corner, then make a long traverse right beneath a roof and belay in an overhanging groove near the right edge of the face.
6. Climb the groove to near its top, then work up and left to a ledge.
7 – 9. Climb up and left to the big corner/chimney of the original *South Ridge* route and follow it to the summit.

10 Optimismus III 9 ★
FA: Walter Fricke and Dan Bench, 1970.
This steep, five-pitch route goes directly up the east face to intersect the *Spiral Route* at the East Meadow. One may continue with a route on the Notch Spire or descend the *Spiral Route*.
When approaching the east face, head for some black water streaks directly beneath the East Meadow. Scramble left up a ramp and cut back right on a ledge to belay beside a large boulder.
1. Climb a sustained crack and chimney in a left-facing dihedral past a roof (crux) and continue to its top. Step right under another roof and belay at the bottom of a right-facing dihedral (9, 130 feet).
2. Climb a right-leaning dihedral/chimney to a large chockstone, then a right-facing dihedral on the left and belay on a ledge (5, 130 feet).
4. Climb straight up a narrow chimney and continue in a right-facing dihedral to belay on a big ledge (6, 160 feet). Move the belay up and right to the bottom of a large, reddish, left-facing dihedral.
5. Climb the dihedral for about 100 feet, then work up and left to the *Spiral Route* (7, 130 feet).

11   White Room   III 11 vs

FA: Roger Briggs and Larry Hamilton, 1974.

This demanding and dangerous route climbs the middle of the east face between the black steaks of *Optimismus* and a smooth wall at right called The Shield. Points of identification are a curved, left-facing dihedral with a large roof at its top, a white patch up and left from the roof, and a large, straight right-facing dihedral at the top of the face. Begin from the talus directly beneath the right-facing dihedral at the top of the face.

1. Climb an easy pitch up and right to reach the curving dihedral (4) or climb a left-facing corner directly into it (7).

2. Climb part way up the dihedral and belay on a small ledge (6).

3. Continue up the dihedral as it leans out to the left (10c), then break out to the right and climb the face to a long ledge (8 s).

4. Do not climb up to the roof, but make a long, rising traverse left, and belay beyond the end of the roof (8 s).

5. Climb past the right end of the white spot (11 s), then continue up and right over unprotected ground to the left end of a grassy ledge (9 s). Above the white spot it is possible to escape left along a ledge to *Optimismus*.

6. Climb straight up a crack (11), then work up and right along a ramp and belay near its top.

7. Traverse left across the blank face (11 s), pass beneath a roof, and climb a crack into the big right-facing dihedral that leads to the top of the face. The dihedral is hardest at the bottom (11) and may require one more belay.

11a. Black Curtains   11c s

FA: Jack Roberts, Tim Coats, and Larry Coats, 1988.

4. Continue up the curving dihedral and climb through the right side of the roof, then step left and follow a crack and corner system to a ledge on the right.

12   Topnotch   III 11c ★

FA: Bret Ruckman, Larry Coats, and Tim Coats, 1988.

This steep route ascends the right side of the east face and follows a difficult crack through The Shield, a smooth face about 150 feet right of the white spot on White Room. Begin about 100 feet left of a gully along the right edge of the face.

1. Climb a short steep wall and a long, curving left-facing dihedral system, and belay on a small ledge (7, 165 feet).

2. Move left and climb a right-facing dihedral with a bush to a stance on a detached block (8, 165 feet).

3. Climb a steep ramp up to the left (9 s) and belay on a sloping ledge beneath The Shield.

4. Jam a finger crack through the middle of The Shield and belay on a ledge at its top (11c). Small TCUs are useful on this pitch.

5. Climb a left-facing corner past a roof, then go right to a ledge with a tree. Work up and left along the right crack of two, and belay on a second ledge with a tree (9 s).

6. Climb the dihedral behind the tree and continue up easy terrain to the top of the face.

13 Pessimismus   III 11d
FA: Bret Ruckman, Kelly Carrigan, Tim Coats, and Lārry Coats, 1990.
This route climbs through the right side of The Shield.
1. Climb the first pitch of *Topnotch* (7).
2. Continue up the corner and belay on a ledge beneath a huge, gaping flake (7).
3. Traverse up and left (8 s) and climb a grey, right-facing dihedral (10a) to a stance with a bolt.
4. Work up the steep face past two bolts (crux) and gain a seam that is followed to a ledge at the top of The Shield (11c).
5. Climb up and left in a steep left-leaning flake/crack (9+) and finish as for *Topnotch*. It also is possible to work right and climb the upper *Northeast Ridge* to the summit.

14 Northeast Ridge   III 8
FA: Larry Hamilton and Dakers Gowans, 1974.
This route ascends the prominent tower at the north side of the east face, then continues up the northeast ridge to the true summit. Begin at the bottom of the steep gully that leads to the notch between the tower and northeast ridge. Scramble several hundred feet and climb a thin crack to gain slabs on the left. Work up and left across the slabs and gain a ledge. Pass a small roof on the left and belay on a ledge beneath a steep wall. Go left from the ledge and climb the wall, then continue up easier ground and belay beneath a head wall. Climb the left of two dihedrals to a roof, then traverse right across the right dihedral, enter a larger dihedral, and climb to the notch between the pinnacle and upper northeast ridge. This notch can be reach more easily by climbing in from the north face. One may also scramble to the top of the pinnacle from the notch. Continue up the northeast ridge for about 500 feet of moderate climbing and gain the true summit.

NORTH FACE

The north face of Notchtop Mountain comprises a vast concave head wall above a dormant glacier. The rock of the head wall is broken and discontinuous and is seldom climbed during summer. The routes described below are normally climbed during fall or winter. The easiest way to reach the north face is to scramble up a chimney in the lower northeast ridge and gain a bench that leads north into the middle of the face. All routes finish at the col between the summit and the Continental Divide whence one may descend via the West Gully or continue up to the Continental Divide and descend via the Flattop Mountain Trail.

NOTCHTOP MOUNTAIN, EAST FACE, DETAIL

10	Optimismus III 9 ★		12	Topnotch III 11c ★
11	White Room III 11 vs		13	Pessimismus III 11d
11a	Black Curtains 11c s		14	Northeast Ridge III 8

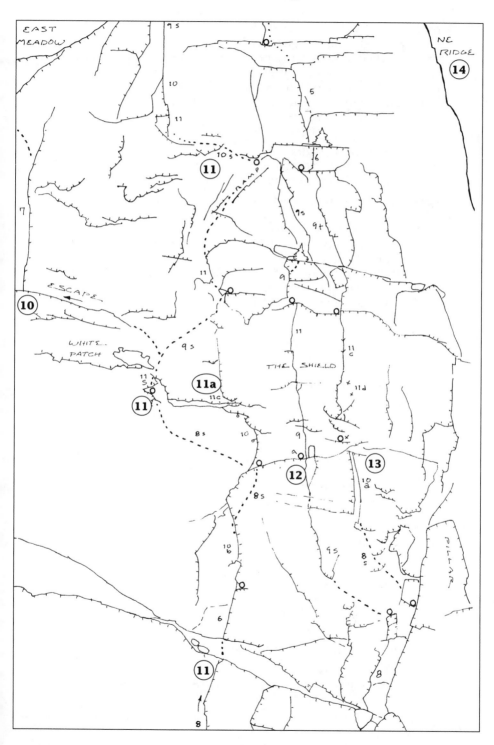

15   North Face Left   III 7 AI4
FA: Doug Snively and Michael Covington.
This route begins at the left side of the north face from a large bench above the one used on the approach. Follow a ramp up and left to a point near the northeast ridge, then follow another ramp up and right into the middle of the cirque and gain the col between the summit and the Continental Divide.

16   Direct North Face   III 8 AI4
FA: Covington and Ketchum.
This line begins a short way right of the preceding route and climbs directly up steep slabs to reach the snow gully at the top of the face.

17   North Face   III 6 WI3 AI4 ★
FA: Tom Hornbein and Bob Frauson, 1952.
Classic. Under optimal conditions, this is an excellent alpine route with steep ice pitches at major rock bands and good snow on the more moderate sections. Beware of avalanche. From the approach, traverse out into the middle of the north face. Climb straight up past several rock bands that are hopefully covered with ice and continue to the col between the main summit and the Continental Divide.

ODESSA GORGE ICE CLIMBS
Below and north of Notchtop Mountain are several ice climbs of merit.

1   Grace Falls   II WI4 ★
The Ptarmigan Glacier drains into the tarn below the south ridge of Notchtop Mountain, which in turn drains into Odessa Gorge. Grace Falls is formed by this steam just above its confluence with the outlet from Lake Helene. Ski or snowshoe to Lake Helene (see Lake Helene Trail under Odessa Gorge). From the north side of the lake, drop down to the northwest and traverse about 0.25 mile to the bottom of the falls. The main column is one pitch. The sheet of ice to the left is WI5; to the left of this is WI3.

ODESSA WALL
Ice sometimes forms on a cliffband to the right of Grace Falls below the north face of Notchtop.

2   Hot Doggie   WI5
FA: Jeff Lowe.
Climb a steep pillar on the lower left part of the cliff.

3   The Hourglass   WI5
This is another transitory feature near to *Hot Doggie*.

4   Guide's Wall   WI2
A moderate ice pitch forms down to the right of Odessa Wall, about 0.25 mile from Grace Falls.

FERN CANYON ICE CLIMBS

The following climbs are reached by hiking the Fern Lake Trail from Moraine Park.

1 Jaws   II WI4 ★

This is a popular and spectacular frozen waterfall about a mile up the Fern Lake Trail. It can be seen through the trees on the north side of the trail just before Arch Rocks. Two large columns of ice hang from a bulging wall with shorter icicles hanging in space between them. Only a glance is necessary to understand the name of the climb. It can be done in one long lead. The left column is usally the easiest. Rappel 50 meters from a large tree.

2 Windy Gulch Cascades   WI2

Moderate ice will be found in a gulch above the trail on the north, about a third of a mile from the trailhead.

LITTLE MATTERHORN

Knobtop Mountain (12331) is the next significant summit along the Continental Divide to the north of Notchtop. The Little Matterhorn is a terminal buttress on a ridge that extends to the east-northeast from Knobtop. It is fairly impressive when viewed from Odessa Lake. Approach via the Fern Lake Trail either from Bear Lake or the Fern Canyon Trailhead. From Odessa Lake, hike directly up to the foot of the buttress. Descend from the top via the *Standard Route.*

1 Standard Route   I Class 4

Scramble up the north or south side of the buttress and gain a notch on the ridge. Traverse east along the exposed crest to the summit.

2 Direct Northeast Face   II 7

The line of this old route is not known. Look for old pitons near the center of the face.

TOURMALINE SPIRE

Gabletop Mountain (11939) is the next summit north of Knobtop along the Continental Divide and, like Knobtop, has a long east ridge that terminates in an impressive buttress (The Gable in this case) above Odessa Gorge. The ridge forms the north side of Tourmaline Gorge and has near its mid-section a phalanx-like spire that has been visited by the occasional cavalier of the arcane. From Odessa Lake, hike west up Tourmaline Gorge to Tourmaline Lake, then scramble north up a steep slope to the objective. Descend via the *North Side.*

1 South Ridge   II 8

FA: Jim Detterline and M. Keeley, 1985.

From Tourmaline Lake, scramble up a steep gully to the bottom of the south ridge (cl4). Climb a dihedral and belay in a chimney/cave (6). Climb an arching crack from the back of the cave (8), then move left and work up the exposed face to the summit.

2   North Side   I 4
FA: Richard Rossiter, 1979.
From Tourmaline Lake, hike up a steep gully to the east of the spire, then climb a chimney on the north side.

HAYDEN GORGE

Hayden Gorge descends northeast from the Continental Divide to join Forest Canyon about 3.5 miles northwest of Fern Canyon. No trail leads into this area, which makes any approach long and arduous.

HAYDEN SPIRE

At the upper south end of Hayden Gorge, between Hayden Lake and Lonesome Lake, is a large complex peak called Hayden Spire. A more remote and difficult to reach climbing objective is not easily found in Rocky Mountain National Park. Hayden Spire is the high point on a ridge that projects northeast into Hayden Gorge. There are at least three more summits along this ridge farther to the northeast. The highest of these is just across a notch from the main summit. The eastern aspect of these towers is about 800 feet high and quite steep.

Approach. The easiest way to reach Hayden Spire is from Bear Lake: Hike over the summit of Flattop Mountain (4.4 miles) and gain the trail junction on the west side. Descend northwest along the Tonahutu Creek Trail for about 2.2 miles, then contour north to Sprague Pass (11708). Climb north along the Continental Divide to the south slope of Sprague Mountain. To reach Lonesome Lake, contour right (northeast) before reaching the summit and pass through a col on the northeast ridge. Hike down a gully for about 800 feet to the east shore of the lake. To reach Hayden Lake, contour across the west face of Sprague Mountain and regain the divide at the beginning to the southwest ridge of Hayden Spire, then descend northwest (for 1200 vertical feet) into the Hayden Lake Cirque.

Hayden Spire may also be reached by following the Continental Divide from Milner Pass (c. 8 miles) or by dropping into Forest Canyon from the Forest Canyon Overlook along Trail Ridge Road, and bushwhacking up Hayden Gorge.

1   Southwest Ridge   I Class 3
From the Continental Divide, follow an easy ridge past a few gendarmes to the summit.

2   Northeast Ridge   II 2
From Lonesome Lake, scramble up a long scree slope and gain the notch at the bottom of the northeast ridge. Follow the crest to the summit. To escape from the summit, reverse the route or return to the Cuntinental Divide via the easy *Southwest Ridge.*

EAST PINNACLE

From the shore of Lonesome Lake, five summits can be seen along the ridge crest of Hayden Spire. The right-most of these is the East Pinnacle.

HAYDEN SPIRE, FROM THE NORTH

3 Northeast Chimney   II 4
FA: Carr and Welleck, 1960.
From Lonesome Lake, scramble up a scree gully and gain big ledge on the northeast side of the summit tower. Climb a chimney to the top.

4 Dihedral Route   I 8
FA: Czecholinski and Wade, 1977.
From Hayden Lake, scramble up the slope and gain a notch behind Hayden Lake Pinnacle. Traverse east through the notch and locate a dihedral formed by the juncture of an orange wall and a tan wall.
1. Climb a sloping ramp and a crack that leads into the dihedral.
2. Climb to the top of the dihedral, then scramble to the summit.

5 Diagonal Route   I 10
FA: Czecholinski and Wade, 1977.
Locate a crack in an overhanging wall about 40 feet right of the orange and tan dihedral.
1. Make difficult move to get started and follow the crack up and right to the edge of the face.
2. Work down and left to gain a crack and follow it past a bulge. Easier cracks lead to the summit.

HAYDEN LAKE PINNACLE

From Trail Ridge Road, a narrow tower can be seem down and right from the main summit — this is Hayden Lake Pinnacle, which rises above the outlet stream to Hayden Lake. To escape from the summit, go down to a notch on the east and rappel 45 meters into a gully. Climb the gully and cross to the right side of the ridge, then descend a scree gully to Hayden Lake.

6 North Ridge   II 7 ★

FA: Czecholinski and Wade, 1977.

Scramble up a gully east of the lake and gain a grassy ledge that runs along the base of the pinnacle. Walk down to the left and begin just west from the prow of the ridge.

1. Climb cracks and short faces up and right to a big ledge (150 feet).
2. Move right and follow cracks and chimneys to a belay on the ridge crest (150 feet).
3. Climb a short face, then continue along the crest past a steep face on the left and belay (100 feet).
4. Climb a short corner and belay on the crest.
5. and 6. Follow the ridge crest for 300 feet to the top.

7 West Face   II 8 ★

FA: Czecholinski and Wade, 1977.

Scramble up to the base of the pinnacle as for the preceding route, but begin beneath a reddish area on the west face.

1. Follow a crack past a small roof in a left-facing dihedral, then work up and left to belay at a large flake (160 feet).
2. Climb directly up easy terrain to the summit.

ICEBERG LAKE WALL

This is a 300-foot headwall above Icicle Lake, about a mile southeast of the Gore Range Overlook and a half-mile northwest of the Tundra Curves on Trail Ridge Road. Park at the Iceberg Lake Overlook and descend snow or scree north to the bottom of the wall.

Iceberg Lake Wall   II 6

FA: Steve Hickman, John Bryant, and Dave Johnston, 1962.

Climb snow up to a prominent chimney system in the middle of the wall.

1. Climb loose rock to a large ledge just left of the main chimney system.
2. Traverse right across the main chimney and climb steep rock to a belay (6, 80 feet).
3. Continue straight up, then angle up and right behind large blocks and belay (5, 120 feet).

Scramble to the top.

Alan Bradley on the *Southwest Corner* route, The Sabre.

Photo: Dan Hare

Mount Chapin   Mount Chiquita   Ypsilon Mountain   Fairchild Mountain   Hagues Peak   Mummy Mountain

THE MUMMY RANGE FROM THE EAST

MUMMY RANGE

Running northeast from Fall River Canyon, the majestic peaks of the Mummy Range dominate the northern frontier of Rocky Mountain National Park. The major summits of the range from south to north are: Mount Chapin (12454), Mount Chiquita (13069), Ypsilon Mountain (13514), Fairchild Mountain (13502), Hagues Peak (13560), Mummy Mountain (13425), Rowe Peak (13400+), and Rowe Mountain (13184). Note that Mummy is connected to Hagues by a long ridge that extends east and south from the summit of the latter and does not reside along the crest of the range. Northwest of Ypsilon Mountain, and connected to it by a high and narrow ridge, are the twin summits of Desolation Peaks (12918 and 12949). The ridge continues northwest for another 1.2 miles to Flatiron Mountain (12335). All of these peaks present gentle slopes that can be ascended as hikes or scrambles, but there are several steep cirques in the range that offer technical climbs on snow or rock. The most spectacular and popular of these is the vast amphitheater on the southeast side of Ypsilon Mountain.

Two trailheads are used to reach destinations in the Mummy Range, both of which lie along Fall River Road. To reach this road, follow Highway 34 from Estes Park to the Fall River Entrance Station, then continue for another 2.3 miles and turn right onto Fall River Road.

Lawn Lake Trail. This popular trail begins in Horseshoe Park (8520) about 0.25 mile west of the turnoff to Fall River Road and travels north along Roaring River to Lawn Lake (10987) at 6.3 miles. This trail traverses along the east side of the range and may be used to reach the Ypsilon Lake Trail, Fairchild Mountain, Hagues Peak, and Mummy Mountain. The main trail ends at Lawn Lake after joining the Black Canyon Trail but a smaller trail continues westward to The Saddle (12398), the broad col between Fairchild Mountain and Hagues Peak.

Ypsilon Lake Trail. This spur begins from the Lawn Lake Trail after 1.3 miles. It crosses Roaring River to the west, then climbs northwest along the crest of a wooded moraine to reach Ypsilon Lake (10530) in 5 miles. This trail provides access to all east-face routes on Mount Chiquita and Ypsilon Mountain. A primitve footpath proceeds westward from Ypsilon Lake along the south side of the inlet stream into the Chiquita-Ypsilon cirque. After the first quarter mile, a steep and rugged branch climbs north along a cascade to Spectacle Lakes (11330); this is the approach to the *Y Couloir* and other routes that ascend the walls of Ypsilon's southeast cirque.

Chapin Creek Trail. This begins about 9 miles up Fall River Road, climbs to Chapin Pass in 200 yards, then descends north along Chapin Creek into the Poudre River Valley.

Mount Chapin Trail. This incomplete trail begins from Chapin Pass (c. 11140) and is reached by hiking the first 200 yards of the Chapin Creek Trail from Fall River Road. From the pass, the trail goes east passing two knolls, then splits near treeline. The right branch starts up the west ridge of Mount

The *North Ridge* route on Spearhead.

The last pitch of the *South Face* route, Petit Grepon.

Chapin, then fades in the tundra. The left branch, which is marked with a
cairn, climbs slowly along the north slope and fades in the tundra before
reaching the col between Mount Chapin and Mount Chiquita. The left branch
is the route of choice for those wishing to reach Mount Chiquita or Ypsilon
Mountain without going over the summit of Mount Chapin. This is also the
easiest line of descent from the summit of Ypsilon Mountain, but if the
ascent was begun from the Ypsilon Lake Trail, a ride must be arranged from
the Chapin Creek Trailhead. Note that Fall River Road is one way going west.

MOUNT CHAPIN
Mount Chapin is the southernmost peak in the Mummy Range. Its summit
may be reached by an easy hike of 1.4 miles up its west slope from Chapin
Pass. See Mount Chapin Trail (above).

MOUNT CHIQUITA
Mount Chiquita (13069) rises to the northeast of Mount Chapin and is about
one mile south of Ypsilon Mountain. It is an easy ascent from any side but its
northeast cirque, which is ascended by a single known route.

1 **Southeast Ridge   I Class 2**
This is the easiest route to the summit of a 13000-foot peak in Rocky
Mountain National Park. Approach via the Mount Chapin Trail (see
above) and gain the saddle between Mount Chapin and Mount Chiquita.
Follow a faint path northwest up the ridge to the summit.

2 **East Ridge   II Class 2**
This is the easiest way to reach the summit from the east side. Hike the
Ypsilon Lake Trail about 4.2 miles to Chipmunk Lake (10660), then
bushwack west for about 0.7 mile to Point 12005, a minor summit at
the east end of the ridge. Follow the ridge crest west and northwest to
the summit.

3 **White Fright   II 9 s**
FA: Salaun, Joseph, and Moderson, 1980.
This route ascends the northeast face of Chiquita, which is about 500
feet high. Approach by hiking west from Ypsilon Lake or from Chapin
Pass and drop over the pass between Chiquita and Ypsilon (12786). A
point of identification is a 120-foot dike of white quartz.

YPSILON MOUNTAIN
Ypsilon Mountain (13514), though not the highest peak of the range, stands
out because of its high visibility from the east and its great southeast cirque
which spans more than 180 degrees and rises 2000 vertical feet. Two deep
tarns known as Spectacle Lakes occupy the floor of the cirque. Most technical
routes are associated with this amphitheater: The two most famous are the *Y
Couloir*, which splits the middle of the headwall, and *Blitzen Ridge*, which
forms the right margin of the cirque. A popular hike ascends the southwest
shoulder of Ypsilon Mountain from Chapin Pass.

Approach all east side routes via the Ypsilon Lake Trail. The easiest descent from the summit is to hike down the southwest shoulder to Chapin Pass, but this requires an auto shuttle for east side climbs. The easiest return to Ypsilon Lake is to descend the south face into the cirque between Mount Chiquita and Ypsilon Mountain. Under the right snow conditions, one may glissade the entire south face (1200 feet) in about five minutes. In late season, some travel on rock and scree is required. One also may scramble down the *Donner Ridge* route.

1 Southwest Ridge   I Class 2 ★
This is a spectacular hike to the summit of a great mountain. Approach via the Mount Chapin Trail and gain the saddle between Mount Chapin and Mount Chiquita. Follow a faint path northeast up the crest of the ridge for about 600 feet, then contour north to the saddle between Mount Chiquita and Ypsilon Mountain. One also may climb the final 400 feet to the summit of Mount Chiquita (12786) and then descend to the same saddle. From the saddle, hike northeast along the west side of the ridge crest to the summit of Ypsilon Mountain (about 3.5 miles from the road).

East Side
The following routes are normally approached via the Ypsilon Lake Trail.

2 Donner Ridge   II Class 3
This is the long, curving ridge that forms the left margin of the southeast cirque. It may be approached from the cirque between Mount Chiquita and Ypsilon Mountain about a half mile west of Ypsilon Lake, or more directly from the south side of East Spectacle Lake (see Ypsilon Lake Trail). The first approach reaches the ridge crest at 12000 feet; the second climbs the entire ridge. Steeper sections may be passed on the left (west). The angle eases off at 13000 feet, whence an easy hike leads northward to the summit.

3 To The Lighthouse   IV 9
FA: George Hurley and R. Bliss, 1975.
This route ascends the middle of the 1400-foot concave wall to the left of the Y Couloir. The line climbs straight above the west end of West Spectacle Lake to a 200-foot white pillar (The Lighthouse) at the top of the wall. Scramble up several hundred feet of scree and set the first belay at a flake beneath a black-streaked dihedral.
1- 4. Follow the dihedral for two pitches, then climb two more pitches up and left to some pinnacles beside a steep crack system.
5. Climb up past several ledges to a steep crack in light-colored rock.
6. Climb up to a small roof and belay.
7. Turn the roof (crux) and wander up to the bottom of The Lighthouse, then go up and left along a ramp to a stance at a short crack.
8. Climb the crack and work up to the top of The Lighthouse. Hike to the summit.

4   Lighthouse Straits   III 7
FA: Hurley and Bliss, 1975.
This route climbs up to the right side of The Lighthouse. Scramble up several hundred feet of scree and set the belay beneath a short, right-facing dihedral about 200 feet up on the wall. Climb up through the dihedral, then do two more pitches up to a roof. Climb through a break in the roof (the Straits) and do three or four more pitches up past the right side of the Lighthouse. Eight pitches in all.

5   Right Chimney   III 8 AI3
To the right of the preceding routes, but still well left of the *Y Couloir*, a chimney system climbs to the right edge of the wall. Follow the chimneys for three or four pitches (often wet or icy), then go up and left in a large gully. Go left around a roof to reach a snow patch and continue up and left along a ramp. The climb finishes near the top of Donner Ridge. Eleven pitches.

6   Prancer Ridge   III 6 AI2+
This route ascends the long ridge that forms the right margin of the great concave wall left of the Y Couloir. Start up the Y Couloir, then work left onto the ridge and follow it to the top of the wall.

7   Y Couloir   III 4 AI4 or steep snow ★
Classic. The 2000-foot wall of the southeast cirque is split into halves by a prominent Y (Ypsilon)-shaped couloir for which the mountain is named. This sweeping couloir provides one of the best snow climbs in Rocky Mountain National Park. The principle hazards on this route are rockfall and avalanche. A large cornice forms at the top of either branch of the couloir and is subject to collapse from early to midsummer. The route is safest from early July through mid August.

Left Branch. From the west end of West Spectacle Lake (11330), angle up and right into the couloir. This lower section is not very steep, but where the angle increases, the gully divides (12300). The left branch maintains a more moderate angle (up to 50 degrees) than the right and curves up to the summit ridge without obstacle but the cornice at its top. The cornice can be tricky and may be passed via rock on the south (2).

Right Branch. The right branch is steeper and leads directly to the summit. A short way above the bifucation, the couloir becomes vertical and forms a deep recess which is usually filled with ice and running water. This can be avoided by a long rock pitch on the left (4) that leads to a ledge where it is easy to re-enter the couloir. Continue directly up

MOUNT YPSILON, SPECTACLE LAKES CIRQUE, FROM THE EAST
2   **Donner Ridge II Class 3**
5   **Right Chimney III 8 AI3**
6   **Prancer Ridge III 6 AI2+**
7   **Y Couloir III 4 AI4 or steep snow ★**
8   **Blitzen Face III 7 or M3**
9   **Blitzen Ridge II 4 ★**

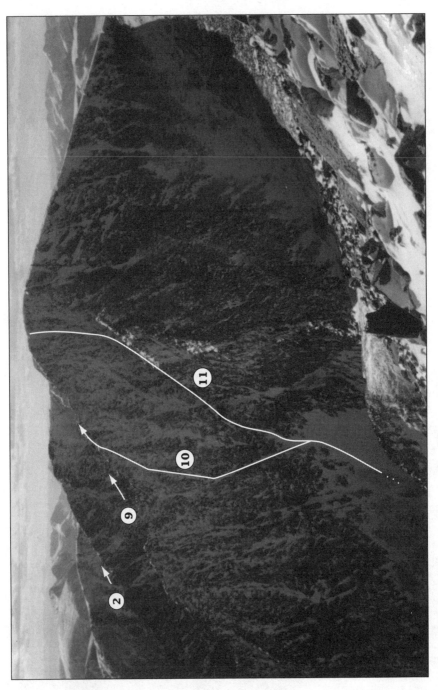

YPSILON MOUNTAIN, FROM THE NORTHEAST

2   Donner Ridge II Class 3   10   BR Couloir II M3+
9   Blitzen Ridge II 4 ★   11   Northeast Couloir II 4 AI3 or   snow ★

the snow, which steepens to about 55 degress, until beneath the cornice at the top of the couloir. The easier and safer option is to exit via a gully at left. For the extremist, it sometimes is possible to climb through the right side of the cornice (snow up to 70 or 80 degrees).

7a Variation

Follow the north branch to the recess and gain a sloping rock ledge at left. Climb straight up the face to the left of the north branch all the way to the summit ridge (7).

8 Blitzen Face   III 7 or M3

FA: S. Thornberg and Scott Kimball.

This route ascends the big spur to the right of the Y Couloir and was first done during winter. Follow a faint rib to where it merges with the face about 300 feet below the crest of Blitzen Ridge (cl4). Climb two or three steeper pitches to the ridge crest (7), then scramble west to the summit.

9 Blitzen Ridge   II 4 ★

FA: Clint Brooks, Charlie Ehlert, Dave Fedson, James Walker, and Phil Ritterbush, 1958.

This classic route rivals the *Exum Ridge* of the Grand Teton in position, scale, and quality. It follows the long ridge that forms the right (north-ern) margin of the great southeast cirque of Ypsilon Mountain. A series of towers called the Four Aces protrude along the ridge crest at about 12500 feet and are generally considered to compose the route's princi-pal difficulties. However, the steep step in the ridge immediately beyond the fourth Ace is no easier. This is a long climb and an early start is advisable. Note that the version of the route described below is from an ascent by Richard Rossiter and Greg Carelli (1995) and varies somewhat from previous descriptions.

From the north side of Ypsilon Lake, scramble up a long grassy gully and gain the crest of the ridge. Hike west and northwest along the nar-rowing crest until the way is blocked by the Four Aces. The first two towers may be passed via narrow exposed ledges that run across their south faces and lead to the notch between the second and third towers (cl4). The third tower is climbed directly via the left of two dihedrals (4). The right dihedral is easier but leads to an overhang where one must traverse into the left dihedral to finish. From the top, downclimb the ridge into the notch at the base of the fourth tower (2). This tower may be climbed directly (7), but it is easier to traverse narrow ledges across the northeast face to the arête on the right (4). From here, an easy traverse across the northwest face leads to the notch between the fourth tower and the upper ridge.

Gain the top of a white boulder on the very crest of the ridge and climb excellent steep rock for a couple of hundred feet, whereafter the angle eases off (4). Follow the jagged ridge crest for another 1000 feet or more to the summit. The easiest (and most aesthetic) line is almost always directly along the crest.

NORTH SIDE
The following routes lie to the north of Blitzen Ridge and are reached via Ypsilon Lake and Fay Lakes Basin.

10   R Couloir   II M3+
FA: Richard Rossiter, solo, 1994.
This alpine route ascends a steep and narrow couloir up the north face of Blitzen Ridge. It is best climbed in early June or winter. Approach as for the *Northeast Couloir* and gain the isolated cirque at its base. Climb an initial snow fan into the narrow part of the couloir, then branch left in a steep and well-formed gully. Climb snow and ice to a bifurcation after several hundred feet. Take the right branch and climb another 500 feet to the crest of Blitzen Ridge. Scramble to the summit.

11   Northeast Couloir   II 4 AI3 or snow ★
The earliest known ascent was made by Rob Mardock and Todd Jirsa during 1992. The following description is based on a solo ascent by the author in mid-June of 1994. This 1500-foot couloir splits the hanging cirque that lies right (north) of upper Blitzen Ridge.
Gain the crest of Blitzen Ridge as described for the Blitzen Ridge route. Do not hike up the ridge, but contour north, passing left of a knoll, to upper Fay Lake. Scramble up the buttress north of the lake to the 11800-foot level, then traverse left along a narrow grassy bench and cross the stream that descends from the hanging valley beneath the Ypsilon-Fairchild col. Hike west into the rugged basin beneath the Northeast Couloir.
Climb into the couloir and continue to where it narrows and bends right. Here, the snow may have melted out exposing slippery wet rock and scree. If this is the case, climb moderate rock on the left side of the couloir for about 400 feet and rejoin the line where the angle eases back slightly. Otherwise, climb straight up the couloir to the same fate. From here, 700 feet of classic alpine snow climbing lead to the cornice at the top of the couloir. This final obstacle may be passed on the left, which delivers one to the very top of Blitzen Ridge, 150 feet from the summit. Note: It is possible to begin the climb with a long ramp to the right of the initial snowfield. The ramp reaches the couloir just above the wet narrow section.

FAIRCHILD MOUNTAIN
Fairchild Mountain (13502) rises to the northeast of Ypsilon Mountain and is among the most remote and least frequented of peaks having technical routes in Rocky Mountain National Park. All routes described are scrambles except those in the Crystal Lake Cirque. Approach via the Lawn Lake Trail. The easiest descent from the summit is via the *Northeast Slope* (see below).

1   East Ridge   II Class 3
This long ridge may be approached from the west side of Lawn Lake or from the south side of Crystal Lake (11300). In either case scramble about 800 feet to gain the ridge crest and follow it to the summit.

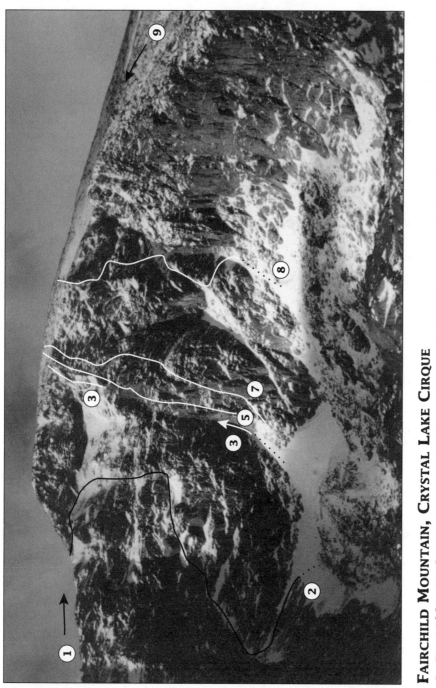

FAIRCHILD MOUNTAIN, CRYSTAL LAKE CIRQUE

1	East Ridge II Class 3	5	Power Struggle IV 11b	8	Lost Buttress III 7 A12+
2	Winterlong III 8 M3+	7	Honcho Boncho Buttress III	9	Northeast Slope I Class 2 ★
3	Abadoo Scronch III 7 M4	7			

CRYSTAL LAKE CIRQUE

The following routes ascend the walls of the Crystal Lake Cirque. To reach these climbs from Lawn Lake, hike up the Saddle trail to a signed junction after about a half mile. Take the left branch and follow it to Crystal Lake. In the middle of the east-facing cirque is a large rib called Honcho Boncho Buttress.

2   Winterlong   III 8 M3+
FA: Dan Stone and Richard Page, 1983.
This route takes the left side of the head wall and was first climbed in winter. Start up and left along a ramp, then cut back right to reach a system of ledges that angles up and right into the face beneath the summit. These pitches end at a big snow ledge. Climb straight up a rib along the right side of a chimney for several hundred feet (crux), then work up and left across a steep snowfield and exit from the face. Continue up the *East Ridge* to the summit or descend to Lawn Lake. Ten pitches.

3   Abadoo Scronch   III 7 M4
FA: Gregg and King, 1964.
This winter route ascends the deep chimney/gully system immediately left of Honcho Boncho Buttress. Avoid a left branch part way up and follow the main gully all the way to easier slopes beneath the summit.

4   Mirage   III WI5? M? ★
FA: Duncan Feguson and Dakers Gowans.
This route is described as "a big ice climb" of four or five pitches near the deep gully left of *Honcho Boncho Buttress*. Its exact location is not known.

5   Power Struggle   IV 11b ★
FA: Doug Byerly and Terry Murphy, 1992.
This route ascends the steep wall on the left side of Honcho Boncho Buttress. Start up the *Abadoo Scronch* couloir, then cut right and set the first belay at the bottom of a large right-facing dihedral beneath a big roof.
1. Hand jam and lieback the dihedral and belay on a slopoing ledge (10d, 165 feet).
2. Traverse up and right, then follow dihedrals to a small grassy ledge in a right-facing dihedral (10c, 132 feet).
3. Stem up the dihedral, make an awkward mantle (10b), and belay on the lower of two ledges beneath an overhanging red headwall (10b, 165 feet). Move the belay to the right end of the lower ledge.
4. Lieback up along the right edge of the red headwall and up a finger crack in a dihedral, then go up and left in a finger crack to a stance (TCUs). Finish with a thin crack and belay on a ledge with boulders (11c, 142 feet). Move the belay right to a cairn at a dihedral with white crystals.
5. Climb up and right via short traverses, then straight up to belay (8, 150 feet).
6. Continue up and right via moderate terrain (7, 165 feet). Descend to the northeast.

Greg Carelli on *Blitzen Ridge*, Ypsilon Mountain.

6 Live With Me   IV+ 11c/d A3

FA: Tom Bohanon and Terry Murphy, 1994. Rack: Typical Diamond aid selection including an assortment of pins up to small angles plus a RURP and a hook.

Locate a smooth 50-meter wall to the right of the initial dihedral of *Power Struggle*. The route begins with the right of two parallel thin cracks.

1. Climb the right crack for about 30 feet, then switch to the crack on the left. Climb for about 80 feet, then veer left to the first belay on *Power Struggle* (11c/d, 165+ feet). Lots of thin gear up to a #2 Camalot needed on this very sustained pitch.

2. Climb straight up a right-facing dihedral to a ledge below a roof (10c, 60 feet).

3. Stem up a short corner, thenjam a hand crack through a 25-foot roof (11c). Belay just above the roof, or traverse right to a right-facing dihedral (*Power Struggle*) and climb another 60 feet to a grassy ledge.

4. Continue up the dihedral, make an awkward mantle (10b) and belay on a long sloping ledge below a steep red head wall (150 feet). Move the belay to a left-facing dihedral at the right end of the ledge.

5. Aid up and left along a difficult crack, jog left (RURP and hook), then continue up and left to a broken arête and climb free to a ledge with boulders (A3, 130 feet). Move the belay about 100 feet right to a corner with white crystals and a cairn.

Finish as for *Power Struggle*.

7 Honcho Boncho Buttress   III 7

FA: Robinson and Johnston, 1964.

This route ascends the large buttress to the right of the preceding route. Hike up along the left side of the buttress to get started, then traverse up and right to gain a large chimney. Follow the chimney for several pitches until it ends in an area of ledges (mostly class 4 with a few harder moves at chockstones). Continue up via short walls and ledges. The line leans right but veers back toward the ridge crest, which is followed to the top of the buttress. Traverse left along a low-angle section and join the *Northeast Slope* a few hundred feet from the summit. This route is described as having 13 pitches, but keep in mind that the maximum height of the head wall is 1000 feet. A direct finish to the buttress should be possible just right of the crest.

8 Lost Buttress   III 7 AI2+

FA: Buckingham and Anderson, 1954.

This route ascends a smaller buttress to the right of Honcho Boncho, but the exact line is not known. If the original route is found, it will feature a "spectacular hand traverse" and be easy for most of its length.

8A Lost Buttress Right   6 AI2+

FA: Greg Sievers, 1993.

This route ascends the right side of the Lost Buttress, but its relationship to the preceding route is not known. Climb snow or slabs up into the gully along the right side of the buttress until it is possible to exit left on easy ledges. Zigzag up the face to a wide, wet crack on the left. Traverse 50 feet right along a narrow, grassy ledge, then follow a beautiful hand crack for 200 feet (6). Fourth class terrain leads to the *Northeast Slope* about 1000 feet from the summit.

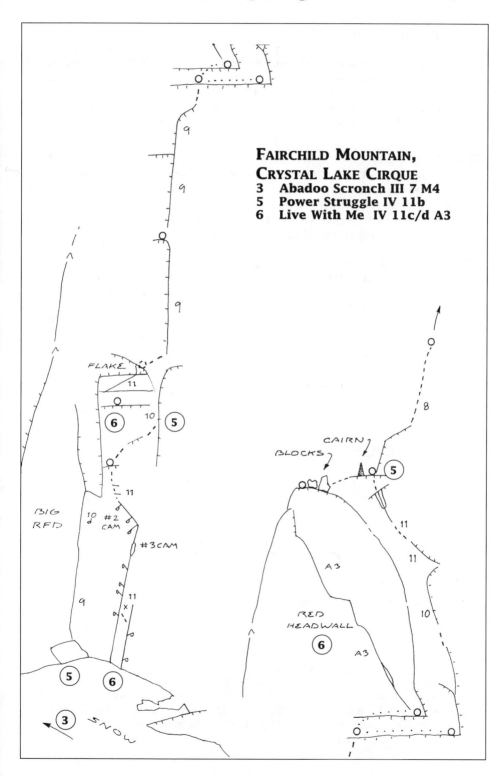

**FAIRCHILD MOUNTAIN,
CRYSTAL LAKE CIRQUE**
3 Abadoo Scronch III 7 M4
5 Power Struggle IV 11b
6 Live With Me IV 11c/d A3

9   Northeast Slope   I Class 2 ★
This is a hike of seclusion and expansive beauty. From Lawn Lake, follow the trail west for 1.6 miles to 12000 feet. Leave the trail and hike
southwest over tundra and talus for 0.9 mile to the summit. One also
may continue to The Saddle (12398) at the end of the trail, and follow
the crest of the north ridge to the summit, which affords spectacular
scenery to the west.

HAGUES PEAK
Hagues Peak (13560) is 1.4 miles northeast of Fairchild Mountain and is the
highest summit of the Mummy Range. It features relatively gentle slopes on
all sides but the west, which drops steeply for 1800 feet into a vast and
rugged cirque above Hague Creek. The Rowe Glacier lies in a smaller east-facing cirque just north of the summit. Approach via the Lawn Lake Trail.

1   Southwest Ridge   I Class 2 ★
From Lawn Lake (10987), follow the trail westward to The Saddle
(12398) and hike the narrow ridge northeast to the summit. From the
summit of Hagues, it is not unreasonable to take in Rowe Peak and
Rowe Mountian to the north. To reach Rowe Peak from Hagues, traverse
the rugged ridge to the north, or more easily, traverse along the east
side of the Rowe Glacier. The ridge between Rowe Peak and Rowe
Mountain is a piece of cake.

2   East Ridge   I Class 2
The crest of the east ridge is easily traversed from the summit of
Mummy Mountain. Approach via the *Southeast Slope* on Mummy.

MUMMY MOUNTAIN
Mummy Mountain (13425) is the eastern outpost of the Mummy Range. Its
familiar profile may be seen from many high places along the Front Range as
well as the plains to the east. The summit is about 1.3 miles southeast of
Hagues Peak and its rugged southwest face rises directly above Lawn Lake.
The easiest descent from the summit is via the *Southeast Slope*.

1   Northwest Ridge   I Class 2
The crest of the northwest ridge is easily traversed from the summit of
Hagues Peak. Approach via the Saddle and Southwest Ridge on Hagues.

2   Mummy Ice   WI4 to WI5+
FA: Duncan Ferguson.
Several ice climbs of varying length and difficulty have been completed
above Lawn Lake, on the rugged southwest face of Mummy Mountain.

3   Southeast Slope   I Class 2
Follow the Lawn Lake Trail for 5.8 miles to its junction with the Black
Canyon Trail. Turn right and follow the Black Canyon Trail for about 0.3
mile to its high point (11000). Leave the trail and scramble north up
talus and tundra to about 11800 feet where the angle eases up, then
head northwest to the summit.

CURSE OF THE MUMMY

Several marathon variations of the Mummy Range are possible. On 31 July 1979, Bill Briggs climbed Mummy Mountain, Hagues Peak, Fairchild Mountain, Ypsilon Mountain, and Mount Chiquita. Obviously, this may be done in reverse, beginning from the Chapin Pass Trailhead and finishing at the Lawn Lake Trailhead, which saves a little on elevation gain. The ultimate one-day event is to include Mount Chapin, Desolation Peaks, Flatiron Mountain, Rowe Peak, and Rowe Mountain, which totals about 14 miles off trail — the Curse of the Mummy!

Powell Peak, Vanquished Buttress, Sky Pond Cirque.

Photo: Michael Bearzi

WEST SIDE

The entire park west of the Continental Divide is unknown to most climbers, however, those weary of the east side trade routes and crowds will find interesting climbing and majestic alpine solitude in this land of the setting sun. Most of the technical climbing is approached from Grand Lake via the North Inlet Trail or East Inlet Trail and is found on two features: Ptarmigan Towers above Lake Nanita and the Aiguille de Fleur above Lake Verna. Farther west, beyond the Colorado River, and less known still, is the long snowy spine of the Never Summer Range — a lonesome peak bagger's paradise. Mount Ida, to the south of Milner Pass, provides one of the easiest and most spectacular summit hikes in Rocky Mountain National Park. The Never Summer Range is not covered in this book.

Mount Ida Trail. Follow Trail Ridge Road to Milner Pass (10758). The trail begins from the east end of a parking lot along the south side of the road, then zigzags up the forest slope to tree line. At about 0.5 mile, a left spur leads northeast to the Alpine Vistor Center. Once out in the open, the Mount Ida Trail climbs along the west side of the Continental Divide and ends after about 3 miles at a cairn in the tundra. See Mount Ida (below).

North Inlet Trail. Reach the town of Grand Lake from the north or south on Highway 34 and turn east on Highway 278. Turn left on a dirt road where a sign indicates the North Inlet Trail and drive 0.25 mile to the trailhead (8500). The trail follows the North Inlet to 9600 feet (about 7 miles), then climbs along Hallett Creek to tree line. It makes several switchbacks to the east, then heads north to join the Flattop Mountain trail. At about 7 miles, a spur breaks right and leads to Lake Nokoni (9.9 miles) and Lake Nanita (about 10.5 miles). It is 12.8 miles from the trailhead to Flattop Mountain and 17.2 miles to Bear Lake.

East Inlet Trail. Turn onto Highway 278 as described above and drive 2.7 miles to the trailhead at the end of the road (8400). The trail climbs up the East Inlet Valley past Lone Pine Lake (5.5 miles) and is maintained to Lake Verna (6.9 miles). A very primitive trail (parts of which may be underwater in early summer) continues along the north shore of the lake. From the east end of the lake, a reasonable footpath continues to Spirit Lake (7.5 miles) and to Fourth Lake (8 miles), then climbs to Boulder-Grand Pass (12061) at 9 miles. It also is possible to ascend the drainage southeast from Fourth Lake to Fifth Lake (9 miles), which lies beneath the imposing north face of Isolation Peak.

MOUNT IDA

Mount Ida (12830) resides along the Continental Divide about 5 miles south-southeast of Milner Pass. Its summit provides fantastic views of Longs Peak, the Mummy Range, the Never Summer Range, the Gore Range, the Ten Mile Range, and more. Yet, unlike Longs Peak and Flattop Mountain, there are no crowds — just silence, haunting beauty, and the ever-present mystic wildness.

1   North Ridge   I Class 2 ⋆
The ascent of Mount Ida via the north ridge (from Milner Pass) is the best easy summit tour in all of Rocky Mountain National Park. Hike the Mount Ida Trail to its end at a cairn in the tundra. The summit is visible to the south-southeast and is about 2 miles away. Continue easily over tundra staying left near the Continental Divide all the way to the narrow summit. During late June and July, the alpine flowers are in full bloom...and...never mind.

2   East Face   I Class 3 AI2 or snow
This route may be approached from Forest Canyon or any other venue that leads to Azure Lake. From the lake, scramble west over talus, then climb snow or bare rock up the middle of the face and finsh with a snow couloir that tops out just north of the summit.

IDA-JULIAN TOUR
From the summit of Mount Ida, descend the southeast ridge to a col, then scramble southeast to the summit of Chief Cheley Peak (12804). Descend the south ridge of Cheley and follow the crest eastward above the south side of Highest Lake where the Continental Divide descends to the south. Continue northeast to the summit of Cracktop (12780), scramble down a steep step east of the summit, then follow the ridge crest northeast and scramble to the summit of Mount Julian (12928). The tour is Class 3 and about 1.7 miles one way.

PTARMIGAN MOUNTAIN
Ptarmigan Mountain (12324) is the western-most peak on the long glacier-carved ridge that runs west-northwest from Mount Alice. Its northeast ridge provides a classic summit scramble and is also the most efficient line of descent to the east. From the summit, a 2 mile traverse along the ridge crest to the southeast allows one to take in Andrews Peak, a mere 12.5 miles from the trailhead. The traverse between the summits is all above 12000 feet and is thoroughly spectacular. This 25-mile tour can be done car-to-car in a long day, but most travelers will want to spend a night or two in the campsites along the North Inlet Trail.

Approach. From Grand Lake, hike the North Inlet Trail and take the right branch to Lake Nokoni. It is not necessary to hike over the pass to Lake Nanita unless a view of Ptarmigan Towers is desired or one plans to climb Andrews Peak from the east and traverse northwest over the summit of Ptarmigan Mountain.

Descent. From the summit, one may descend the *North Ridge*, the *Northeast Ridge*, or the *Southeast Slope* as desired.

PTARMIGAN TOWERS
Ptarmigan Towers is the name given to five large and precipitous pinnacles on the east side of Ptarmigan Mountain, a short way west of Lake Nanita.

PTARMIGAN TOWERS, VIEW FROM THE EAST ACROSS LAKE NANITA

1 Southeast Slope I Class 4
2 Northeast Corner III 9 ★
3 Rocky Rangers III 7
4 Sunshine Ledges III 4 or 6 ★
5 Northeast Ridge I Class 4 ★

These impressive towers reach heights of 800 feet and are visible from many points along the Continental Divide inside the park. That few routes have been developed on these features is due to the very long approach up North Inlet. For those who desire solitude and the chance to explore new terrain, Ptarmigan Towers should not be overlooked. Note that in this book the towers are described Five through One, from left to right, though only three routes have been documented on two of the towers. It is likely that other routes have been climbed and not recorded. Any new route on the south or east faces of these towers is likely to be difficult.

Approach. From Lake Nokoni, follow the trail over the pass to the south and descend a short way until it is obvious to break west to the bottom of the towers.

Descent. Downclimb off the north side of any of the towers, then hike down the northeast ridge of Ptarmigan Mountain to the saddle between Lake Nokoni and Lake Nanita.

1   Southeast Slope   I Class 4
This is a useful route of return after an ascent of Ptarmigan Towers Five, Four, or Three, but it also affords a fine summit scramble on easy terrain. Hike over the pass to the southeast of Lake Nokoni, then break right and hike along the base of the very impressive Ptarmigan Towers. Scramble up around the west side of Tower Five and join the *Northeast Ridge* route just below the summit. The route is all Class 2 but for the last 75 feet to the summit.

TOWER FOUR

2   Northeast Corner   III 9 ★
FA: Larry Hamilton and T. Griese.
This route ascends the northeast corner of Tower Four, then climbs the right of two distinct chimneys to finish on the east side of the summit. This route is directly across a deep gully from *Sunshine Ledges*.
Begin with a short dihedral near the left edge of the face, then work up and right to the bottom a steep, 50-foot dihedral. Climb the dihedral to a ledge, then traverse right and climb another dihedral to a higher ledge. A long pitch leads to the bottom of a 40-foot column. Work left and climb a rotten left-facing dihedral to moderate terrain, then angle up and left past steep walls and gain a big ledge that may have a cairn left by the first ascent party. Work up and left to a belay in the right of two chimneys. Climb the chimney (9, loose in places) and continue to the summit.

TOWER TWO

3   Rocky Rangers   III 7
FA: Richardson and Schneider, 1986.
A distinct gully separates Tower Two and Tower Four; Tower Three lies recessed between these two at the head of the gully. *Rocky Rangers* apparently begins to the left of *Sunshine Ledges* and climbs part way up Tower Four, then works up the gully, and eventually joins *Sunshine Ledges* on Tower Two for the last pitch.

Begin left of the gully and ascend a short wall. Continue up a left-facing corner to a roof, then traverse right. Cross the gully between Towers Two and Four, cross a steep wall, and belay. Climb broken rock for a pitch and belay around on the east face (7, 150 feet). Work right across the east face, then climb a crack up the left side of a short wall and finish with a gully and a short chimney. Climb a left-facing dihedral and join the last part of *Sunshine Ledges*. Good luck.

4   Sunshine Ledges   III 4 or 6 ★
FA: Sandy Kline and Janis Aldins, 1970. Direct Start: R. Rossiter, solo, 1994.
This is the "standard route" on Ptarmigan Towers featuring seven or eight leads on varied terrain. The route ascends the southwest corner of Tower Two, then traverses a ledge across the east face and finishes on the northeast side of the summit. Be careful of loose rock.
Begin about 6 feet left of a deep slot at the bottom of the gully between Tower Two and Tower Four.
1. Climb straight up a small buttress for about 100 feet until it is possible to exit right into the gully — this is the best pitch on the climb (6, 150 feet). The original start works in from the left along a flake/ramp (3).
2. Cross the gully, then work up and right and gain the southwest corner of the pinnacle (4).
3. Climb steep cracks and chimneys to the end of the rope (4).
4. Continue up the southwest corner to a big ledge with trees (4, 150 feet).
5. From the west end of the ledge, work up and right for 100 feet to a higher ledge, then traverse right beneath an overhanging chimney and belay beneath a large, right-facing dihedral (cl4, 120 feet).
6. Climb the dihedral and gain the crest of the ridge (4, 150 feet).
7. Follow the crest westward for about 100 feet to the summit (cl3).

4A   Tundra Turkey Crack   8
Begin right of the gully between Towers Two and Four, beneath a grungy chimney. Climb up and right over a steep wall and gain a distinct crack. Follow the crack for two pitches, then work up and left to join *Sunshine Ledges*.

5   Northeast Ridge   I Class 4 ★
This is an excellent scramble up the ridge just behind the Ptarmigan Towers. Nearly the entire route is visible from the east shore of Lake Nokoni. Follow the trail to the saddle between Lake Nokoni and Lake Nanita, then hike southwest up the broad, grassy ridge and gain a small saddle behind Tower Three. The gully above here is loose and dangerous. It is best to angle up to the right and climb grassy ramps and ledges along the ridge until one is forced into the talus on the left. Scramble west and pass through a notch in the ridge crest. Traverse along the north side of the crest to another notch below the summit block. Climb directly up moderate rock (cl4) to the summit plateau or ascend a slot about 50 feet to the right (cl3). The summit is marked with a cairn and has a register in a glass jar.

The author on the ninth pitch, *Birds of Fire*, Chiefs Head.
Photo: Bonnie Von Grebe

On the first pitch of *Vanquished*, Sky Pond Cirque.

Photo: Michael Bearzi

6 North Ridge   I Class 2
From the north shore of Lake Nokoni, hike northwest, eventually along a faint path, and gain a saddle on the ridge crest. Follow the ridge as it curves around to the south, and finally hike east to the broad, grassy summit.

ANDREWS PEAK

Andrews Peak (12565) lies 2.5 miles west of Mount Alice along the same ridge that terminates farther to the northwest with Ptarmigan Mountain. The most dramatic aspect of Andrews Peak is the steep northwest face above Lake Nanita. The moderate south slope rises above Lake Verna in East Inlet. The high-flying summit is graced by a seven-foot cairn that draws the eye from afar and calls to the intrepid . . . if for no other reason than to find out what's sticking up on top of the mountain. Andrews Peak may be approached from North Inlet or East Inlet, either of which offers a long and arduous trek.

1 Northeast Couloir   II Class 3, moderate snow
This remote route climbs Andrews Peak from the northeast and is most easily approached from North Inlet and the trail to Lake Nanita. Hike southeast from Lake Nanita along a fading path and gain a col east-northeast of the summit (c. 11400), then descend into the basin east of the peak. Climb slabs for 300 feet and gain a broad couloir that leads to a col south of the sumit. Scramble northwest up the ridge to the summit.

2 Notch Box   II 7
FA: Sandy Kline and party, 1970.
From Lake Nanita, hike south into the cirque beneath the northwest face. Climb short walls via cracks and chimneys followed by 600 feet of steep scrambling, and gain a notch on the ridge north of the summit, then hike to the top.

3 West Ridge   I Class 2 ★
This beautiful tundra ridge is likely ascended most often via the spectacular two-mile hike from the summit of Ptarmigan Mountain. However, at least two other options exist. Three northeast-facing cirques are cut into the ridge between Andrews Peak and Ptarmigan Moutain. The middle of these cirques is headed by a col that is directly southwest of Lake Nanita and north-northwest of Lone Pine Lake. The col is marked by a small cairn and is reached more easily from Lake Nanita. From the col, hike 1.2 miles east to the summit of Andrews Peak.

AIGUILLE DE FLEUR

The granite monolith of the Aiguille de Fleur (c. 11940) rises dramatically to the south of Lake Verna in the East Inlet valley and provides the best technical rock climbing on the west side of Rocky Mountain National Park. The tower features relatively long routes (up to 1000 feet high) on good granite and in exquisite surroundings. The name Aiguille de Fleur, which can be translated from French as "flower tower," apparently is a reference to the large and improbable summit plateau that is covered with grasses and wildflowers.

ISOLATION PEAK AND AIGUILLE DE FLEUR, VIEWED FROM THE SUMMIT OF ANDREWS PEAK

Approach. From Grand Lake, hike the East Inlet Trail to its end at Lake Verna, then continue along a primitive path toward Spirit Lake. Just before reaching Spirit Lake take a right branch in the path and follow it along the west end of the lake to the outlet stream. Cross the stream on a log and bushwhack directly up the steep forest slope to the slabs at the foot of the north ridge.

This eight mile approach typically necessitates a camp or bivouac. Several designated campites exist along the East Inlet Trail including one at Lake Verna which is strategically ideal. If none of these sites is available or one prefers to awaken nearer to the objective, an excellent bivouac can be made in the alpine valley on the east side of the tower. For the very athletic (and those like me who hate to carry overnight gear), an ascent can be made car-to-car in a single ass-kicking day — an 18-mile round trip.

Descent. See *South Ridge*.

1   **South Ridge**   I 4 ★

This is an excellent mountaineer's route to the summit of a spectacular tower; it is also the easiest line of descent. Hike around into the high basin on the east side of the tower and continue south until beyond the east face, then scramble west up a couloir that leads to the sharp notch south of the summit plateau. Note that this couloir holds snow into July. From the col, climb a steep 50-foot wall on the north, then scramble to the summit plateau. Hike north to the highest point which is marked by a cairn. To descend, downclimb or rappel back into the col. The couloir that descends to the west from the col presents no obstacle but a short chimney 100 feet below the top.

2   **East Face**   III 9

FA: Ken Trout and party, date unknown.

The steep and secluded east face is about 700 feet high and consists of high quality granite. This route ascends a long dihedral system located a bit right from the center of the wall.

1. Work up and right along a ramp until below and right of the dihedral system.
2. Climb a difficult pitch up and left to a ledge at the base of the dihedral.
3. and 4. Climb the dihedral for two or three steep and sustained pitches.
5. Turn the roof at the top of the dihedral and belay on a big ledge.
6. A moderate chimney leads to the summit plateau.

3   **North Ridge**   III 7 ★

FA: Filip Sokol and Peter Hull, 1969. Data is from a solo ascent by R. Rossiter, 1994.

The north ridge of the Aiguille de Fleur, which provided the first route on the tower, is easily 1000 feet high and appears in profile from the west end of Lake Verna. The ridge consists of three sections: a 400-foot apron of beautiful slabs, a very steep mid-section, and a lower angle crest that soars another 400 feet to the summit. A grassy ledge contours right from the bottom of the east face to a large terrace on the

Aiguille de Fleur, from the Northwest
3 North Ridge III 7 ★
5 West Face III 8 ★

crest of the ridge above the initial apron. This ledge continues all the way around beneath the west face and allows easy access from one side of the tower to the other. Note that the route described includes the initial apron, whereas the original ascent began from the terrace on the ridge crest.

Climb three or four pitches up the slabs at the bottom of the north ridge, beginning with a left-facing dihedral, and gain a large terrace. Scramble up to the bottom of the steep middle section and set the belay toward the left side of the ridge. Stem up a steep inset, step right, and climb a vertical crack to easier ground (7, 160 feet). About four more pitches up to 6 in difficulty lead to the top of the ridge. When in doubt, stay toward the left side of the ridge.

4   Greenie   III 7

FA: Hodges and Boon, 1974.

Begin from the bottom of the north ridge. Climb three or four leads up the granite apron at the bottom of the north ridge and gain the terrace that spans the tower. Traverse right to the first dihedral on the west face, then follow a steep crack system for three pitches to a big flake (6). Traverse left (7) and climb straight up to a belay. Continue straight up for another pitch to a big ledge. Follow a crack system up and right for three more pitches and gain the summit (7).

5   West Face   III 8 ★

FA: Dan Hare and Jim Sauder, 1978.

Two, long parallel cracks run along the left side of a large flake near the north edge of the west face; this route ascends the right of the two cracks, which leads to a long left-facing dihedral high on the wall. Its relationship to the previous route is unknown.

1. A short easy pitch leads to a big ledge.
2. Just left of the main crack, climb a shallow left-facing dihedral, then move back right to the crack and climb to a stance (7, 160 feet).
3. Climb the crack past a wide spot and belay.
4. Continue up the crack and pass an overhang.
5. Angle up and right toward the long left-facing dihedral that can be seen from the terrace at the bottom of the wall, pass a bulge, and climb a thin crack along the left side of a steep wall (8).
6. Start up the long dihedral, pass an overhanging section on the left, and belay where the angle eases off (7). Scramble to the summit.

PTARMAGAN TOUR

During late August of 1994, I completed the following tour carrying a pack with food and water, storm gear, and 10 pounds of camera equipment: North Inlet Trail to Lake Nanita, free solo *Sunshine Ledges* on the Second Ptarmigan Tower, traverse summits of Ptarmigan Mountain and Andrews Peak, back over summit of Ptarmigan, down *Northeast Ridge,* then out North Inlet Trail. Thirty miles. It took all day, but I was slowed considerably by having to identify all the routes on Ptarmigan Towers and photograph every climbing feature in the area. Note: After reaching the summit of Andrews Peak, it would be easier and perhaps more interesting to descend the southeast slope to Lake Verna and hike out the East Inlet Trail.

INDEX

Index 297

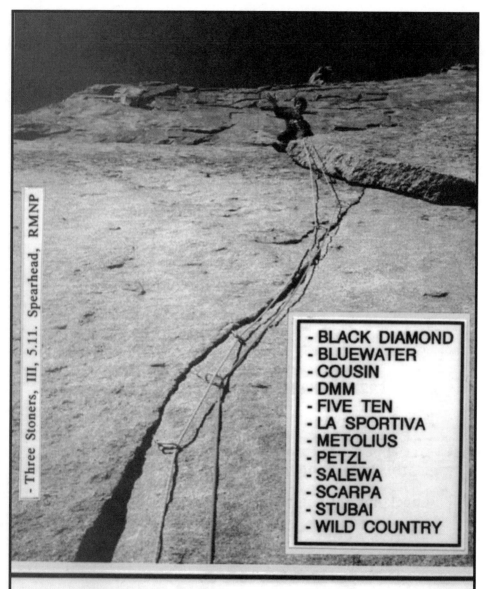

- Three Stoners, III, 5.11. Spearhead, RMNP

- BLACK DIAMOND
- BLUEWATER
- COUSIN
- DMM
- FIVE TEN
- LA SPORTIVA
- METOLIUS
- PETZL
- SALEWA
- SCARPA
- STUBAI
- WILD COUNTRY

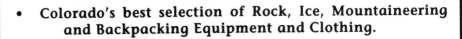